# PRAISE FOR *RE*
# *REPUTATIONAL*



'The authors have examined trust in business through the lens of reputational risk and identified themes that really matter. Their well-illustrated commentary is a good read for business leaders at all levels.'
**Dame Alison Carnwath, Company chair, Audit Committee chair, NED and Supervisory board member**

'*Rethinking Reputational Risk* is a helpful book not only for those involved in business but for all organizations and institutions, including the Church. It highlights the inevitable vulnerability of all personal and corporate leadership and the common inability of such leadership to recognize and act on the possible consequences of such vulnerability. The themes of this book are timely and pertinent for all.'
**John Stroyan, Bishop of Warwick**

'This publication does indeed rethink reputation risk. It provides an accessible, readable discourse on the subject and, unlike many of its ilk, combines expertly theory, example and practice. The latter is key to help companies improve, and the addition of practical questions does this.'
**Philippa Foster Back CBE, Director, Institute of Business Ethics**

'This book is a must-read for all risk managers. It covers the critical issue of human behaviours and culture and how inappropriate behaviours can seriously damage an organization's reputation and therefore the organization itself. This way of looking at the matter is new to the repertoire of books on reputation risk.'
**Trevor Llanwarne CB, UK [Chief] Government Actuary 2008–2014**

'This excellent book plugs gaps in and is a much needed contribution to our understanding of how reputational damage can wreak havoc on a business and its stakeholders.'
**Simon Osborne, Chief Executive of ICSA: The Governance Institute**

'*Rethinking Reputational Risk* serves as a powerful and timely reminder for all organizations not to use their risk management systems and processes to provide a false sense of security. If just one of the many questions to mull included in the book encourages you to stop, reflect and act on potential vulnerabilities in your organization, it will have helped you on the journey to build greater resilience.'
**Charles Tilley, Chief Executive, Chartered Institute of Management Accountants (CIMA), 2001–2016**

'It can be difficult to identify reputational risks because perceptions are subjective. However, no organization can or should ever be risk-free because innovation should be

encouraged and human fallibilities are inevitable. Leaders need to walk this precarious tightrope, and this book offers valuable insights to help them.'
**Michal Izza, Chief Executive of the Institute of Chartered Accountants in England and Wales**

'This is an inspiring, insightful and definitive guide for both companies and their investors. A deeper understanding of human behaviour is at the heart of a deeper understanding of corporate and investment resilience.'
**Andy McNally, author of *Debtonator* and Chief Executive of Equitile Investments**

'Take well-researched insight into the anatomy of reputational risk, add a dash of social anthropology, a handful of provocative questions and you've got a recipe for success. This book will give you the academic rigour behind the latest thinking on reputational risk as well as the practical advice you need to start applying what you learn.'
**Jennifer Janson, author of *The Reputation Playbook***

'How refreshing to find a book on business that recognizes from the start that we as human beings , and especially as leaders and managers, do not behave rationally and have an infinite capacity to fool ourselves into complacency. Fitzsimmons and Atkins speak from experience and their powerful array of examples and war stories should get your attention.'
**Mark Goyder, CEO, Tomorrow's Company**

'This book provides a fascinating bridge between individual-based psychological principles and an understanding of organizational systems. This opens up a wealth of opportunities for the application of psychology into an area where it has perhaps been undervalued.'
**Dr Lizzy Atkins, NHS Consultant Clinical Psychologist**

'Effective use of traditional management metrics is a given for many organizations, but Derek and Anthony's valuable reference work illustrates that sustainability requires an equal focus on the risks associated with people and their behaviours. This fresh thinking is most welcome.'
**Diane Walker MBA, FCII, Managing Director, InTouch**

'There was a time when the whole business world was based on long-lasting, pure and undefined ethics and reputation. This is a great book bringing to the surface what this business world we live in has tried to ignore and hide away for so long, thus creating so much damage in the process.'
**Stavros Stavrou, Former Chairman of Cyprus Airways, MD, Oilinvest BV and Executive Vice President of the Cyprus National Hydrocarbons Company Ltd**

'This new highly readable book, with its forceful stories of board shortcomings, is a timely reminder of directors' responsibilities.'
**Bernard Cook OBE, portfolio chairman**

'Internal auditors need to have a place at the table when reputational risks are discussed. This book is not only relevant to risk managers but also to professional internal auditors. *Rethinking Reputational Risk* is a book that will never become obsolete.'
**Eman Hafedh, CIA, CISA, CRM; Head of Internal Audit**

# Rethinking Reputational Risk

## How to manage the risks that can ruin your business, your reputation and you

Anthony Fitzsimmons and Derek Atkins

KoganPage

First published in Great Britain and the United States in 2017 by Kogan Page Limited



2nd Floor, 45 Gee Street
London
EC1V 3RS
United Kingdom

c/o Martin P Hill Consulting
122 W 27th Street
New York, NY10001
USA

4737/23 Ansari Road
Daryaganj
New Delhi 110002
India



ISBN 978 0 7494 7736 3
E-ISBN 978 0 7494 7737 0

**British Library Cataloguing-in-Publication Data**

A CIP record for this book is available from the British Library.

**Library of Congress Control Number**

2016961398

Typeset by Graphicraft Limited, Hong Kong
Print production managed by Jellyfish
Printed and bound in Great Britain by CPI Group (UK) Ltd, Croydon CR0 4YY

*For Kristina and Diana*

# CONTENTS

# FOREWORD

Professor Daniel Kahneman, the American academic acclaimed across the world for his best-selling book *Thinking Fast and Slow* (2011), won the Nobel Prize for Economics in 2002 for his pioneering work into how people make decisions in conditions of uncertainty. He must be the only holder of that honour who consistently prefers to describe himself as a psychologist rather than an economist.

This is not an affectation. The curse of economics is that it assumes people are entirely rational, markets are perfect, and everybody at all times knows everything they need to know about the situation in which they find themselves. This allows academics of a certain bent to construct elegant mathematical models that purport to describe how the economy and businesses behave, but at the same time makes the science of little use as a practical guide to business and everyday life.

Psychology fares rather better. Understanding how people think, what it is that makes them do what they do, how they behave with others, how they will react under pressure and why they will choose one course of action over another can all be very useful indeed.

One ironic conclusion from his work is that people are very bad at investing, and the flaws that make this so also make one question their ability to run a business.

The first characteristic is that people have too much confidence in their own ability, and this confidence not dented by reality that suggests the opposite. In investment this means buying and selling too much and failing to register that what is sold usually does better than what has been bought. The parallel in business is the constant search for new blockbuster ideas, and a failure to nurture and get the best out of the familiar and the established.

The second mistake in investment and business is to fall in love with one share or business and focus on these rather than on the performance of the whole portfolio. This is known as narrow framing and among other things it shows people to feel disproportionately hurt by a loss with the result that that they devote far too much effort to supporting losers so as to avoid having to admit to a mistake. A rational approach to running a portfolio is summed up in the phrase 'you win a few and you lose a few'. That is not the view most people take.

The third flaw is to apply hindsight in a way that convinces us that we did in fact vaguely expect or anticipate some happening when in reality we had totally failed to foresee it. Most people in business today will say that the 2008 financial crash was inevitable and have convinced themselves that they also thought this at the time. Applied across the board this prompts people to think the world is far more predictable than it actually is, which leads them to advocate actions on the flimsiest of evidence. It leads them to deny the real uncertainty that actually dominates most of our lives.

Now the point is that this is not just how investors behave; it is how people behave. And notably it is how people in top management behave. Those whom head-hunters and boards have painstakingly selected for their intelligence, their experience their vision and their rationality are as subject to over-confidence, narrow framing and an inability to cope with uncertainty as the rest of us. The decisions they take will not always be emotional, but neither will they always be rational – and a lot of the problems in modern business and many of the disasters that overtake most companies at some point in their history result from a failure by boards to spot the difference, let alone deal with the consequences.

This is a sensitive area. Given how much evidence these authors have uncovered that failures in senior management, business culture and the boardroom lie behind most business disasters, there has been surprisingly little candour about the subject.

Just as economists find it easier to assume people are rational, so the people who write business risk manuals find it easier to think companies behave in predictable ways like a machine.

The reality is that companies are collections of people and are anything but predictable because, for all sorts of different reasons, good people also make mistakes. But because this does not fit leaders' perceptions of themselves and is difficult to evaluate, this area is largely ignored.

That is why this book, which explains how normal human behaviour makes organizations predictably vulnerable, is such an important addition to the literature of how organizations really work. It delves into an area that has been neglected and ignored for far too long.

*Anthony Hilton*

# PREFACE

Explosions, fires and corporate crashes. Conspiracies, leaks and cover-ups. Crises, scandals and scapegoats. Reputations in tatters as innocent people suffer.

Reputational crises combine tragedy and farce. Their histories, when revealed, often verge on the unbelievable. Shareholder value, the Holy Grail of so many business leaders, evaporates as reputations are destroyed.

Leaders are regularly removed after debacles like these. Many are left with lifelong guilt about any human casualties, and a damaged personal reputation that can lead to public pillory and enforced retirement.

When this book's authors met, we had each dissected dozens of crises, looking behind the headlines and witch hunts for the deeper causes. As we brought our knowledge together, we found patterns. Repeating across otherwise unrelated sectors (healthcare, energy, financial and more) was a flaw in how people think about reputational risk.

Not only that: we identified a large gap in the system used by leaders and their risk teams to find and manage risk: risks from the individual and collective behaviour of people. This gap matters because it explains why well-respected organizations suffer reputational crises that shock leaders and outsiders alike.

The Financial Reporting Council's 2014 *Guidance on the Strategic Report* now expects boards of UK quoted companies to report annually on 'principal risks and uncertainties,' whether they originate from 'strategic decisions, operations, organization or behaviour, or from external factors over which the board may have little or no direct control'. Its 2015 *Guidance on Risk* developed the theme. In May 2016 Andrew Bailey, then the Chief Executive of the Bank of England's Prudential Regulation Authority and now Head of the Financial Conduct Authority, gave a speech[1] forcefully directing attention to this area with an unusually robust focus on the role, attitudes and behaviour of leaders.

One way to avoid disasters is to learn lessons from the painful experience of others. Our aim is to make those lessons accessible to all: executives, boards, risk teams, internal auditors and regulators. And pioneering professional investors are showing interest too.

Our book is divided into three parts. Part One systematically explains our insights derived from combining our knowledge and experience with the work of behavioural scientists. We discuss what reputations are and how they are lost before turning to reputational risk – explaining the gap in classical risk management systems, and discussing how to fill it.

You, like us, will want evidence. We have written many studies of crises and read scores more. In Part Two we describe some of the most recent crises that have hit our headlines, and some older stories that remain valuable. Reading these tales, you will find illustrations of just about every risk phenomenon we discuss. We have supplemented them with questions you can use to illuminate risks in your own organization.

Having identified an important gap in risk management, we thought it important to outline a practical solution, and this is the role of Part Three. We considered providing a detailed process. Sadly, processes readily turn into tick-box cultures that lull users into complacency and a false sense of security before a preventable disaster shatters the delusion. This is why we decided to provide instead a structure and principles – and to counter complacency we have included questions you can use to challenge yourself and your colleagues to keep reality in sharp focus.

We have included a glossary with succinct explanations of technical terms and abbreviations as well as a bibliography and ample endnotes so that you can easily find our sources.

## Note

**1** Bailey (2016).

# PART ONE
# **Rethinking**

# Introduction 01

## Learning from crises

As two-year-olds, our children discovered the question: 'Why?' They discovered how much it could irritate their parents, particularly as bedtime approached. But they also learnt how persistently asking that question revealed valuable insights into how cause and effect drive the world's workings. Now in their thirties and beyond, they retain the ability to ask the world's most penetrating question. That is partly because we, too, retained it and know that it provides the most valuable route to understanding anything, including the anatomy of failures.

As we began to ask 'why' about crises, the first answers were specific to the particular disaster. A refinery blew up because an operator cut a corner. A fairground ride crashed because procedures were not followed. A hacker disrupted a computer system because its security failed. A firm hosted a rogue trader because supervision was ineffective. A plane crashed because of a maintenance error.

But these are not satisfying answers; we wanted deeper insights. We were not alone. Academic researchers and safety analysts were also studying human error in accidents. And at the other end of the telescope, we met PR directors and company secretaries some of whom muttered darkly that things were not really as good as they seemed from the outside.

What we wanted to discover was:

- Why do some crises tip into reputational catastrophes whereas others do not?
- Are common factors at work?
- To what extent are reputations predictably vulnerable?

## Anthony's story

Through offering legal support to businesses in crisis, Anthony saw 30 years' worth of calamitous events from the inside. He saw, at close quarters, the emergence of the compensation culture, the 'blame game' and 'infotainment'.

As a liability and insurance lawyer, Anthony was trained to look for something called the 'proximate' cause of the accident – an event, error or omission but for which the accident would not have happened. That means looking for the event closest to the accident of which you can say: 'Aha! But for that, the accident would not have happened.'

This process is as convenient for leaders as it is misleading because it tends to blame lowly Fred or Freda who made a mistake – such as pressing a button at the wrong moment. Partly through his experience working with aviation – an industry that took a different approach – Anthony began to feel that a proximate cause was not enough. As Anthony Hilton, the leading City columnist put it, 'inquiries focus on the processes within an organisation until they find some hapless individual or group who departed from the manual. Identifying that person becomes a proxy for solving the problem'.[1]

Blame them: sack them: job done. This is where most inquiries into crises stop. They fail to delve to deeper discoveries, such as: 'Why did they make that mistake?' 'To what extent did the system drive them to it?' Root cause risks remain unidentified, unmanaged and ready to strike again.

Always close to the insurance market, Anthony was also involved, decades ago, in groups that were chewing over dietary fat, sugar and genetically modified organisms, reputations and other risks that were difficult or impossible to insure. In those days few lawyers understood much about reputations let alone reputational risk.

But Anthony had not begun his career as a lawyer. His degree in engineering had given him a particular kind of curiosity. Dealing with the liability and insurance consequences of major accidents, he was left with a big puzzle: why was it that even after crisis lawyers had minimized legal liabilities and maximized insurance pay-outs, businesses still struggled to recover fully from a crisis?

Clues began to emerge from the aviation industry. Aviation does things differently. The difference explains why airline flights have become so safe – though it was not ever thus and the path to safety was long and deliberate.

An early pointer emerged from the British Midland Airline's 1989 crash at Kegworth. Forty-seven people died and 74 were badly injured. Its Chief Executive Michael Bishop focused on the plight of those affected and learning the lessons of the disaster. His response is widely credited with putting British Midland on the map as a 'good' airline.

For Anthony, one practical insight was that the humanity and generosity shown to the victims of crises, plus demonstrably learning from mistakes, were not only morally right: they were economically right too. With judicious juggling it was possible simultaneously to meet the expectations of victims, liability insurers and future customers and minimize the damage to the reputation of the airline that had caused the victims' misfortune.

Michael Bishop's handling of the Kegworth crash was a first insight into reputational risk, and one Anthony began to put into practice, helping clients in crises to do what they saw as the 'right thing' in both moral and business terms. A challenge was to avoid upsetting their liability insurers who, encouraged by their lawyers, often resisted any expression of sympathy for victims lest it be construed as an admission of legal liability.

But astute insurers, well briefed, increasingly saw the potential benefits. Victims and their families treated with humanity typically seek recognition of any wrong done and fair compensation, and want the lessons to be learned. Relatives of victims dealt with callously are more likely to want revenge as they try to punish the perpetrator by delivering a lesson that is both expensive and painfully memorable. Insurers discovered that treating victims fairly was not just morally right, it cost less too. And it pleased many that the only losers were lawyers, who lost the opportunity to earn fees as fractious fencing dragged on for years.

Meanwhile, 1990 saw the publication of 'Human error in the cockpit',[2] a paper from Swiss Re, one of the world's thought-leaders among reinsurance companies. It set out from the observation of Stanley Roscoe, an aviation psychologist, that a finding of 'pilot error' after a crash was 'in no sense an explanation of why the accident occurred,' but merely 'the substitution of one mystery for another'.[3]

Various air crash investigations had concluded that communication failure among the flight crew had been an important cause of accidents. A junior crew member knew something important but was unable to communicate that fact so that the captain understood it. Reasons included the complexity of unfolding events and unspoken hierarchical rules that seemingly made it impossible for a co-pilot assertively to tell the captain that he (in those days it almost always was a 'he') might be making a serious mistake, even though they, their passengers and crew were facing imminent, avoidable death.

## Derek's story

Derek's decision to study engineering was, if not a rebellion, at least a decision to be different. With a father who worked as a public relations (PR) manager at the *Daily Mirror* newspaper group, reputation was a regular feature of Atkins family life.

Derek went on to complete a doctorate and began his career at the UK Patent Office, a role with engineering, not reputation, at its heart. But, following the 1974 Flixborough disaster, an explosion at a UK chemical plant that killed almost thirty workers, and the introduction of the Health and Safety at Work Act a few months later, the insurance sector was under pressure to change.

Derek moved to the City of London, where he joined one of the UK's leading insurance companies. His boss there had been a Major General in the Royal Electrical and Mechanical Engineers (REME), the Corps that still keeps the UK army's kit working on battlefields. The REME had become thought leaders in risk management and his boss had been headhunted to bring that expertise to the insurer and its clients.

Derek spent the next 30 years managing crises for his company. For 20 years he was on call as first responder, part of the team dealing with business continuity and crisis management for the company. He had plenty of real crises to deal with, including bombs (exploding and threatened), demonstrations, Legionnaires' disease, rogue employees, computer breakdowns and floods. There he came to appreciate that customer complaints are the most valuable source of feedback for improving products and service: previously they were seen more as a nuisance. In time Derek became UK Strategy Director.

Having seen and managed crises at first hand, Derek too became fascinated by them. In parallel to his insurance career, he became a teacher of aspiring insurance company managers at London's Cass Business School. He found time to write and co-write over a dozen books, including the insurance industry's own textbook on how to manage insurance companies and books covering risk and risk management.

An early inspiration for Derek's thinking on reputational risk was a conversation with a colleague, Ian Bates, a long-experienced internal auditor who asked Derek a penetrating question: 'Why do people seem to behave and make decisions at work in a way that is different from how they would these do things at home? When they get on the train to commute to the office, do they undergo a personality change or is there something about the work environment that causes a difference?'

Derek, Ian and Lynn Drennan, a public sector risk management specialist, went on to research the subject and the result was one of the first books on reputational risk, published in 2006. It took the important step of linking reputation to stakeholder expectations in respect of performance and behaviour. It concluded that reputation needed active risk management before something went wrong: until then, it was widely seen as a PR issue to be dealt with after things had gone wrong.

A few years later, Derek and Anthony were introduced by a mutual friend, John Hurrell, a man steeped in risk know-how who had become the Chief Executive of Airmic, the Association of Insurance and Risk Managers in Industry and Commerce.

We realized that between us we had extensive experience of crises, crisis management and the blame game that often follows. But working together we began to find patterns that illuminated why crises happen; and why some became disasters whereas others did not.

## Combining our insights to reveal hidden truths

A turning point was a major study that dissected a score of crises and systematically catalogued underlying causes of reputational damage and corporate failure. These crises had caused damage that no amount of PR could fix. At best, the business was able to carry on, but with a tarnished reputation that left the organization and its leaders more vulnerable to the next crisis. At worst, the organization was financially damaged, taken over or destroyed. Leaders were frequently ousted, often in disgrace.

The research emerged as *Roads to Ruin*,[4] the Cass Business School's report for Airmic. Working in a team with Professor Alan Punter and led by Professor Chris Parsons, we identified a previously under-recognized family of underlying risks that not only caused crises but also tipped them into reputational catastrophes. Most of these risks emerged from perfectly normal human behaviour. We now call these 'behavioural' and 'organizational' risks. John Hurrell was to describe the report as 'the best piece of research I have seen in this field for many years'.

Back at Reputability, the firm in which we work together, we went on to double the cohort of studies and focus on the role of leaders in failure. Our results emerged as *Deconstructing Failure: Insights for boards*.[5] We showed that five varieties of board-level failure were involved in at least half of the 42 crises we studied, with some apparent in almost all the crises. It took time to understand this finding, but we came to recognize that the problem was not that leaders were bad: it was their influence. Influence and power magnify the consequences of errors.

## Why study crises?

One of the biggest challenges in this field is to discover what is really going on inside an organization. Even with the internet, large volumes of inside information are hard to find unless there is a disgruntled insider, and these may not be reliable. That said, insiders who gain an audience can change the climate, as the US, UK and Panamanian governments and many organizations and individuals have discovered following revelations by Chelsea Manning[6] and Edward Snowden,[7] and leaks from Mossack Fonseca.[8]

When a crisis happens, everything changes. Everyone is eager for information. Leaders must take crises in their stride, and their actions and inactions speak volumes. Information flows fast. If a leader's message is misleading, prompt public rebuttal is likely. To cap it all, severe crises regularly lead to statements, inquiries, investigations, depositions, litigation and reports, rich sources of reliable information.

That creates unrivalled opportunities for the inquisitive to observe the inner workings of organizations. For a leader, high-quality case studies focused on the causes of crises are an excellent opportunity to learn how, and why, apparent success can conceal the seeds of destruction.

For this book we have dissected eight crises, mostly since 2010. This is partly to provide evidence for what we say and to illustrate what happens in real life if root cause risks like these are not found and tackled before they cause harm. But we are also keen to provide our readers with a painless way to learn from the excruciating misfortunes of others.

## Outsiders can see more clearly than insiders

Before we take you to the meat of this book, we must introduce you to a theme that may be unexpected: the root cause risks that lead to reputational crises are often more easily visible to outsiders than to insiders, especially leaders.

Why should this be? The reasons have to do with the way in which groups of people work and think. Pierre Bourdieu, a leading anthropologist, concluded that those on the inside of cohesive groups often share unarticulated cultural norms and mental maps that leave them with shared perspectives and assumptions. These remain un-discussed because they are so deeply embedded as to be invisible, or if visible then unquestionable[9] – though a supervening crisis may lead to their questioning. This observation fits with those of psychologists who use concepts such as group dynamics, social norms, groupthink and polarization to explain how intelligence is no bar to risk blindness and lemming-like tendencies in cohesive groups.

Whatever the rationale, the phenomenon means that insiders, and particularly leaders, have difficulty in seeing important risks. Richard Feynman, the physics Nobel Laureate who went on to disentangle the cultural as well as physical root causes of NASA's *Challenger* disaster, put it pithily: 'The first principle is that you must not fool yourself – and you are the easiest person to fool.'[10] Daniel Kahneman, the psychologist and winner of the Nobel Memorial Prize in Economic Sciences, later wrote: 'We are often confident even when we are wrong, and an objective observer is more likely to detect our errors than we are.'[11]

The counterpart is the extent to which a detached but observant outsider can see these problems in advance. We were far from alone in realizing, from the outside, that something fishy was happening inside the Independent Insurance Company long before it collapsed and its leaders were jailed for fraud.[12] We and other students of BP[13] have little doubt that BP was visibly ripe for a crisis turning into a reputational disaster well before the *Deepwater Horizon* blew up. Terry Smith, an independently thinking fund manager, correctly saw aggressive accounting at Tesco as a reason to avoid investing in them, explaining why in the *Financial Times* a few weeks before Tesco's accounting crisis emerged.[14]

When working with clients, we have the privilege of being trusted 'inside-outsiders', the approach often used by anthropologists to discover what is really going on inside groups of people. We add inside information to our initial 'outsider' analysis to help clients visualize an un-blinkered inside-outsider's view of the extent to which, and why, the organization is vulnerable to, resilient to or even likely to benefit from shocks that might damage others. Armed with a trusted outsider's view of what is really going on within, leaders are well equipped to manage what are often unrecognized, systemic vulnerabilities well before they cause harm.

## What is in it for whom?

The benefits for insiders such as leaders and executive teams are obvious. Leaders cannot make the decisions needed to bring these risks to light and manage them if they lack sufficient understanding of their roots and a shared vocabulary to describe them. Risk and internal audit teams, charged with finding these risks, need both, together with analytical techniques and a safe environment in which to look for and report on them. So too do public relations, marketing and human resources teams. We satisfy these needs.

But outsiders can benefit too.

The best regulators are increasingly keen to anticipate human behaviour that may cause a regulatory incident. Some are now using their powers to demand informed analysis of these risks and we provide a valuable new framework for their investigations.

Insurers of boards can use a similar approach to determine which boards should pay higher premiums for their directors and officers liability (D&O) insurance; and which companies should pay more for their liability or casualty insurance.

Investors would prefer to avoid the share price drop that often accompanies a reputational crisis. Many of the factors that make a company vulnerable are visible in advance from the outside if you know what to look for and are able to see beyond the herd's consensus. Whilst outsiders lack insider knowledge successfully kept secret, it will not take long for a thoughtful investor, knowing what to look for, to assemble a picture showing the extent to which, and why, a seemingly attractive investee is predictably vulnerable.

That kind of information benefits short-term investors too. BlueMountain, a hedge fund, used it to make money at the expense of JP Morgan, whilst the latter's leaders remained in the dark as to what their very own 'London Whale' was doing.[15]

## Notes

1 Anthony Hilton: There's no strength in ignoring flaws, *Evening Standard* 17/7/2013 http://www.standard.co.uk/business/markets/anthony-hilton-there-s-no-strength-in-ignoring-flaws-8714019.html accessed 11/3/2016.

2 Swiss Re (1990).

3 Roscoe (1980).

4 Atkins *et al* (2011).

5 Reputability (2013).

6 https://en.wikipedia.org/wiki/Chelsea_Manning accessed 18/4/2016.

7 https://en.wikipedia.org/wiki/Edward_Snowden accessed 18/4/2016.

8 Panama Papers leak highlights global elite's use of tax havens, *Financial Times* 4/4/2016 http://on.ft.com/1M90M9s accessed 18/4/2016.

9 Bourdieu (1977).

10 Feynman (1974).

11 Kahneman (2011), p 4.

12 Insurance bosses jailed for fraud, BBC News 24/10/2007 http://news.bbc.co.uk/1/hi/business/7059381.stm accessed 7/6/2016.

13 Such as Raj Thamotheram and Maxime Le Floc'h (2012) The BP crisis as a 'preventable surprise': Lessons for institutional investors, *Rotman International Journal of Pension Management*, 5 (1), p. 68, and Hopkins (2012).

14 Terry Smith, *Financial Times*, 2/9/2015, http://on.ft.com/1oM7WxH accessed 7/6/2016.

15 Tett (2015); Chapter 8 tells the story.

# Reputation basics 02

*The purest treasure mortal times afford*
*Is spotless reputation; that away,*
*Men are but gilded loam or painted clay.*

SHAKESPEARE, *RICHARD II*

We all know that a good reputation is valuable. But in our experience, few know enough to be able to manage reputational risk. As a result, most reputations, including leaders' personal reputations, are at greater risk than their vigilant, diligent custodians believe. And we regularly find responsibility for reputation split in ways that leave cracks through which reputational crises can emerge.

The trouble is epitomized by the long-running squabble over the nature of reputation risk. Some see it as the ultimate result of the failure of the organization to manage other risks properly. For example, if you pollute, you can expect to have to pay to clean up the mess and compensate victims and may suffer consequential reputational damage. Others see it more directly: 'If we cause pollution we may suffer reputational damage.'

What unites both groups, and business leaders, is the knowledge that reputational damage, whatever it is, can destroy apparently solid, reputable organizations and end leaders' careers.

Our research shows that both sides are right so far as they go. But neither sees the complete picture; neither offers a practical solution that gives reputation the robust protection it needs and deserves; and few organizations allocate sufficient resources to protecting what is often the organization's single most important and valuable attribute.

It is not possible to tackle reputational risk (which we explore in Chapter 4) effectively without a comprehensive understanding of the nature of reputations. So we will begin by answering two fundamental questions:

- What is reputation? and
- What are the implications of this definition?

## What is a reputation?

There are many definitions of 'reputation'. The *Financial Times* business lexicon defines 'corporate reputation' as:

> Observers' collective judgments of a corporation based on assessments of financial, social and environmental impacts attributed to the corporation over time.[1]

This is inadequate because it is based on the notion that little counts beyond financial performance and activities in the realms of corporate social responsibility.

The *Oxford English Dictionary* is better, hinting at the multiple judgements involved:

> The general opinion or estimate of a person's character or behaviour etc.; the relative esteem in which a person or thing is held.[2]

But even so this needs translating to a world that includes organizations and some extra breadth. Our definition follows the *Oxford English Dictionary* pattern but spans personal and corporate reputations:

> Your reputation is the sum total of how your stakeholders perceive you.

This deceptively simple statement incorporates six important observations:

- Your reputation is not about how you perceive yourself; it is about how your stakeholders perceive you.
- Your reputation is about how others perceive you to be, not the reality of your true nature.
- Since your stakeholders hold that critical perception, if your stakeholders come, rightly or wrongly, to perceive you in a different way, your reputation changes.

- That 'sum total' can vary depending on which stakeholders are most relevant or influential at any particular time.
- It is therefore important to understand all your stakeholders, including when their perceptions may become more or less relevant, influential or vocal.
- You lose your reputation when stakeholders come to believe, rightly or wrongly, that you are not as good as, or are worse than, they previously believed you to be.

This raises the question: what do we mean by 'good' and 'worse'? The *Oxford English Dictionary* definition correctly hints at the answer with its reference to 'a person's character or behaviour etc'. Based on our research, we believe that what matters most is attributes such as character, trustworthiness, humanity, skill, experience and competence. For organizations we must add culture and whether it is coherent or dysfunctional including as to its relations with outside stakeholders such as suppliers and subcontractors. When it comes to individuals, particularly leaders, perceptions of their personal character, integrity and motivation matter too. Perceptions of history also play an important part.

The case studies in Part Two provide many illustrations of stakeholders who changed their minds, downgrading well-respected organizations' reputations from 'excellent' to 'junk' in days or weeks.

In many cases reputations are justified by reality. But what if stakeholders get it wrong? Whether they give you an undeservedly better or worse reputation, you, not your stakeholders, have a problem.

We are all sensitive to having a reputation worse than we feel we deserve and likely to be proactive in dealing with correcting the misapprehension. But what about a reputation that is undeservedly good? The temptation is to grab this unlooked-for bonus, but this is a mistake. The risk is that when stakeholders discover that you are not as good as they thought you were, they do not blame themselves for getting it wrong: healthy humans resist blaming themselves. They are more likely to blame you for over-egging your strengths and downplaying your weaknesses; and they may also put you on a spectrum running from untrustworthy to downright dishonest.

## How is a good reputation valuable?

A good reputation confers opportunities that are often hard to value. For example, it may give you the opportunity to charge a premium price; make you a seemingly more desirable trading partner or support your 'social licence to operate' relatively free of interference by (or with support from) society such as local people, regulators and lawmakers.

The concept of 'social licence to operate' was pioneered by Jim Cooney, a former executive with a large mining company that was concerned about the ability of local communities to block mining projects. It can be thought of as a social contract with local stakeholders under which they allow the company to operate as a trusted provider of benefits (such as employment and infrastructure) that sufficiently outweigh dis-benefits (for example noise and pollution) in their field of operations. A reputation for trustworthiness is an essential component: if stakeholders do not trust you to deliver future benefits, stakeholders will give those benefits no value and the trade no longer works.[3]

## The unrecognized role of heuristics

As we go about our daily lives, we all use heuristics, or mental short cuts, to simplify daily decision-making. In strict logical terms, a decision as seemingly simple as 'what shall I eat for lunch?' involves vast numbers of options and even more permutations; but we make the decision in seconds or minutes, not hours.

Recognition and reputation are foundations of heuristics that help us all to decide, quickly, whether a person or organization is friend or foe, reliable or untrustworthy as well as whether they are a welcome member of society or someone with whom we have, grudgingly, to work, holding them at arm's length.

Heuristics such as these save us from having to research the question every time we have to deal with someone new. A good reputation implies recognition and summarizes assumptions about qualities such as trustworthiness and perhaps warm feelings. Augmented by the full range of other feelings, which range from desirability to dread, these help us to make even the simplest decisions.

In his book *The Brain*,[4] neuroscientist David Eaglesham tells the sad tale of Tammy, an intelligent lady who lost her orbitofrontal cortex, the part of the brain that integrates feelings into decision-making. Whilst she retains the ability to analyse choices, her inability to integrate analysis with feelings leaves her unable to make the seemingly simple decisions (such as what to buy for lunch) that would take you seconds.

We all use mental shortcuts like this constantly and without noticing. Gerd Gigerenzer, a leading thinker about decision-making, has concluded that what he calls 'fast and frugal' – but contextually appropriate – heuristics are what make the human race smart.[5]

In his book *Thinking Fast and Slow*,[6] Nobel Memorial Prize Laureate Daniel Kahneman explains his 'dual system' model to help understand how we all make decisions. Whilst work on modelling decision-making continues, we will use his model in our book.[7]

## Systems One and Two

Kahneman's System One is fast, unconscious and frugal. A machine that has evolved effortlessly to jump to conclusions, that is what it does. It is impulsive, automatic and effort-free and it does not stop to ponder whether the decision is right or wrong.

In contrast, System Two is slow, conscious and logical. It is the only check we have on System One: but using it needs mental effort. Frequently we do not use System Two to query the instant decisions made by System One: because it takes time and energy. System Two is, however, the only way we have to behave like homo economicus, the relentlessly rational human created by classical economists.

When thinking fast, we all use heuristics to extrapolate and interpolate, to create plausible stories, to solve problems using analogies, instinct, experience and prejudice, in order to arrive at quick, pragmatic answers.

But whilst many heuristics – built on experience, approximations, assumptions, gut feeling and other short cuts – work much of the time, they can be treacherous when they are not well adapted to the nature or complexity of the question. And they are doubly so because they are so well integrated into our thinking that we kid ourselves that we are being rational even when we have taken a short cut that is contextually inappropriate. We need to be alert to the risks inherent in the heuristics we constantly use if we are to have any chance of avoiding the pitfalls they create.

### Availability heuristic

Are left-handed people sinister or gauche? Are power or wealth aphrodisiacs? And why, do many of us temporarily fear flying after an airline crash?

Your authors are glad that bias against the left-handed is scarce nowadays. But many of us are led by newspaper headlines about unfaithful politicians and celebrities into perceiving that their power and wealth lead to excessive infidelity. Aircraft crashes are dramatic and dreaded – though they are so infrequent that that five times more people die in UK road accidents than in a typical year's global airline accidents.

What is going on here? One of the ways in which we judge probability is to estimate frequency – how often something happens. A common short cut, when we don't have proper frequency data to hand (which is most of the time), is to think how easily we can call examples to mind. Welcome to the availability heuristic.

It often works but this useful tool can mislead, for example when:

- we try to compare the probability of rare but dramatic, dreaded events (such as airline crashes) with tragedies with which we are more familiar (such as car crashes that rarely make the national press); or
- something makes it easy to bring examples to mind, such as advertising or newspaper headlines about celebrity infidelity.

If you have a good reputation, you are readily seen as a trusted, welcome member of society. Contrariwise, a bad reputation works in the opposite sense. A reputation for untrustworthiness and cynical exploitation of customers and society generally led many to regard all banks and bankers as predators or pariahs with little social value.

This effect too is not a matter of strict logic. Few of us rigorously research people and organizations before we decide our attitudes towards them. We use our feelings – something behavioural economists call the affect heuristic.

### Affect and recognition heuristics

We love all things Apple, but should we buy Apple shares?

In rational (System Two) mode, we would analyse factors like Apple's history, profits, assets, debts, business model, competitive advantage and management before making a decision. If we replace that difficult fact-finding and analysis with a simple question: 'Do we like Apple?', answer: 'We *love* Apple', and buy the shares, we are under the influence of the affect heuristic.

Something similar happens when fear is involved. Some of us were brought up surrounded by adorable dogs and even dote on Dobermans. Others were bitten and feel fearful. These feelings drive our behaviour when we meet an unknown dog – leading us to approach or avoid it.[8]

Recognition itself matters too. There is evidence that when we recognize one of a number of choices but have no better information, we are likely to put a lower value on the option we do not recognize. This heuristic can produce a sensible result (think of the old adage 'better the devil you know') but it is particularly unreliable when recognition is increased by advertising and the like – or our own PR.

## The value of a good reputation

Bankers lost their reputation for rectitude and responsibility, and with it their societal licence to operate. The result is heavy regulation and widespread backing for regulators to mete out heavy fines – reinforced by regulators' own licence to operate, which has led some to feel that society expects them to impose heavy punishments. Banks' lost reputation has also made it far easier for 'claims farmers' to demonize them and profit from large portfolios of aggrieved bank customers.

John Cridland, interviewed by the *Financial Times* just before his retirement as Director General of the Confederation of British Industry, clearly thought that the demonization of banks had indirectly damaged trust in business as a whole. He felt that the Volkswagen (VW) diesel emissions crisis, which had erupted shortly before his interview, only made things worse and that the loss of trust would take decades to fix.[9]

When we first reflected on the subject, we readily concluded that a good reputation was likely to be a well-respected organization's most valuable asset.

Figure 2.1, showing the share price of VW, whose sorry tale is one of our case studies, is typical of what happens to the share price of a respected quoted company hit by a reputational crisis. Companies regularly lose 30 to 40 per cent of their share price when their reputation is badly damaged, so we take 30 to 40 per cent of market capital as a first estimate of the financial value of a well-regarded company's reputation. This agrees broadly with estimates emerging from those who specialize in valuing reputations from a more quantitative perspective. So, for example, a 2015 report from Reputation Dividend suggested that 27 per cent of the stock market value of the participants in the UK's FTSE 350 Index consisted of the value of their reputations.[10]

**Figure 2.1** VW share price normalized to 100 on 16 September 2015

A good reputation is also an important non-financial attribute of an organization whatever the sector. It underpins its licence to operate because having stakeholders who trust you and allow you a social licence to operate are a benefit just as being untrusted is a disadvantage. You can think of the associated goodwill as reputational capital even though, if home grown, it is not in your balance sheet. All organizations should consider how changes in stakeholder attitudes would affect stakeholder relationships.

For organizations that depend on public support, such as regulators and branches of government, the attitudes of governments and voters, are critical. Similarly charities rely on support from donors. Many reputable or politically influenced donors will shun or denigrate an organization with a damaged reputation. There is also a growing trend for reputable organizations seeking funding to worry about donations from the tarnished for fear that the association will taint their own reputation.

## Whose reputation is it anyway?

As we mulled the consequences of reputational crises, we increasingly thought it odd that when a quoted company's reputation is damaged, the share price may plummet but the loss does not usually appear in the balance sheet.[11] Nor does the value of a home-grown reputation appear in balance sheets. So we asked a more fundamental question: is 'your' reputation truly yours? Let us revisit our definition:

> Your reputation is the sum total of how your stakeholders perceive you

and three implications:

- Your reputation is not about how you perceive yourself; it is about how your stakeholders perceive you.
- As it is your stakeholders who hold that critical perception, if your stakeholders come to perceive you in another way, your reputation changes.
- You lose your reputation when stakeholders come to believe, rightly or wrongly, that you are not as 'good' as they previously believed you were.

These suggest why the value of an organization's reputation should not appear in its balance sheet. Your reputation is the collective perception of your stakeholders, as to how 'good' you are, taking into account whatever factors affect your stakeholders' views. Your own opinions are irrelevant to your reputation.

In other words, your reputation is a construct – albeit an important one – in the collective minds of your stakeholders. If the consensus is to hold you in high regard, you benefit from their high esteem. This is 'your' good reputation. If you fall in their estimation, they hold you in lower esteem: in plain English you lose 'your' reputation.

The implication is that what we routinely think of as 'our' reputation is not in fact ours in the sense that we own it. Whilst we are undoubtedly the beneficiaries of our stakeholders' warm feelings towards us, 'our' reputation only exists in the minds of our stakeholders, who effectively lend us the benefit of their shared perception.

It follows that if – for good reason or bad – your stakeholders change their collective opinion so that you fall in their estimation, they will impose on you, against your will, a tarnished reputation. You feel the downgrade as reputational damage. Stakeholders' lowered opinion will tend to reduce your freedom of movement in markets, restrict your ability to operate unhindered by interference from society at large and its proxies and affect how your owners (or equivalents) value you. Equally, if you rise in stakeholders' estimation, so your reputation improves, whether their changed view is correct or misguided.

In the next chapter we will turn to how reputations are lost, laying foundations for rethinking reputational risk itself, in Chapter 4.

### Questions to mull

- What is your organization's reputation worth? And its licence to operate?
- What would your organization's future look like if it acquired a poor reputation?
- What is your personal reputation worth to you?
- What would your future look like if, deservedly or not, you lost your reputation for competence, humanity or ethicality?

## Notes

1 http://lexicon.ft.com/Term?term=corporate-reputation accessed 7/6/2016.

2 Oxford University Press (1993) *The New Shorter Oxford English Dictionary*.

3 http://www.bcbc.com/content/1708/EEBv7n2.pdf accessed 7/6/2016.

4 Eaglesham (2015).

5 For more on this see Gigerenzer *et al* (1999).

6 Kahneman (2011).

7 For an alternative approaches, see Kruglanski and Gigerenzer (2011).

8 For more see Loewenstein *et al* (2001).

9 Departing CBI chief: 20 years to restore trust in UK business, *Financial Times* 3/11/2015 http://on.ft.com/1iz4LO0 accessed 7/6/2016.

10 *The 2015 UK Reputation Dividend Report*, Reputation Dividend http://reputationdividend.com/index.php/download_file/view/101/112/ accessed 7/6/2016.

11 An exception may occur when the reputation is in the balance sheet as goodwill acquired with an acquisition.

# How reputations are lost 03

It seems that 'stakeholder' is a term coined at the Stanford Research Institute in 1963 to describe:

> Those groups without whose support the organization would cease to exist.[1]

Milton Friedman, our third Nobel winner, forcefully argued[2] that a corporate executive's main duty was to carry out the wishes of the owners of the business. If owners sought profit maximization, the duty was to strive for it to the maximum extent legally and ethically permitted by society. Anyone arguing for businesses to show a social conscience was, wrote Friedman, 'preaching pure and unadulterated socialism'; and an executive delivering socially beneficial activities was 'spending other people's money'[3] when they ought to be spending their own.

The argument became fashionable but Ed Freeman, an American philosopher and management professor, challenged[4] Friedman's approach, arguing that companies need to pay attention to stakeholders generally, not just shareholders.

Freeman thought that core 'stakeholders' included employees, customers, suppliers, financiers and shareholders, as well as 'society'. But he also recognized that others can support or obstruct the organization, including governments, pressure groups, competitors and unions. He recognized that potential adversaries, as well as friends, are important to the delivery strategy. And he recognized that the perspective, power and relative importance of each stakeholder are components of any good evaluation of strategy. To put it brutally, if a firm fails to pay enough attention to its wider community of stakeholders, it risks putting itself out of business and shredding its shareholders' investment.

## Stakeholders in crises

Freeman's basic principles are sound and his book *Strategic Management: A stakeholder approach*[5] is still in print 30 years later. Our research shows that the relative importance of stakeholders also depends on the context, particularly when it comes to crises. Crises regularly stimulate stakeholder reactions that are extreme and, though not expected from a peacetime mindset, are predictable when looking through the lens of a crisis. So when considering strategy and risk, it is essential to analyse stakeholders' potential attitudes as much, and at least as deeply, in adversity as we do in normal times.

Many large organizations recognize the importance of politicians. They try to curry favour with them, perhaps supporting re-election campaigns and favourite causes. These organizations expect support from those they pay and politicians regularly deliver. But faced with unacceptable revelations in a crisis involving an important corporate funder, politicians have to balance loyalty to those who finance them with the opinions of their own stakeholders, the media and their electorate. It may not take much for a politician to side with electorates and ditch funders. Understanding our stakeholders' stakeholders can be crucial in gauging stakeholder loyalty in adversity.

At the other end of the spectrum, a lonely whistle-blower with a grievance may be a manageable minor irritation in good times, and one who can be contained or sacked and made unemployable. But given the right (or wrong) circumstances, that long-ignored, lone whistle-blower's message can become the spark that turns a pile of seemingly pulpable pronouncements into a furious inferno as their now pertinent, plausible message becomes topical, feeding manna to the media.

One of the phenomena that can help transform what seems, logically, to be a manageable mishap into a serious crisis is social amplification. Research suggests that amplification is likely to be triggered if an event that could affect many creates a sense of fear and arises in circumstances that create moral outrage.[6]

## Confidentiality evaporates in a crisis

Before the arrival of the internet, it was fairly easy to keep the inner workings of an organization private. Loyal employees expected a 'job for life' from equally loyal employers, so they were reluctant to publicize their employer's inner weaknesses; and any who wished to publicize unacceptable practices usually lacked the means to disseminate information widely. This made it a credible crisis strategy to sit tight and wait until the newspapers became bored and it all 'blew over'.

Major crises have long provided an exception. Before the internet became ubiquitous, journalists would descend on local pubs and bars, hoping to collect inside information. Many scoops were based on a journalist's anonymous discussion with a disaffected employee over a drink or three. Even then, the Establishment had many opportunities to protect its own, influencing, if not always controlling, the news agenda.

If the crisis was sufficiently serious, particularly if people were killed, there might be a formal inquiry. Inquiries commissioned by the organization have a limited value in discovering what has gone wrong because the organization sets its terms and selects the inquisitor, often more domesticated cat than lynx. A variety of factors, ranging from lack of skill to strong incentives and outright bias, can prevent such inquiries delivering an impartial root cause analysis into what has gone wrong.

Government-backed inquiries can be more effective. But they are often ponderous and can take years. In the UK such inquiries have been most effective when led by forensically and technically skilled inquisitors with the power to demand answers to seemingly impertinent questions – and to reach conclusions on real root causes without the disincentive of worrying who will give them their next job.

Since the arrival of the internet that landscape has vanished. Journalists no longer need to risk their livers at the local bar. Armed with a laptop, a Twitter feed and access to the blogosphere, they can rapidly discover what people say is going on – often a good story in itself as a crisis begins.

Nowadays information flows freely. With near-universal access to social media, anyone can become a global news outlet. When someone with inside knowledge, topical news or an agenda to push, feels the need, or wish, to share what they know or want to say with the public, they are literally one click away from broadcasting the information. If the conditions are right to trigger social amplification, the crisis may begin to grow on social media.

Whether the information is picked up by journalists is not a matter of chance. Tweets trend and it is easy to direct a message to journalists and broadcasters who, in a crisis, are especially receptive to new information – especially inside information.

## Crises as a public stress-test of leaders

Leaders have to manage crises. Their actions are so instantly visible that a crisis is often a live public stress-test of leaders' competence and values. As events and reactions unfold in real time, the reputations of all involved are constantly re-evaluated.

This exceptional flow of information is why crises provide ideal opportunities for research into how and why reputations are made and lost, and into the rise and fall of organizations and their leaders. It is also why our case studies tell the stories of organizations in crisis.

Each crisis has its own special features. Given that there is no opportunity to know what would have happened in parallel crisis-free universes, we cannot test causation rigorously, and we have to reduce hindsight bias as far as we can. But in our research dissecting to root causes, what we do find is patterns that repeat time and time again. Typically a crisis has multiple root causes, often systemic, that remained unrecognized and unmanaged but gradually accumulated, unnoticed over years, to make the organization vulnerable to crises generally; and, when a trigger materialized, to this one in particular.

## Crisis dynamics

One pattern concerns the dynamics of crises and the way that they lead to a reassessment of reputations.

**Figure 3.1** Crisis dynamics simplified

We have summarized our observation of many crises into a simplified model that provides a framework both for analysing crises and for planning to deal with them (Figure 3.1).

Your organization and its leaders begin with their existing reputation, whatever it is, based on how your stakeholders perceive you, how they feel about you and what they remember of your history. Past public relations campaigns will play a part in this as they will affect what comes to stakeholders' minds and how they feel – the recognition, availability and affect heuristics at work.

Individual stakeholders will have different perceptions, views and recollections. For many, recollections will be vague. Your reputation may be what you deserve or undeservedly good or poor. Stakeholders are neither omniscient nor infallible. 'What you deserve' may be debatable. And we are all influenced by what Phil Rosenzweig calls the 'halo effect'[7]: we over-praise those who are doing well, overlooking their weaknesses whilst heaping ordure on those who are not, emphasising their weaknesses and overlooking their strengths.

## The trigger

Then something happens to make your organization newsworthy and puts your reputation into play. It might be something dramatic – an explosion or scandal directly affecting you. There may be a crisis elsewhere, for example at a competitor, a supplier or even a competitor's supplier. Or it could be a slowly developing issue that has reached a tipping point. Some triggers are naturally newsworthy. Others are less obviously so but gain attention, perhaps through social amplification.

### What is a trigger event?

The trigger event for the 1666 Great Fire of London occurred when a hapless baker forgot to dampen down his bread oven overnight. The bakery fire spread to the rest of the City, densely built using timber and roofed with thatch; and the Mayor delayed demolishing houses to create firebreaks that might have stopped the fire's spread.

Fortunately, those who rebuilt the City eventually avoided jumping to the wrong conclusion about the cause, though not before a demonstrably innocent scapegoat had been hanged. They didn't ban bakers; they addressed the underlying cause and introduced regulations requiring that buildings be made of fire-resistant materials spaced further apart.

## Stakeholders and media engage

The next phase dawns with stakeholders and the media showing heightened interest. It provides ideal conditions for good communication of information that leaders would have preferred to keep private.

Before the arrival of the internet, companies facing a crisis could at least hope to control the flow of information about the incident. Nowadays this is virtually impossible. In a typical case, information starts to flow freely immediately there is a major incident or accident. It takes little internet expertise for an individual to become a news outlet and commentator rolled into one. With the media constantly trawling for information, the internet often provides the first spark of a major story.

## The back story

Before the internet, newspapers kept extensive files on newsworthy organizations and these were reporters' first port of call in a crisis. If the company had 'form', the epithet 'troubled company' was applied before a résumé of its past sins, misdemeanours and other problems. When facts were scarce, this 'back story' provided instant padding.

Nowadays, the history is instantly available on the internet. The Wikipedia entry for many organizations includes a section for embarrassing episodes. For example, the entry for BAE Systems,[8] the UK defence company, currently includes sections on corruption investigations and other criticisms. The entries for Exxonmobil,[9] the oil company, include sections covering their environmental record and 'criticism'. That for BP catalogues a series of environmental issues, health and safety concerns and charges of market manipulation.

Even for those that do not (and at the time of writing, the main Volkswagen Wikipedia entry[10] contains no reference to the 2008 sex, bribery and corruption scandal that led to the conviction of a member of the supervisory board and a former personnel director[11]), information about an organization's past is freely available. Anyone with an internet connection can assemble a plausible history in minutes and a detailed one within an hour or so. It might even be accurate!

That history, brought back to stakeholders' consciousness through interested pressure groups and the media, colours stakeholders' perceptions. At best, an unappealing history merely frames how stakeholders perceive new information as it becomes available. At worst it forms a pattern, in which case critical questions emerge, typically: Has this happened before? Have they learned from experience? If not, why not? And what does this tell us about the organization and its leaders?

As the story develops, insiders may leak unflattering information. Such leaks can carry substantial weight with outsiders. A former employee with a grudge may spread information (or untruths) and may spin it against the organization. Those caught by the wake of the crisis may try to separate themselves from any perceived wrongdoing. The Volkswagen story illustrates this too.

When the scandal of Volkswagen's cheating diesel engine software broke, the initial focus was on Volkswagen. But people soon wondered how many other manufacturers of diesel-powered cars were up to the same tricks.

Whilst VW's share price fell about 30 per cent during the early days of the crisis, Daimler's also fell, by about 15 per cent (Figure 3.2).

When it emerged that Bosch had supplied the software, their share price dropped by 13 per cent; but this recovered when Bosch demonstrated that it had warned Volkswagen not to use the software in production cars.

**Figure 3.2** Share prices of VW, Daimler and Bosch normalized to 16 September 2016

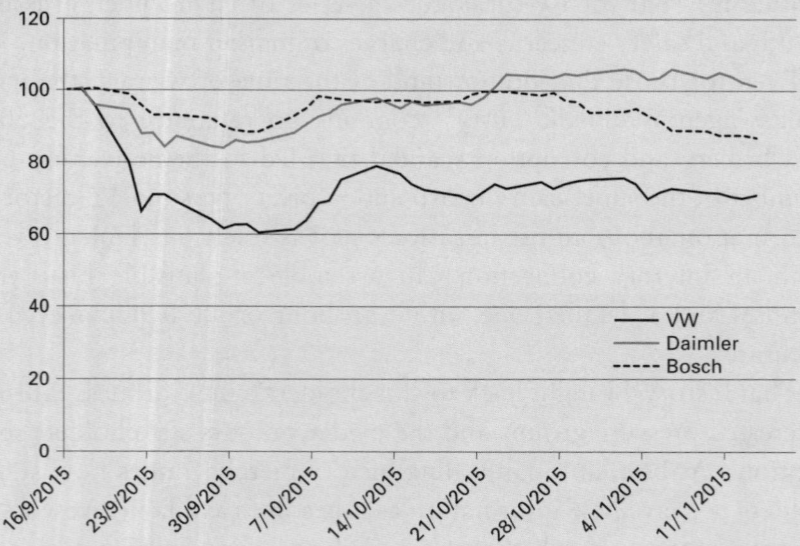

Whether the information is accurate or not, its flow is outside the control of the organization at the centre of the maelstrom. There was once a notion that injunctions and libel laws could help to keep inaccurate or damaging information away from the public eye. That day has passed because once information, right or wrong, is on the internet it is almost impossible to erase it. And the effort involved in attempting to remove it may give the information greater publicity and credibility.

## Leaders are not necessarily trusted

Whilst, with a well-rehearsed crisis plan, it is occasionally possible to get ahead of public perceptions and influence the way they change, the best many organizations can do is to correct errors and provide accurate information. Whether they are believed is, however, another question that depends on whether the organization and its leaders have a reputation for honesty.

Edelman's annual *Trust Barometer* measures the extent to which various groups are trusted. In 2016 they reported that only 49 per cent of respondents regarded a chief executive as a credible spokesman,[12] so a chief executive officer (CEO) trying to rebut a story in a crisis faces an uphill battle. Independent experts carry more weight.

## As stories develop, reputations evolve

As information flows, commentators, amateur and professional, spread their opinions. Their personal reputations and networks determine whether their opinions carry influence. With commentators constantly commenting, the atmosphere can be febrile.

Typically there are two narratives. People want facts. What happened? Who suffered? How badly? How are victims being treated? Are there heroes or villains? This is the first story to emerge, along with the back story about the organizations involved.

But it is the second story that has the larger effect on reputation. Once the immediate impact has been assimilated, four questions come to dominate. Why did it happen? Who is to blame? What lessons need to be learnt? And what does this incident tell us about the organizations involved and their leaders?

A complicating factor is the potential for outrage, one of the triggers for social amplification. According to Professor Art Markman of the University of Texas at Austin:

> Outrage is an emotion that has three components. First, it has negative affect. That is, it is a bad feeling. Second, it has high arousal. That is, it is a strong and powerful emotion. Third, it occurs when people experience a violation of a moral boundary.[13]

This 'moral boundary' typically has to do with a belief or tenet that people will not allow to be violated. That boundary explains why the death of eleven people in the high-profile *Deepwater Horizon* explosion provoked outrage whereas the death of over 600 people[14] every week on US roads passes with barely a comment.

Sometimes those involved in a crisis start to blame each other. This is dangerous unless you are certain of winning. The media adores the ping-pong blame game because it creates self-perpetuating news stories. Blaming others may also be seen as a reflection of leaders' inability to see their own faults. A demonstrable lack of self-awareness and self-criticism readily damages the reputation of both a leader and the organization they lead.

If the story has national interest, politicians will wade in. Those local to the organization may support it; those local to the crisis may attack. If the crisis is sufficiently newsworthy, national politicians may become involved; and, as we have mentioned, politicians' own stakeholders may shift politicians' allegiances.

As the second story develops, stakeholders continuously reassess their perceptions of the organizations involved. And it is those revised perceptions that become the current reputation of the organization.

We are now ready to explore the real nature of reputational risk. That is the subject of the next chapter.

### Questions to mull

- What does your organization have to lose in a crisis?
- How might your financiers (including shareholders) react if your reputation was badly damaged?
- Which of your stakeholders might desert you in a crisis? Why?
- Which of your stakeholders would stick with you through the worst crisis? Why?
- What would an intelligent but sceptical journalist write about the history and track record of your organization and its leaders if a crisis made it relevant?

## Notes

1. According to Freeman and Reed (1983).
2. Friedman (1970).
3. Steve Dunning (2013) The origin of 'the world' s dumbest idea': Milton Friedman, *Forbes* 26 June, http://www.forbes.com/sites/stevedenning/2013/06/26/the-origin-of-the-worlds-dumbest-idea-milton-friedman/ accessed 20/4/2016.
4. Freeman (1983).
5. Freeman (1983).
6. For a succinct introduction to this, see Environment Agency (2002).
7. Rozenzweig (2014).
8. https://en.wikipedia.org/wiki/BAE_Systems accessed 15/4/2016.
9. https://en.wikipedia.org/wiki/ExxonMobil accessed 15/4/2016.
10. https://en.wikipedia.org/wiki/Volkswagen accessed 15/4/2016.
11. VW sex and bribery scandal: Sentences handed down in corruption affair, *Spiegel* http://www.spiegel.de/international/business/vw-sex-and-bribery-scandal-sentences-handed-down-in-corruption-affair-a-537137.html accessed 15/4/2016.
12. Edelman (2015).
13. Markman (2008).
14. 32,717 road deaths in 2013, Wikipedia https://en.wikipedia.org/wiki/List_of_motor_vehicle_deaths_in_U.S._by_year accessed 15/4/2016.

# What is reputational risk? 04

Reputational risk is less well understood than most people believe. Some see it as the ultimate result of the failure of the organization to manage other risks and thus not a risk in its own right. Others see it as a distinct category of risk. This is a deeper issue than it first seems to be and we will begin with the protagonists because their arguments contain important but incomplete truths.

Reputational damage often flows from a failure to manage underlying risks. The problem is that, in the real world, what the protagonists mean by 'other risks' is risks that are identified and being managed. Clothing retailers now know that if they are discovered using child labour to make clothing, they will suffer reputational damage. They put 'child labour in the supply chain' on the risk register. They may also list it as a reputational risk for good measure. Many will put a ban on using child labour into their corporate principles and have an auditable contracting process designed to keep children out of their supply chain.

Similarly, the concept of reputational risk as a risk in its own right is useful even though we agree that reputational risk is in a sense a derivative or composite risk that needs to be broken down into its components. This is because asking the question 'What could cause reputational damage?' can yield exceedingly valuable insights – provided that the question is pursued with sufficient rigour. That said, those who subordinate dealing with underlying risks to protection from reputational damage create a new risk of reputational damage when outsiders learn of that warped priority.

But the real problem with current approaches to reputational risk is that they only scratch at the surface. Reinforced by cognitive biases, this leaves organizations with the dangerous delusion that they have reputational risk under control, when little could be further from the truth.

## Cognitive biases and their consequences

Most of us are brought up to think of ourselves as rational beings, and those who studied classical economics had the notion reinforced by the idea of homo economicus with rational, profit-maximizing tendencies.

We humans have awesome mental processing power but it has limits that are more constraining than we realize. We regularly use all kinds of heuristics and are subject to unconscious biases in directions that are often predictable but unacknowledged. We have world views that are more subjective and idiosyncratic than we realize, yet we use those perspectives to interpret information and make assumptions and decisions. And our self-esteem colours our views about ourselves.

Just as fish are probably unaware of the water in which they live, we are mostly unaware of the heuristics and cognitive biases that constantly affect our decisions. Unless we set out systematically to recognize and neutralize these ingrained drivers, our behaviour will be less rational than we believe. Overcoming them can bring us up against the limits of our processing power.

## How cognitive biases and heuristics lead us astray

Please do not get us wrong. We agree with Gerd Gigerenzer that effective heuristics provide useful mental short cuts. But when we use heuristics and biases in the complex world we now inhabit – and that certainly includes our modern world of work – they can be inappropriate and lead us to make mistakes that are so systematic and surprisingly predictable that Professor Dan Ariely, a behavioural economist, has written a book called *Predictably Irrational*[1] to illustrate how and why.

**Luck and the self-serving bias**

How did you achieve this outstanding success? If you come from an individualistic western culture you are likely to attribute success to your skill.[2] But asked why you produced a disappointing result, the odds are that you will claim that blame bad luck played a part.

Attributing success to skill and failure to bad luck are examples of self-serving biases. Another is the tendency to reject criticism. These help most of us to maintain our self-esteem.

Self-serving bias doesn't just affect 'other people': it affects all who believe themselves successful. It is one reason why successful people are less inclined to investigate the reasons for their own success than why others failed. But by believing their success is largely due to skill, they lose the opportunity to discover both the extent to which their success is underpinned by luck: and how to improve the odds.

## A better definition of reputational risk

In Chapter 2 we observed that:

> You lose your reputation when stakeholders come to believe, rightly or wrongly, that you are not as 'good' as they previously believed you were.

A simple definition of reputational risk would therefore be:

> The risk that your stakeholders come to believe that you are not as good as they thought you were.

Whilst straightforward, this does not explain what 'good' means. Our research, some of which we share in Part Two, will give you a broader feel for what 'good' means in practice; but the most important aspects of 'good' are about what you achieve, how you achieve it and at what cost. So we prefer to refine this simple definition:

> Reputational risk is the risk of failure to fulfil the expectations of your stakeholders in terms of performance and behaviour.

Many risks from failure to 'perform' are captured by enterprise risk management, but few risks from individual or organizational behaviour are captured by classical risk analysis. This field includes risks from weaknesses in ethos, culture, trustworthiness, humanity, skill, experience and competence as well as from the organization's coherence, complexity or dysfunctionality and from its relations with stakeholders such as staff, suppliers and subcontractors. When it comes to individuals, particularly leaders, weaknesses as to character, integrity and motivation matter. Perceptions of history also play an important part.

## Follow those root causes

Our definition takes account of stakeholder unreasonableness; and many have double standards of which we are only dimly aware.

Many people want inexpensive food and clothing but do not think about the implications of retailers' low prices. Many expect some degree of retailer ethicality and if enough stakeholders feel that sources of supply do not meet expectations of ethicality, the disparity can damage the retailer's reputation.

Issues of this kind have layers of complexity that are rarely explored with the public or their proxies, the media. So to follow through the child labour example, the retailer faces reputational risk from issues such as:

- using child labour at all;
- paying exploitative rates of pay;
- depriving children of education.

But let us look through those immediate causes to deeper causes. The use of child labour may be the result of:

- strategy ('buy as cheaply as we can');
- ethos ('source cheaply – we won't ask questions');
- incentives (including executive bonus schemes that do not put ethicality ahead of profit margin);
- leaders who do not think about ethicality at all.

These causes may have yet deeper origins, such as:

- inadequate leadership education;
- recruitment or promotion practices that favour undesirable aspects of character;
- external stakeholders such as investment managers with strong short-term incentives.

Understanding the deepest causes, including why undesirable choices are made, and dealing with them will not just prevent a recurrence of the same problem – the unacceptable use of child labour. It will also prevent new problems with similar root causes, especially if you improve choice architecture by reducing the attractiveness of undesirable choices. Thus if you find and tackle a root cause – such as an unrecognized incentive that puts profit above ethicality – you will help prevent not only known consequences of those root causes – such as bribery, mis-selling and installing cheating emissions software – but also other consequences you have not even thought of.

## Latent weaknesses incubate slowly

The 'root cause' route approach to analysing accidents is relatively recent. An early investigator was Barry Turner. A chemical engineer turned academic sociologist, he immersed himself in studying large-scale accidents and disasters, and a result was his book *Man-Made Disasters*.[3]

Turner analysed over 80 accidents and disasters between 1965 and 1975, including mining disasters, railway accidents and collapsing bridges. Two were pivotal. The Summerland fire, in which 50 revellers were killed as they enjoyed an evening in a night club, led to changes in how buildings were constructed in the UK.[4] And the 1966 Aberfan disaster, which killed 116 children and 28 adults when a colliery spoil heap slid downhill and flattened the nearby primary school, changed the attitude of the UK's National Coal Board, now long defunct, to safety.

Turner showed that most accidents incubate slowly. Our research, which we shall describe in Chapter 13, suggests that most major accidents incubate for more than three years, with more than 25 per cent taking longer than eight years to emerge.

Analysing these long incubations, Turner found steady accumulations of tell-tale events that were not acted upon. Some were overlooked or misunderstood for reasons ranging from wrong assumptions to a failure to understand the complexity of the system. Others were ignored because people refused to accept just how bad the consequences could have been if the mishap had not been a 'near miss'.

Turner also saw cases where the key information was known in the organization but not to the right person. He highlighted the importance of organizational learning, encouraging contrarian ideas, learning from mistakes and avoiding groupthink if accidents are to be reduced. His were early descriptions of what are now called behavioural and organizational risks. One is groupthink.

## Groupthink

In his early study of groupthink, Irving Jannis analysed a series of US governmental level decisions with outcomes ranging from success through near-miss to fiasco. He developed the theory that fiascos had their roots in failed group decision-making and a phenomenon he named 'groupthink'.[5]

He thought teams are most vulnerable to groupthink when a cohesive group strives for consensus or unanimity and, as a result, loses its ability to think rationally about alternatives. Self-censorship of dissenting views may occur. He thought groups particularly vulnerable when:

- they lack sufficient diversity of thought and perspectives;
- there is a leader who is not impartial or is power-seeking; and
- they are working under stress or time pressure.

He suggested that groupthink can be reduced by:

- explicitly acknowledging the risk of groupthink;
- avoiding characterizing dissenters and opponents as 'the enemy';
- using a 'devil's advocate' systematically to put contrary views – though it is important the 'devil's advocate' is neither alienated nor domesticated.

## Turner's innovative equation

Turner also concluded that for a disaster to happen, errors have to be combined with the potential for large consequences. Having investigated mostly physical accidents where the release of energy is a factor that determines the scale of events, he proposed the general principle:

Disaster = energy + misinformation.[6]

This is an interesting equation. It needs re-working outside the world of physical disasters; but it hints at an important truth about power and influence. The consequences of an error depend partly on the influence of the person making it. Leaders' mistakes can often cause much more damage than a similar error made by a junior person because they can affect the system. We shall return to this in Chapter 14.

## Lessons from Three Mile Island

The Three Mile Island nuclear power station accident happened on 28 March 1979, a year after Turner's book was published. Following a series of mishaps, one of the nuclear reactors lost the supply of cooling water to its hot radioactive reactor core. As the core began to overheat, operators had difficulty in understanding exactly what was going wrong. This was mainly because the reactor control system and its instrumentation were complex and internally interlinked in ways that they did not fully understand.

The reactor had a partial meltdown, making it the world's first famous civilian nuclear reactor accident. Escaped radiation was estimated to cause barely a single additional cancer death in the surrounding population. But the collateral damage to the reputation of nuclear power, socially amplified by dread of radioactivity, was enough to stop its growth in the USA.

President Carter set up a commission to investigate the accident, and Charles Perrow, a sociologist, was asked to write an organizational analysis of the disaster for the commission. His paper grew into *Normal Accidents*,[7] our second milestone.

Perrow argued that wherever there are complex systems, such as in aircraft, nuclear power stations, nuclear missile systems and bacteriological laboratories, people are generally vigilant as to recognized risks and consequences. However, people find it much harder to predict how failures may interact, let alone what failures may evade the risk management system.

## Complex systems fail in complex ways

Perrow's core thesis was that complex systems are likely both to fail and to do so in complex – and unexpected – ways. After failure, this complexity may make the aftermath hard to predict. Complexity is thus a risk that both causes incidents and makes their consequences harder to manage.

This is particularly so where the system is what engineers and sociologists call 'closely coupled'. If you connect your garden hose to a tap at one end and fit a spray head to the other end, you have set up system that is linear and loosely coupled. Turn on the tap and water flows to fill the hose. When water reaches the end, it emerges from the nozzle. The nozzle and the water pressure dictate how much water flows from the nozzle. If a two-year-old holding it gets out of control, there is a simple, infallible solution: turn off the tap.

Contrast a school. The head teacher leads the school and appoints teachers who teach the children.

Teachers may like or loathe the head and they will react accordingly. Children may criticise a teacher and complain to their parents. Parental attitudes to the head and particular teachers will affect their attitude to the school, how they react to their children's complaints and the extent to which they support teachers. Parents may complain to the authorities. If enough complain, the head may feel threatened; the school may be closed, with consequences for other schools in the area. And that is before we get to the interactions of government and school regulators, not forgetting that these answer to politicians who in turn answer, every few years, to electorates.

This is a complex system with multiple feedback loops. Whether the school is stable, succeeds or fails depends on how those involved respond to feedback from within and without.

Any large organization will be complex, but we are surrounded by unseen systems that are as invisible to most insiders as water is to fish. It is also worth mulling the extent to which leaders are aware of the interlocking complexity of the developed world's systems for delivering energy, water, food, finance and communications, not to mention international treaties facilitating trade.

### 'Insiders' and 'outsiders'

As organizations grow, so do teams. A good team can achieve more than its participants could on their own. Well run, they foster shared goals and cooperation, sharing team experience.

Groups may form based on function, hierarchy, location, background and much else. The work of Robin Dunbar,[8] an evolutionary psychologist and anthropologist, suggests that as human group size extends beyond about 150, if not well before, groups tend to divide. As groups grow and multiply, so do group identities and purposes.

Those in one group readily come to see those in another as outsiders, even rivals. Cooperation can become more difficult as interests diverge or conflict. Communication and cooperation between groups rapidly becomes unpredictable. And predicting the dynamics of interactions between groups, particularly under stress, becomes increasingly difficult.

## 'Normal' accidents

Larger organizations contain more, often overlapping, groups. Each has its own identity and purposes; and with scale comes increasing complexity. This does not just make large systems prone to accidents. When something goes wrong in a complex, tightly coupled system, the consequences are harder to predict and therefore more difficult to manage. Perrow concluded that we should expect complex systems to fail. He considered the risk of failure of complex systems was so high that we should categorize accidents in such systems as 'normal', as opposed to unexpected, accidents.

Those who lead, or regulate, such organizations and markets should therefore expect system failures as a part of their normality. This insight should motivate leaders to make considerable efforts to find and understand the unrecognized latent systemic vulnerabilities over which they preside and deal with them before they cause harm.

Before 2007 the financial sector was widely seen as a beacon of success, earning large amounts of money and generating substantial tax revenues for governments. Few questioned the extent to which the apparent success of this huge, closely coupled system was real or due to luck. So it is no surprise that politicians and regulators globally failed to foresee the crash of 2007/8 let alone to be ahead of events as they unfolded. Whilst a few leaders did see the impending disaster, even profiting from it, most did not and were shocked that such a catastrophe could engulf their industry, let alone their firm or country.

Airline accidents used to be worryingly normal. Anthony's father was an early aeronautical engineer who spent the Second World War 'repairing bent Spitfires'. He did not have a nervous disposition. Nonetheless, Anthony vividly remembers when, in the early 1960s, his father told him where to find his parents' wills. The reason: they had to fly together on the same aircraft following a family bereavement. Flying was seen as high risk.

How things have changed. Flying on modern aircraft is arguably a much lower risk than driving. Two factors make that a surprise to many people. First, some believe that flying is still dangerous. That is partly due to the availability heuristic. Air crashes are dramatic and always make the headlines, so most of us can easily recall a recent air crash. If we fear flying, that fear can be reinforced.

Reality is different. Comparing fatality rates across modes of transport is not straightforward, but in the US passengers travel about 7 trillion km per year[9] and about 32,000 were killed on US roads in 2013.[10] Globally, air passengers travel about 4 trillion km per year.[11] Global deaths on Western-built commercial jets for 2010 to 2014 from aircraft-related causes (so excluding terrorism, military action and the like) averaged less than 300 per year.[12] That makes about 4,600 US road deaths per trillion person miles every year, compared with about 75 deaths per trillion passenger miles for commercial jets.

# Overconfidence and optimism

The second factor is System One's overconfidence bias, which leads us to believe that we are better than other people, and optimism.

## Overconfidence bias

When experimenters ask random selections of drivers how they rate their driving, it is common to find a substantial majority rating their driving as 'above average'.[13] A US survey[14] asked new entrepreneurs the probability that a business like theirs would succeed. Their answer: about 60 per cent. When asked about their own business the percentage rose to about 80 per cent. Yet the cold statistics show that only about 35 per cent of new businesses survive even five years.

Overconfidence bias doesn't just affect drivers and entrepreneurs. It applies at the highest corporate level in the C-Suite, too. Daniel Kahneman tells how, over years, Duke University collected over 11,000 chief financial offer (CFO) predictions as to how the Standard & Poor index would perform over the next year. It is no surprise that, just like the rest of us, the CFOs had absolutely no idea where the index would go.

What was alarming was their overconfidence. Participants were asked to give the upper and lower levels that they were 90 per cent confident would not be breached by the market. If CFOs got this right, 20 per cent of their predictions would be outside this range. In fact, 60 per cent were outside their range. Kahneman described the cohort as 'grossly overconfident'. And CFOs who were more overconfident about the S&P were also overconfident about their own firm's future performance.[15]

## Optimistic bias

Optimists don't just enjoy life: many make good company, they feel happy to take risks because they believe they can bounce back from adversity. Success breeds admiration and reinforces the effect.

But whilst optimists are nice to know, their optimism can make them risky companions or colleagues. Optimists may have unrealistic expectations that good things will happen to them; and we all tend to delude ourselves that bad things are less likely to happen than a realist would consider.

Taken with self-serving bias and overconfidence bias, this helps us to understand why leaders, particularly those enjoying success, can be blind to important risks that others can see.

## The role of human error

James Reason, a professor of psychology at Manchester University, took the analysis of errors to new levels. The central thesis of his book *Human Error*[16] is that the valuable human ability to use simplification and approximation to solve complex problems at speed comes with distinct disadvantages:

- Fast mental processing makes errors inevitable.
- We hold vast amounts of knowledge in our mental database. Since we organize our knowledge around mental models such as theories, we risk skewing our thinking to fit theories that may not be applicable – leading to the risk of confirmation bias.
- The way our mental retrieval system works may lead us to give too much weight to patterns from the past when we shape our expectations for the future.

### Confirmation bias

How do we decide what to believe? The answer is surprising but intriguing.

Our fast, unconscious and frugal System One is programmed to try to make sense of what it learns and believe it if it can. Given time and energy, System Two will test System One's answer. System Two tests mainly by searching for evidence that confirms what System One believes. So when we are analysing a problem and have a hunch, System Two's natural tendency is to scour the available material to back up the hunch. Because it is not effortless, most of us are not consistently sceptical.[17]

Scientists are trained to adopt the opposite approach: to look for evidence to disprove a hypothesis. This is much harder and needs much more energy and time for contemplation.

This why we are inclined to believe what is asserted confidently and we tend to seek evidence to back initial hunches and conclusions, not to disprove them. It is also one reason why we make worse decisions if we are tired or distracted; and why even well-trained scientists are more vulnerable to believing what they see on the television after a long, hard day.

## The problem of systemic weakness

James Reason extended his thinking from the individual to complex organizations. He considered that for what he called 'technological organizations' humans were still able to make individual mistakes that were the direct cause of an accident.

But he thought that a proper investigation – what we call a root cause investigation – would reveal latent systemic weaknesses in the organization. He likened these to bacteria and viruses in humans – omnipresent, capable of being benign for years but equally capable of flaring up to kill. He regarded these latent conditions as 'present in all systems' and 'an inevitable part of organizational life'.[18]

Our own research has concluded that a large majority of crises we have studied involved latent conditions that incubated over periods stretching from years to decades, before emerging, often to catastrophic consequences including a damaged or destroyed reputation. We shall discuss this further in Chapter 13.

## Enter the Swiss cheese model

In an organization that manages risk, errors are resisted by multiple layers of defensive measures. If these were perfect, there could be no accidents. One of Reason's better-known insights is that all real-life defensive measures have weaknesses, particularly when pitted against human frailty and ingenuity. The challenge is to find unidentified weaknesses before they cause harm. Reason devised his 'Swiss Cheese' model to illustrate the point.

Emmental is a Swiss cheese riddled with large holes: every slice contains holes. If we think of each layer as a defensive measure and put the slices together, we may find that none of the holes align in which case the 'defences' work. But if some of the holes align, then we have a weakness through which an accident can happen. Figure 4.1 illustrates this.

**Figure 4.1** The Swiss cheese model (after Reason, 1990). Multiple layers of leaky defences can make an impervious whole

▲ Four defences with faults presented as slices with holes

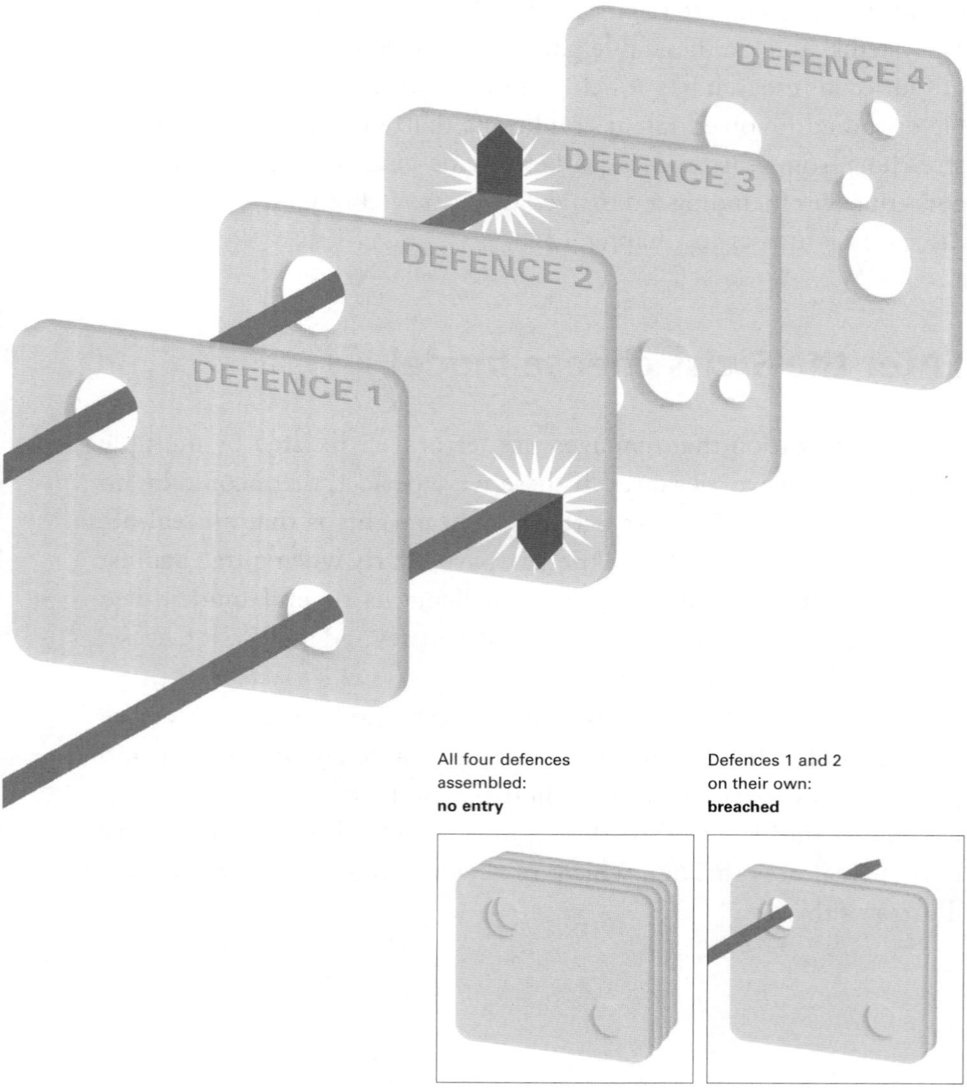

However our research has led us to realize that there is a more fundamental problem. Classical risk management is good – even very good – at managing the risks it manages, and for those risks there will be multiple defences. But classical risk management has a systemic weakness. That is the subject of our next chapter.

### Questions to mull

- How would you investigate the relative importance of skill and luck in your organization's greatest current success?
- What 'normal accidents' should your organization expect?
- Try estimating the number of groups with their own identity in your organization. Then divide your organization's total headcount by 100. How do these numbers compare?
- What barriers to communication are there between groups to which you belong and those immediately above, below and alongside you?

## Notes

1. Ariely (2008).
2. Hooghiemstra (2008).
3. Turner (1997).
4. https://en.wikipedia.org/wiki/Summerland_disaster accessed 26/8/2016.
5. Though widely accepted the concept is not without academic controversy. See J Rose (2011) Diverse perspectives on the groupthink theory: A literary review, *Emerging Leadership Journeys*, **4** (1), pp 37–57 http://www.regent.edu/acad/global/publications/elj/vol4iss1/Rose_V4I1_pp37-57.pdf accessed 26/8/2016.
6. Turner (1997), p 157.
7. Perrow (1984).
8. See Dunbar *et al* (2005) Chapter 7 for an introduction.
9. US NHTS (2012) Travel profile of the United States 2009, http://nhts.ornl.gov/2009/pub/profile_2012.pdf accessed 26/8/2016.

10 https://en.wikipedia.org/wiki/List_of_motor_vehicle_deaths_in_U.S._by_year accessed 26/8/2016.

11 IATA (2015) Air passenger market analysis 2015, http://www.iata.org/whatwedo/Documents/economics/passenger-analysis-dec-2015.pdf accessed 26/8/2016.

12 Boeing (2014).

13 Svenson (1981).

14 Cooper *et al* (1988).

15 Kahneman (2011), p 261 et seq.

16 Reason (1990).

17 Kahneman (2011), Chapter 7.

18 Reason (1990), pp 10–11.

# 05 The hole in classical risk management

Risk management isn't new. It's been an evolutionary force beyond human memory. Communities of marmots learn it from experience when a sibling becomes an eagle's lunch and warn each other of possible predators as they roam steep alpine slopes. They don't call it risk management, but they have a simple risk management heuristic: if it looks like an eagle's shadow, warn everyone and run for cover.

Humans have long been wise to identifying risks, assessing their likelihood and potential impact before accepting them or trying to avoid or mitigate them. The Egyptians developed fire brigades, Augustus added fire watchmen and the Phoenicians invented what we now call insurance.

For centuries, much of the expertise in managing risks was found in military and religious institutions keen to maintain their dominance, but the modern discipline of risk management took off after the Second World War. When soldiers returned to civilian life, they began to apply military risk management ideas to business life. Civilian risk management took root in the United States before moving to Europe and beyond.

High-risk industries, such as chemicals, pharmaceuticals, oil and gas, were early adopters often learning from the aftermath of the biggest disasters but risk management gradually spread to other industries. A major stimulus was the increase in insurance premiums in the mid-1970s, which drove companies to give more attention to risk mitigation.

Risk management became more sophisticated in the 1990s and began to focus more on corporate, especially financial, risks. Companies began to make more use of techniques such as hedging, business continuity and crisis management. A recurring frustration was coordination – or rather the lack of it. Most companies had a hotchpotch of plans and analyses, some overlapping and some conflicting. More seriously, some identified risks were ignored because they were nobody's specific responsibility.

Enterprise risk management (ERM) was an attempt to address this patchwork. From the early Noughties, some companies adopted a more comprehensive enterprise-wide approach, encouraged by stricter codes of corporate governance and a perception of an increasingly risky environment.

Risk management has not yet taken the further evolutionary step, of incorporating behavioural and organizational risks. For reasons that we will explain in Chapter 14, it will not do so until boards, and particularly chief executives and chairmen, demand that their talented risk teams tackle these unfamiliar risk areas and give them the necessary status and authority to do so.

## Where 'three lines of defence' fails

The 'three lines of defence' risk management model sounds robust, but it contains a systemic weakness that is not yet widely recognized.

Despite its name, 'Three lines of defence' usually has four layers:

- Line managers deal with risks as they take them.
- Centralized teams monitor and report on risk to the CEO's team and the board.
- Internal auditors bring an independent view.
- The whole system is overseen by non-executive directors, typically the audit or risk committee.

The UK Parliamentary Commission on Banking Standards, set up to investigate the 2007/8 banking crisis, severely criticized the 'three lines of defence' model for promoting a 'wholly misplaced sense of security',[1] blurring responsibility, diluting accountability and leaving risk, compliance and internal audit staff with insufficient status to do their job properly. They thought much of the system had become a box-ticking exercise.

The Parliamentary Commission correctly identified a failure in implementation of the model, but it has two deeper, more dangerous flaws. It takes no account of the risks from perfectly normal human behaviour that investigators regularly find at the root cause of major accidents; and it fails to recognize the 'risk glass ceiling', an effect that gives rise to 'unknown knowns': things that are known in the organization but unknown to its leaders.

## Normal human behaviour

John Stuart Mill proposed the idea that man is capable of judging the comparative efficacy of means for obtaining wealth.[2] This developed into the idea that we could expect the butcher, brewer and baker to make available the food for our dinner not as a result of their benevolence but 'from their regard to their own interest'.[3] This developed into the concept of homo economicus, shorthand for the idea that humans rationally seek out the best for themselves.

For decades, most economists and business schools seem to have operated as though *homo economicus* represents real people and not an assumption or approximation. The truth, as we all know, is that we humans are not always strictly rational. Beyond widely recognized human behaviours such as love and altruism, we regularly use heuristics to make decisions at speed, and we have a variety of biases that influence even our more rational 'System Two' thinking, assuming we actually use it.

As any psychology student learns, all of us make errors that are predictable. This departure from strict rationality is no abnormality: quite the reverse, it is a crucial part of being a properly functioning human. Yet it is only in recent years that business schools have even begun to teach this area of knowledge, with the result that many, perhaps most, current business leaders and their boards lack systematic education in this area.

Most of us can 'do' logic and strictly rational thinking when we need to. But we also have characters, emotions and principles and intuitively use heuristics and biases to make life practicable.

Confronted by an aromatic array of freshly baked bread, do you carry out a comparative analysis of the nutritional content of each type of bread, a blind taste test, and a survey of other bakers to ascertain local prices (taking into account the transport and time costs) and whether they have other breads on offer that, acting rationally, we ought to consider? That would use time and energy that we refuse to allocate; choosing selection criteria would be a can of worms; and in any case, the bread we most crave would have gone by the time we had barely begun the research.

Enter heuristics and biases. We follow our eyes, our noses and our predilections rapidly to choose what we feel is the best choice: today a crisp baguette; tomorrow a seedy sourdough loaf – and if you have a sweet tooth you might treat yourself to the sugary, jam-filled deep-fried doughnut that you know your ought to resist!

Emotions, heuristics and biases affect our decisions and this is normal, healthy, sane behaviour, not a symptom of abnormality. We all do it, at home and at work. Intelligence doesn't come into it. As our colleague and behavioural economics mentor Professor Peter Ayton wittily put it,

> *Birds do it*
> *Bees do it*
> *Even educated PhDs do it*
> *Why not violate the normative rules of rationality?* [4]

These basic features of human behaviour are ubiquitous, but they have not yet found their way into the lexicon of risk outside a few sectors. Heuristics and biases lie at the roots of many behavioural and organizational risks. And when these and other deep-seated, but unrecognized, systemic risks emerge, after what is usually a long period of incubation, they regularly lead to reputational damage. Insiders are shocked by events. Leaders wonder why neither they nor their risk managers saw it coming. In contrast, outsiders cannot believe that insiders were so incompetent as to allow latent vulnerabilities to languish, unrecognized and un-remedied, for so long.

## The hole in classical risk management

The public is quick to recognize failings and downgrade their collective assessment of the organization concerned. But the root cause risks involved are not only neglected in superficial investigations: they are equally outside the scope of classical risk management. The opportunity to find them before they cause what can be severe harm is therefore lost.

We discovered this hole in risk management when, in 2010, we participated in a research project at the Cass Business School in London for Airmic, the London-based association for those responsible for risk and insurance. The aim was to investigate the origins and impact of major corporate crises.

Four of us, Professor Chris Parsons, Professor Alan Punter and your authors, studied a score of substantial crises on which a large amount of relatively reliable information was available in the public domain. The seemingly disparate crises chosen ranged from fires and explosions, through product and supply chain crises to fraud and information technology (IT) failures. They involved large, well-known and generally respected organizations. The team estimated that the combined pre-crisis assets of the companies involved totalled over US$6 trillion. We had little real idea of the causes of the crises and set out to discover the extent to which they shared common features and the extent to which insurance helped.

Consequences went far beyond the main event:

- In 11 cases, the chairman and/or chief executive lost their job.
- Shareholder value was destroyed on a prodigious scale. Seven companies faced bankruptcy, though two were bailed out by governments. Luckier shareholders merely suffered a large drop in the value of their shareholdings and lost most or all their expected dividend income for a number of years. Others lost everything.
- Survivors generally suffered severe reputational, financial and operational damage, with insurance playing a limited role.

The report emerged as *Roads to Ruin*,[5] the Cass Business School report for Airmic. It showed how, despite the disparity of industries and the different types of crisis, they shared a spectrum of underlying vulnerabilities.

These vulnerabilities did not just make the organizations concerned especially vulnerable to crises. They also made it more likely that a crisis would escalate into a reputational disaster. Almost all these vulnerabilities related to the way organizations and their systems were structured and the way people behaved, both individually and collectively. We now call these risks 'behavioural' and 'organizational' risks.

Derek and Anthony went on to extend the research to over 40 failures. We wanted to discover the extent to which the activities of boards – executives and non-executives – were causes of the failures. Reputability's report *Deconstructing Failure: Insights for boards*[6] concluded that boards were heavily implicated in the root causes of every crisis we studied, On average, four of the seven risk factors we analysed were present in each failure. We explain the details and implications in Chapter 14.

Regulators began to recognize this in 2002 when a study of insurance failures by European insurance regulators concluded that 'management problems appear to be the root cause of every failure or near failure, so more focus on underlying internal causes is needed'.[7] This and the huge experience of financial sector failures led Andrew Bailey, now head of the UK Financial Conduct Authority, then Chief Executive of the Prudential Regulation Authority, to observe:

> *My assessment of recent history is that there has not been a case of a major prudential or conduct failing in a firm which did not have among its root causes a failure of culture as manifested in governance, remuneration, risk management or tone from the top. Culture has thus laid the ground for bad outcomes, for instance where management are so convinced of their rightness that they hurtle for the cliff without questioning the direction of travel. We talk often about [financial risks and] conduct risk in its several forms. You can add to that, hubris risk, the risk of blinding over-confidence. If I may say so, it is a risk that can be magnified by broader social attitudes. Ten years ago there was considerable reverence towards, and little questioning of, the ability of banks and bankers to make money or of whether boards demonstrated a sufficient diversity of view and outlook to sustain challenge. How things have changed. Healthy scepticism channelled into intelligent and forceful questioning of the self-confident can be a good thing.*[8]
>
> Andrew Bailey
> © Bank of England, 2016

For now, the point is simple: there is no widely available process that sets out to find risks of these kinds at board – or any other – level.

## The 'Swiss cheese' model has a hole!

Every organization is run and led by humans. A system of risk management that does not provide defences against risks from commonplace human behaviour and from the way that organizations are organized has a major flaw.

This is not a hole of the type described by Reason's 'Swiss cheese' model. It is a systemic lacuna that is better represented as a hole drilled from one side of the block of cheese to the other (Figure 5.1).

**Figure 5.1** The Swiss cheese model meets a systemic flaw

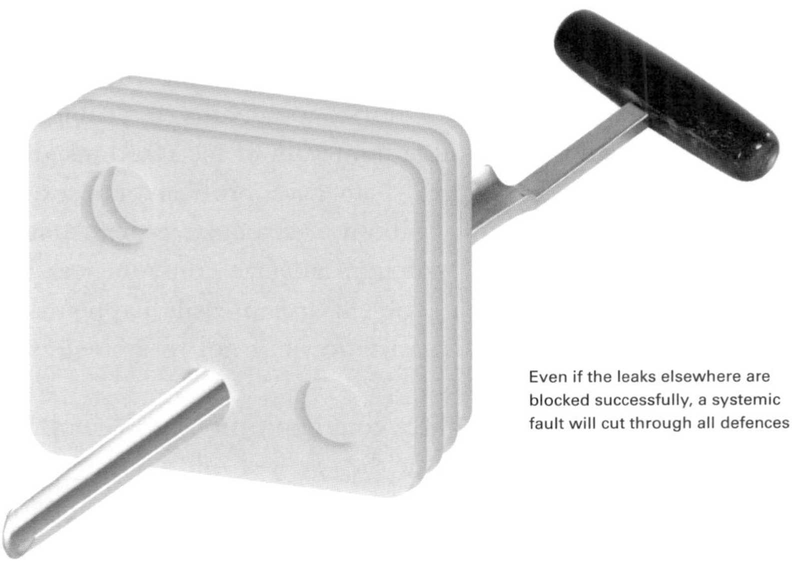

Even if the leaks elsewhere are blocked successfully, a systemic fault will cut through all defences

## Boards in the dark: unknown knowns and the risk glass ceiling

We have frequently seen crisis-struck boards devastated to discover that 'such a thing' could happen in their organization, let alone on their watch. Before the crisis incontrovertibly proved them wrong, they believed that 'disaster could not happen here' because 'we are not like that'. Leaders are doubly concerned when they learn that people below them – and sometimes outsiders – could see that the disaster, or something like it, was waiting to happen.

Donald Rumsfeld was unfairly ridiculed for explaining unknown unknowns. 'There are things we know that we know. There are known unknowns. That is to say there are things that we now know we don't know. But there are also unknown unknowns. There are things we don't know we don't know.'[9] Insurers have used this terminology for decades but neither they nor Rumsfeld had thought about the fourth permutation. Some things are known within organizations but unknown to its leaders. We call these 'Unknown knowns'.

We highlight three varieties. First, to identify a problem, you need to assemble, in one mind, a minimum of facts and insight that makes it possible to recognize them as a problem. For example, an individual needs to know of both a particular practice (such as a procedural short-cut) and potential adverse consequences before the practice is identified as a problem. It can easily happen that all elements are known in the organization but not to a single person able to recognize the problem.

At first blush this sounds like a communication problem. But that is too superficial. We must pursue the two-year-old's question: why?

The answers can be revealing. For example, information may not be communicated upwards because a subordinate does not regard the information as important, for a reason such as ignorance, complacency or an inability to see longstanding normality as potentially dangerous. A superior may have been told but was distracted, a poor listener, habituated to the state of affairs or insufficiently experienced to see its implications.

The effect can also result from distortion of information as it passes up the corporate hierarchy, rather as in the game known as 'Chinese whispers' in the United Kingdom or 'telephone' in the United States. As information passes upwards, each recipient receives it, reinterprets it from their perspective and passes it on. The more hierarchical and complex the organization, the more layers – and with each comes another opportunity for reinterpretation. The recipient may struggle to fit the information in to their own mental model of events around them. There may be recipients who find the incoming message unpalatable for some reason. They may misinterpret or massage it before passing it on. The end result is that leaders do not receive what the originator sent.

### Mental models

We summarize the way we believe things work into mental models and use them to make predictions and simulations.

Some think thermostats control the amount of time that the heating is turned on; some that they control the amount of heat that is produced; and others that they turn the heat source on and off depending on the temperature. These are mental models of a thermostat, though only the last is accurate.

Another possibility is that the subordinate believes their superior does not wish to know of the problem. For example, there may be a culture in which leaders give the impression that targets should be achieved by whatever means necessary – but they don't want to know about short cuts taken. There may be a culture where leaders only want to hear good news. Subordinates may expect that their leaders will not listen or will react badly to unwelcome news, whether denial, contradiction, not listening, or reprisals ranging from social exclusion to blocked promotion or worse. So the subordinate does not bother.

This shades into a second variety: the subordinate both knows of the practice and understands its risk implications, but is not willing to share the insight with superiors. Why the silence? They may prefer not to reveal a peer's weakness or misdeeds because loyalty to peers outweighs loyalty to the organization. It may be lack of status. We have been told by individuals that they will not tell those whom they perceive to be 'in power' about a problem they can clearly see, because it is 'beyond their pay grade' or would upset a person with power over them.

A tragic variety of the status problem concerns co-pilots who, whilst realizing that the pilot in command was unwittingly flying their airliner into the ground or a mountain, nonetheless remained unable to assert themselves sufficiently to correct their superior's mistake.

Then there is fear: fear of the anger of a superior who is a bully or reacts badly to unwelcome news; through to the knowledge that the chief executive's bonus depends on a certain pattern of behaviour and that endangering that bonus is a recipe for personal disaster.

We know a former senior internal auditor at a large company who was required to submit all his audit reports to an executive who would decide which could be shown to the board audit committee without embarrassing management.

When the auditor complained to the CEO, he was told, 'That's the way we do things round here.'

So he resigned. It took a year to get another job because he was marked out as a potential whistle-blower and some appeared to fear a risk professional who was prepared to tell the board the unvarnished truth.

Contrast 2016, when two Bank of England leaders delivered papers emphasizing the importance of internal auditors, and risk managers, being effective and independent of management.[10]

Whatever the cause, the result is that those in charge, with the power to act, remain ignorant. Boards are left with a worrying question: we know that good news travels fast. But to what extent can we be confident that unwelcome news will arrive before it is too late?

For risk-aware leaders, this is a double worry. First they know a 'risk glass ceiling' causes risk blindness as to important risks, leaving them unable to deal with them before they cause harm. Second, they know that if such a risk materializes with severe consequences, they will face particularly severe criticism, for presiding over a dysfunctional organization where leaders do not know what is going on. They, as well as their organization, will face serious reputational damage.

**Risk glass ceiling**

A 'risk glass ceiling' is a barrier, often caused by culture, incentives or social norms, that prevents risk information from reaching the top of the organization.

Leaders who are not risk aware represent our third variety: these unfortunates do not even realize that they are in the dark about unknown knowns. At least those who know they may have blind spots can make decisions in that light, including acting to bring unknown knowns into daylight. Warren Buffett tackles this head-on:

> *Somebody is doing something today at Berkshire that you and I would be unhappy about if we knew of it. That's inevitable: We now employ more than 250,000 people and the chances of that number getting through the day without any bad behavior occurring is nil. But we can have a huge effect in minimizing such activities by jumping on anything immediately when there is the slightest odor of impropriety. Your attitude on such matters, expressed by behavior as well as words, will be the most important factor in how the culture of your business develops. Culture, more than rule books, determines how an organization behaves.*
>
> Warren Buffett, 2010, letter to his senior managers[11]
>
> (© Berkshire Hathaway/Warren Buffett: reproduced with permission)

## Unwanted incentives affect risk managers

The reporting structure of risk teams is itself a source of risk because it can cause systemic blind spots in risk areas that are rich causes of reputational damage. Only boards can ensure that such blind spots are eradicated.

Some risk teams report to the finance director. Few people readily accept being told by an equal, let alone a subordinate, that they have vulnerabilities, still less that they are a source of risk. Any risk manager can see the risk in telling a superior that some of their activities should be added to the risk register. This is no theoretical problem. A small error by a junior clerk is likely to have minor consequences. The errors of leaders such as the CEO, CFO or the board can have systemic consequences.

Other risk teams report to the company secretary. Some company secretaries are focused on compliance and procedure; some are risk aware individuals with considerable knowledge of the deeper problems of the organization, including problems from board and leadership personalities and dynamics. Some see themselves as servants of the chief executive; others feel they serve the chair or are fiercely independent-minded individuals who see their duty as serving the long-term interests of their company as opposed to those who currently lead it.

Risk managers reporting to company secretaries at one end of the spectrum may find themselves in the same position as those who report to the finance director. Those who report to the independent-minded variety may find themselves able to function much more effectively.

## Protecting chief risk officers

Following the 2007/08 banking crisis, the UK's Walker Review considered this problem in the context of huge banking risk teams that had failed to recognize the seeds of their banks' destruction. Sir David Walker recommended that the board of a bank or other financial institution should be supported by a chief risk officer (CRO) with authority to 'participate in the risk management and oversight process at the highest level on an enterprise-wide basis and have a status of total independence from individual business units'.[12]

He recommended that in addition to internal reporting lines to the chief executive or finance director, the CRO should report directly to the board risk committee and have unfettered direct access to the chair of the committee. To buttress the position of the CRO, Sir David also recommended that the board, not the CEO, should decide on the employment and sacking of the CRO, with CRO pay to be approved by non-executives.[13]

In theory this ought to deal with the problems we have outlined above. In practice it solves some but still leaves weaknesses. CROs have told us that because they work so closely with the chief executive and finance director, they find it very difficult to discuss their colleagues' activities from a risk perspective without undermining valued working relationships.

Some CROs seem reluctant to focus the board risk committee's attention on such subjects, let alone on questions flowing from how the board operates. This is perhaps less of a surprise given that these non-executive board members who protect CROs from executives cannot protect CROs from any ire non-executive directors (NEDs) feel.

This reluctance may also involve a question of status because board performance is the chair's responsibility at least in the UK. Chairs are rarely risk specialists. Anecdotal reports suggest that many remain reluctant converts to the notion of robust, independent board performance evaluations. Recognizing the board as a source of risk may be a step they find too difficult to contemplate.

That being so, it is no surprise that few chairmen have focused on reputational risks emerging from their board. As we will show, the board is an important source of risks that can result in severe reputational and other damage to the organization: not because boards are 'bad' but because they are influential.

## Questions to mull

- When did you last consider behavioural and organizational risks in your organization? With what results?
- How would you set out to assess the nature and extent of behavioural and organizational risks in and around your board? What do you expect to find?
- What gap in your knowledge do you most fear? Why is it there and how can you plug it?

# Notes

1. Parliamentary Commission on Banking Standards (2013), Volume I, para 20.
2. Mill (1836) and (1874), Essay 5, paras 38 and 48.
3. Smith (1776), p 119.
4. Ayton (2000).
5. Atkins *et al* (2011).
6. Reputability (2013).
7. McDonnell (2002).
8. Bailey (2016).
9. Rumsfeld (2002).
10. Mills (2016) and Bailey (2016).
11. Buffett (2010).
12. Walker (2009), recommendation 24.
13. Walker (2009), p 12.

# Stakeholder behaviour 06

Are politicians more or less unfaithful than lawyers? If you are like us, and like Daniel Kahneman and Amos Tversky, your first reaction is probably that politicians are less faithful. After all, we regularly read about politicians' peccadillos. But there's a clue: we may be giving politicians a poor reputation for fidelity because we can recall examples of politicians caught in flagrante but we can't think of so many examples of lawyers.

Why is that? It is partly because reporters like to report on politicians who preach family values but practise infidelity: hypocrisy is newsworthy. In contrast, a lawyer's infidelity will often be an irrelevance to most and remain unreported.

But it is also because the availability heuristic is at work. 'How often do lawyers and politicians cheat on their spouses?' needs decent statistics for a proper answer. To get there quickly, we subliminally replace the question with a related question that we can answer: such as 'what examples of cheating lawyers and politicians can we think of?' If we can only recall cheating politicians, politicians win the unfaithfulness contest. Their reputation goes with the answer.

The availability heuristic is an important factor in reputation – what real stakeholders actually think of you, whether right or wrong. What comes easily to mind matters. That is one reason why advertising works (another is the recognition heuristic). And if all we can remember about a company generates a warm glow, the affect heuristic will help lead us to think it is good.

But there is a risky side to this: what if the media starts to report unpleasant things about you? Just as the availability and affect heuristics help generate warm glows when we can only recall endearing facts, if what we remember paints an unsavoury picture, our starting point is low esteem and a dubious reputation or worse.

Newspapers have notoriously long memories. They have long filed facts and figures for future use and had them ready to parade as padding when a company was having a bad day. The media still do it, but, as we observed earlier, that archive is now public and available to all through the internet, with Wikipedia providing convenient compendia of controversies and convictions for most large organizations.

## How does this work in practice?

When promoted to lead BP after the Texas City explosion, Tony Hayward promised to 'focus like a laser' on safety.[1] Then the *Deepwater Horizon* exploded, killing 11 crew, injuring 16 more and causing extensive pollution.

As ever in a crisis, the first focus was on the victims and the drama. But within days the media was full of BP's history: the deadly explosion at Texas City; the promises to learn; oil leaking from pipelines in Alaska; dodgy dealing in the gas markets: and, to cap it all, a six-month-old citation[2] from the US Occupational Safety and Health Administration (OSHA) claiming 439 'wilful' safety breaches at Texas City in violation of the safety settlement agreement.

Our brains process the most readily available information as the easy way to form or revise our views – a good practical reaction provided the data is balanced and correct. With a back story like that in the public arena BP was in difficulty on reputation if it hit the headlines.

But here is the point. Once the OSHA citation was published, in October 2009, any stakeholder detached enough to make a dispassionate analysis could see that the risk of reputational damage at BP was severe, as was the risk of something going wrong to cause a crisis. As Professor Andrew Hopkins put it in his excellent study of the Deepwater Horizon crisis, 'The blowout in the Gulf of Mexico on the evening of 20 April 2010 caught everyone by surprise, although it shouldn't.'[3]

For a contrast, let us turn to airline safety. Airliners crash. Boeing publishes data on accidents to western-built jet airliner. In 2014 the world fleet ran to over 23,000 such aircraft and there were 25 million departures. There were three major accidents globally.[4] Only two involved fatalities on board the aircraft: there were no injuries in the third.

When an airliner crashes, there is a burst of reporting. But there is rarely an extended discussion. It helps that the airline industry almost never plays the blame game. But the main reason is that there is a shared understanding, inside and outside the aviation industry, of how the aftermath of an air crash should be managed. The understanding endures because it is widely known that when an aircraft crashes, a thorough analysis of its root causes is almost invariably carried by a fiercely independent team of specialized investigators whose findings are published promptly and acted upon globally. Better still, the global industry assiduously collects information from incidents that might have been serious but were not – and learns from them too.

So when an airliner crashes, what springs to mind? Empathy for the victims and their families of course; perhaps a spike in fear of flying. But most people soon remember that commercial aviation is kept safe by a long track record of 'honest and thorough' investigations from which lessons are learned and applied globally[5] – though war and terrorism, designed to create fear through acts that cause carnage, generate risks and fears that are beyond the industry's power to resolve alone – which is why Boeing's statistics do not capture them.

## Reputational capital and reputational equity

Whilst each airline has its own track record when it comes to factors like customer service, punctuality and value for money, the industry's record on safety and its rock solid reputation for learning from incidents and accidents combine to give it a distinct advantage when it comes to crises.

When stakeholders share positive feelings towards an organization, we say that the organization has 'reputational capital' – and as with the airline industry, reputational capital can be shared by many.

Some include consequent effects on share price as a component of reputational capital, but we prefer to use the separate term 'reputational equity' for any related share price effect.

## Unduly good reputations

The aviation industry deserves its reputational capital, but those with unduly good reputations can come badly unstuck.

Readily available warm feelings, whether from past promises, a recent marketing campaign or the chief executive leading the response to a crisis with palpable competence and humanity, may lead us to feel a warm glow about an organization coping heroically with difficulty.

But if there is a bad back story, it will usually emerge. If it adds up to an organization that did not deserve its good reputation before the crisis, the result is likely to be a downgraded reputation. The downgrade is likely to be even greater if stakeholders conclude that the organization had been making unjustified claims of virtue or promises that were not kept.

## Stakeholders in peacetime

Without stakeholders you could have no reputation, only self-esteem. Your reputation grows as your stakeholders come to like or love you and declines as your stakeholders lose confidence, or come to despise you. The extent to which they are justified in trusting you affects how enduring your reputation is likely to be.

As we mentioned earlier, the Stanford Research Institute's definition of 'stakeholders' was: 'those groups without whose support the organization would cease to exist'.

This is a good place to start, but where does it lead? Ask a company board to list stakeholders and most will begin with shareholders, if it has them, and customers, closely followed by employees. If you do not have shareholders there will usually be a group in an equivalent position. As an arm of the state, this may be politicians. If a charity, those who provide your funding may take that role.

Pressed, you will soon be listing other groups, such as those with whom you cooperate, the media, those who lend you money, suppliers, regulators and sections of the public affected by your activities. You may include pressure groups, perhaps some politicians.

## Stakeholders in a crisis

A list like that often seems adequate. But what if your organization hits trouble? This is where many come unstuck. Because in a crisis three things regularly happen:

- The attitudes of normally active stakeholders may change.
- Stakeholders who are normally quiescent may become active.
- Some stakeholders may not just desert you but may turn against you when things go badly in particular directions.

## Insiders are stakeholders too

It begins inside the board. In a crisis, the personal interests of the executive team and the chairman readily diverge from those of the organization itself. If a burgeoning crisis looks likely to involve reputational damage to leaders as well as to the organization, leaders will react.

Some will blame others, seeing themselves as blameless or unlucky. Survival instincts may kick in, though many manage, as they ought, to put and keep their organization's interests ahead their own.

Employees may turn on their leaders if they disapprove of their actions. They may become defensive, attack leaders or leak information, especially if they feel they may be blamed or that the public is being misled.

This is something that good company secretaries and crisis lawyers strive to keep in mind as they work to protect the interests of the organization. It makes things much easier in a crisis if the chair, executive team, board and employees are explicitly on the list of stakeholders that has been analysed and understood in the context of a crisis – before one arrives. Because if unattractive behaviour emerges in a crisis, it is likely to rebound, increasing reputational damage to both the organization and its leaders.

## Licence to operate

We have explained how your licence to operate without undue interference from society depends on being widely accepted as a good citizen. Many types of organization, for example most of the mining, aviation and financial sectors, have to obtain an actual permission or licence from a government or regulator in order to be allowed to operate.

However, even organizations that are able to trade more freely benefit from being seen as 'good citizens'. That is one reason why so many organizations go out of their way to have corporate social responsibility programmes. These are often designed to build reputational capital by showing good citizenship. One result can be that potentially unfriendly stakeholders trust you enough to become quiescent stakeholders.

Everything changes when things go wrong. Quiescent stakeholders question and challenge. Whether you retain trust depends largely on the extent to which your stock of reputational capital remains intact and the extent to which the crisis is attributed to your organization or its leaders. It is essential that you understand, in advance, who may become active if you take unpopular steps or if things are going wrong, and why. This is a crucial part of crisis planning and essential to crisis strategy.

In a crisis it is not uncommon to find usually supportive stakeholders switching sides. For example, the US oil industry could usually rely on considerable support from many politicians; and oil companies do not usually criticize each other. But in the heat of the *Deepwater Horizon* crisis, BP, a well-connected oil company with a huge US business, found itself on the receiving end of hostility from the political class including President Obama and from other oil companies. Obama's concerns no doubt reflected the attitudes and expectations of his own stakeholders, the American electorate; and oil companies wished to distance the quality of their standards from the media's portrayal of those at BP.

## Stakeholder expectations

Your reputation is the collective perception of stakeholders. So, what if your stakeholders' expectations are based on erroneous facts? And what if they are just plain unreasonable in their expectations?

The first answer to both questions is that if your stakeholders' expectations are ill founded or unreasonable, that is your problem and not theirs. You have to deal with how your stakeholders actually see you and their expectations, however ridiculous or unfair they seem to you. Your reputation is their perception of you, not yours.

### *Stakeholders underestimate your virtues*

If your stakeholders see you as less good than you really are, you are dealing with the consequences of another risk problem: the risk of failing to communicate effectively with your stakeholders. You have a strength that they do not perceive.

Whether putting this right is easy or difficult depends on the extent to which your stakeholders trust you. By and large it takes years, not months, to build a better reputation. This is partly because stakeholders trust the reliable evidence of actions and tangible results more than they trust words. Actions and results usually take longer to deliver.

There is an additional problem: the public distrusts business leaders. The 2015 Edelman *Trust Barometer*[6] found that CEOs were among the least trusted sources of information when forming an opinion about their company. CEOs from developed countries shared a particularly bad reputation for trustworthiness, being trusted by only 31 per cent. Whilst the 2016 survey[7] showed some revival, CEOs were still trusted by less than 50 per cent overall. Boards fared worse.

Sometimes, however, there is an opportunity to demonstrate, by actions, that the organization deserves a better reputation. The British Midland airline crash at Kegworth, introduced in Chapter 1, is a good example. Michael Bishop, its Chief Executive and largest shareholder, was rapidly on the scene. He had practical experience: 20 years previously, it had fallen to him to tell the families of 40 victims of another crash that their loved ones had died. Nassim Taleb might have seen British Midland as 'antifragile'.

## Antifragility

We are all familiar with the spectrum that begins with fragile and vulnerable and continues towards robust and resilient. Taleb's insight was that we did not have a word that extends the spectrum beyond the robust and resilient towards states that 'benefit from shocks' or 'thrive when exposed to volatility, randomness, disorder and stressors and love adventure, risk and uncertainty'.

Taleb coined the term 'antifragile' to describe such a characteristic and wrote his book *Antifragile*[8] 'to explain it at greater length.

Since Bishop knew all the crew he really did understand how friends and relatives must be feeling, and as he gave his first interview on his way to the airport, this was clear. Throughout he showed empathy and humanity, visiting victims in hospital and constantly speaking to reporters.[9] He promised to find out what had gone wrong and acted accordingly.

The problem began when one engine failed. The official air accident investigation showed that a series of human errors led the crew to shut down the functioning engine instead of the failed one. The captain was paralysed in the accident and subsequently retired. The co-pilot was dismissed after the investigation reported.

As is typical of air accident investigations, many lessons were learned globally, not just within the airline. Some were technical, but we meet one every time we fly: the modern 'brace' position to be adopted if an aircraft is about to crash. Less visible to passengers, the way crew are trained and tested in handling abnormal situations was also changed.

Fine words, real empathy and constant competence shown through a crisis all help limit reputational damage. But Bishop went beyond that. Traditionally, organizations in a crisis clammed up and refused to talk of compensation, and this was certainly the overwhelming paradigm of liability insurers and their lawyers at the time. But Bishop took compassion to his wallet. He offered each affected family £5,000 as an interim payment to help tide them over the financial stress that many faced.

That step not only showed that he cared – and as 50 per cent owner of the airline he was not paying with what Professor John Kay has called 'other people's money'.[10] It was the precursor of the aviation victim compensation scheme that is now built into the laws of the USA, European Union and beyond.

By his humane and competent handing of the accident and its aftermath, Bishop established a good reputation for British Midland. The airline could have been destroyed, but instead ticket sales held and gradually grew. This lesson has been learned widely. Merlin's handling of the Alton Towers roller coaster accident is one of many more recent examples of good practice. Within days, Merlin's Chief Executive had apologized, admitted liability and set in train a process for compensation and rehabilitation of those injured.[11]

## If stakeholders overestimate you

Occasionally you will hear a chief executive or public relations specialist proudly explaining that their communications team has built an excellent reputation, betraying a hint of the idea that their reputation is perhaps better than they deserve. More often we encounter organizations with a good reputation that they believe they deserve: but we can see that their reputation has flawed foundations. Such organizations are predictably vulnerable.

Having a reputation that is better than you deserve is a reputational risk, for two reasons. First, there is the obvious risk that your reputation will fall to the level you actually deserve. That might be called getting your just deserts. But more insidious is the risk of overshoot – the risk that your reputation overshoots to fall below the level of reputation you actually deserve.

Downward corrections are often the result of an event that reveals hidden flaws. It takes time for stakeholders to find the correct level for your re-rated reputation. The process can involve over-correction as easily as under-correction. But there can be two other elements behind an overshoot:

- If stakeholders feel they were misled, they may also feel that you are untrustworthy. In that case you can expect to be marked down to correct both the misapprehension and reduced trustworthiness.
- If stakeholders feel that you should have known of the flaw but didn't, you can expect to be marked down for not knowing what is going on in an organization now categorized as 'dysfunctional'.

## Stakeholders' unreasonable expectations

Unreasonable stakeholder expectations are also a reputational risk. There is a tendency for leaders to think in terms of what is reasonable and we were as guilty as anyone else. The law is full of 'reasonableness' tests; and we once thought that you only needed to meet the 'reasonable' expectations of your stakeholders.

In a perfect world, in which all stakeholders are rational and reasonable, meeting the reasonable expectations of stakeholders would be the right test. But if there is only one lesson that emerges from behavioural economics, it is that none of us are consistently 'reasonable'. We all show qualities that defy strict logic and these lead to valued human qualities such as tolerance and altruism as well as to irritating behaviour such as 'unreasonableness', a description that is often a question of perspective.

That is why we concluded that the notion of failure to meet only the 'reasonable' expectations of shareholders is an inadequate definition of reputational risk. You have to meet – or deal with – their unreasonable expectations too: their unreasonableness is your problem, not theirs.

## Owners and their proxies

Stakeholders who represent ownership have a particular power over an organization and its leaders. Ultimately this derives from their power to dismiss leaders.

As regards businesses, this means the investing public and their proxies, the fund management industry. Their confidence in the ability of the company to deliver consistent performance matters. If growth or earnings falter, their opinion of the company – part of its reputation – will fall, often taking the share price down too.

Investors' time horizons matter. In his review of UK equity markets John Kay wrote, 'short-termism is a problem in UK equity markets, and... the principal causes are the decline of trust and the misalignment of incentives throughout the equity investment chain.'[12]

Professional investors are directly responsible for what can amount to large blocks of a company's shares, so any incentive driving 'bigger returns now' readily translates into a corresponding pressure on the investee company, its chief executive and its finance director. We regularly hear NEDs complain of this pressure. It readily drives board short-termism and presents risks to the reputation of the investee company. These short-term incentives conflict with what many believe are the wishes of the ultimate investors in most shares – retail investors and current and future pensioners – actually want, which is steady performance over years, even decades, not months.

The world of privately owned companies is different. Many long-lived family-owned companies aim for long-term sustainable growth and enduring mutually owned companies may be able to pursue similar objectives, which is not to say that they will succeed. And for companies bought by private equity, to be 'improved' in some way before being sold on, owners' wishes may be different again.

For the organization's leaders, what matters is to understand stakeholders and what motivates them. Differences between their expectations, reasonable or not, and what is realistic should be assessed for reputational and other risks.

Not all organizations are privately owned. In many countries, governments devolve functions to separate agencies. The UK's National Health Service (NHS) is one example. The NHS does not have shareholders. It delivers services to the UK electorate on behalf of government. Politicians know that if the NHS does not perform adequately in the eyes of voters, politicians will be held responsible and suffer reputational damage eventually reflected in the ballot box.

The NHS structure is hierarchical, with increasingly distant devolved layers of management. This creates a series of intermediate leaders who can be blamed when things go wrong. These potential sacrificial lambs can be used as firebreaks between failed service and the reputations of politicians and their parties, though if these leaders gain strong reputations with the public, the tables may be turned.

Since the public ultimately holds politicians responsible for the NHS, politicians regularly act as the ultimate owners of the NHS. Equally their behaviour, often short-termist and electorally driven, drives reputational risks to the NHS as does the complexity of the organization they have created in the quest to protect their reputations.

## Regulators: stakeholders with multiple agendas

The best regulators selflessly set and enforce standards that meet the reasonable expectations of the public and protect the sector from the more unreasonable demands of the industry's other stakeholders.

Regulators have stakeholders who usually include arms of government and thus politicians who commonly wish to avoid blame whilst spending the minimum possible on regulation. Other stakeholders include the industry they regulate as well as their supposed beneficiaries, often 'the public' in some form. These relationships should always be understood since they often become critical in a crisis.

Weak or incompetent regulators are a reputational risk to the sector they regulate. Their ineptitude may lead the organization to feel it has regulatory backing for inadequate standards. But when this comes to light in a crisis, the organization risks additional reputational damage if it is found to have encouraged weak regulation or subverted the regulator. If such a history comes to light, the regulator is also likely to suffer reputational damage, be defenestrated by politicians and replaced by someone more muscular and endowed with stronger teeth.

This leads to the second problem: even inadequate regulators wish to survive. This can lead them to regulate with an eye to survival that distracts from their primary aim, for example by grandstanding in the hope of growing reputational capital.

### Questions to mull

- On what is your organization's reputational capital based? How strong are its foundations?
- Who are your stakeholders? Which of them may be only fair-weather friends?
- On what and whom does your licence to operate depend? How strong are its foundations?
- To what extent does your organization deserve its reputation? What worries you?
- To what extent are your regulators and owners (or equivalents) allowing or encouraging behaviour that would be embarrassing if it was discovered in a crisis?

## Notes

1 *Financial Times* 6/6/20 http://www.ft.com/cms/s/0/9b484cc4-6e8e-11df-ad16-00144feabdc0.html#axzz3pbzV5mpS accessed 27/8/16.

2 October 2009 briefing https://www.osha.gov/dep/bp/BP_Citation_Willful_All.html accessed 27/8/16.

3 Hopkins (2012), opening words.

4 Boeing (2014). These capture losses from aircraft-related causes, not external causes such as terrorism, military action and the like.

5 Kay (2015).

6 Edelman (2015).

7 Edelman (2016).

8 Taleb (2012), Prologue, p II.

9 http://www.mediafirst.co.uk/our-thinking/kegworth-plane-crash-25-years-on-a-media-first-analysis/ accessed 27/8/16.

10 http://www.johnkay.com/2015/06/15/other-peoples-money-introduction accessed 27/8/16. The origin of the phrase is Adam Smith's: Smith (1776) Book V Chapter 1 Part III Article 1: 'The directors of [joint stock] companies, however, being the managers rather of other people's money than of their own, it cannot well be expected, that they should

watch over it with the same anxious vigilance with which the partners in a private copartnery frequently watch over their own... Negligence and profusion, therefore, must always prevail, more or less, in the management of the affairs of such a company.'

**11** Honourable Merlin gives a lesson in responsibility after Smiler crash, *Evening Standard* 9/6/2015 http://www.standard.co.uk/business/markets/jim-armitage-honourable-merlin-gives-a-lesson-in-responsibility-after-smiler-crash-10308001.html accessed 29/6/2016.

**12** Kay (2012), p 9, https://www.gov.uk/government/uploads/system/uploads/attachment_data/file/253454/bis-12-917-kay-review-of-equity-markets-final-report.pdf accessed 17/3/2016.

# 07 Risks from failing to communicate and learn

Failures of communication and learning are rarely a root cause risk but they are a revealing symptom of deeper behavioural and organizational risks at work.

When communication failures are a cause of a crisis, leaders are regularly accused of presiding over a dysfunctional organization and, if they were in the dark, of not knowing what is going on in their organization. This readily translates into reputational damage because stakeholders expect organizations to be 'joined up' inside and leaders to know about all that matters in their organization. Leaders are unlikely to avoid blame by arguing that they cannot know everything of importance: large and unwieldy organizations are created and maintained by leaders.

## Upward communication failures

We frequently find that important information is not passed upwards efficiently. There are three problems here:

- Unwelcome information does not travel upwards as quickly as good news.
- Information becomes distorted as it travels up through the organization.
- Leaders fail to listen to those below them or to absorb what they are really being told.

## *Unwelcome information*

Good news travels fast. Everyone likes to talk about success: it spreads pleasant feelings and may even trigger a celebration and praise for the messenger.

Passing on bad news is different. Messengers feel uncomfortable even if they are not to blame: too many attack those who bring bad tidings. Ostrich-like recipients do not want to hear the news. Some may not listen. Others may hear it but fail to understand or internalize the message. Unhappy at best, they may be rude, angry or vengeful.

As for 'whistleblowing', so many innocent whistle-blowers have faced sanctions that it is widely seen as career-threatening. Whistle-blowing is rarely more than an unreliable residual safety valve that may be used when normal internal communication channels have failed to report bad news to the top.

When it comes to passing on unwelcome news, the cultural climate matters. Warren Buffett recognizes this.

*If you see anything whose propriety or legality causes you to hesitate, be sure to give me a call....*

*As a corollary, let me know promptly if there's any significant bad news. I can handle bad news but I don't like to deal with it after it has festered for awhile. A reluctance to face up immediately to bad news is what turned a problem at Salomon from one that could have easily been disposed of into one that almost caused the demise of a firm with 8,000 employees.*

Warren Buffett, 2010 letter to his senior managers[1] (© Berkshire Hathaway/Warren Buffett, reproduced with permission)

Someone who is to some extent responsible for bad news may have an incentive to hide it. They may be reluctant to volunteer it unless they feel it is safe to do so and, to the extent that they are to blame, they will be treated fairly.

Unreported unwelcome news presents a risk, and this risk lies at the root of the 'unknown knowns' problem we explained previously. Any reluctance to pass unwelcome news upwards creates what can be a systemic series of risk glass ceilings that leave boards in the dark about important information. Board risk blindness is one of the most frequent features of major failures. It also represents a lost opportunity to fix the problem before it causes damage.

## *Distortion*

As we described in Chapter 5, messages can become distorted as they pass upwards. The more hierarchical and complex the organization, the more layers there are, each bringing the opportunity for another layer of misunderstanding and reinterpretation.

Distortion may be innocent, for example because the news is subconsciously squeezed to fit with the recipient's mental model. But there will also be recipients who find the incoming message unpalatable. These may deliberately misinterpret or massage it into something more acceptable, before passing it on.

## *Risk glass ceiling*

Fear of aggression, ostracism or reprisals prevents important risk information from reaching leaders and can deter even risk professionals from passing unwelcome news to their superiors. Derek has personal experience of the glass ceiling.

In the 1980s Derek's job included preparing a regular market briefing for the main board.

On one occasion he explained analysts' serious concerns about the company's potential over-exposure to mortgage indemnity insurance as house prices were falling rapidly. The report was passed as usual to the C-Suite for pre-issue approval, but within minutes he was summoned by a very senior executive, now long dead.

This much-feared man demanded that Derek withdraw his report. When Derek remonstrated that it was important and represented an accurate picture of how the company was regarded by the investment community, he was told that it was not suitable to be shown to the board. The executive continued, 'Let me give you some advice. When you deal with people as senior as I am, you have a duty to agree with them!'

We have already mentioned that even chief risk officers may lack effective status and authority to manage all important risks effectively, and this is another root of the risk glass ceiling.

In the United Kingdom, the Financial Reporting Council Guidance on Risk Management now recommends that the board should 'consider whether it, and any committee or management group to which it delegates activities', which includes risk teams, 'has the necessary skills, knowledge, experience, authority and support to enable it to assess the risks the company faces and exercise its responsibilities effectively'.[2]

This guidance primarily flags the issue of whether risk teams have the skill to assess all kinds of risks: many will find they have skills gaps as regards behavioural, organizational and reputational risks. But it also flags the crucial question of authority. Even if a risk team sees and understands a behavioural or organizational risk issue emanating from board level, they will not deal with it if they lack sufficient status and authority, leaving an internally recognized risk unknown to leaders. We believe that very few, if any, risk teams have the status or authority to raise board-level behavioural or organizational risks discovered incidentally, let alone the skills to analyse such risks systematically.

As a result of the Walker reforms in the aftermath of the 2007/08 financial crisis, it is increasingly common for financial companies to have a CRO set in a protective environment and some other large companies have followed suit. Even so, most CROs work sufficiently closely with the executive team that they feel a part of it even if they are in theory somewhat apart.

Gillian Tett is best known as a *Financial Times* journalist, but she also has a doctorate in anthropology. In her book *The Silo Effect* she discusses an important observation of Pierre Bourdieu, an influential anthropologist: that cohesive groups form mental maps of their world. 'Groups' includes boards and leadership teams as much as hockey teams, political parties, tribes and nations. Two crucial insights for us are that those maps define who is an 'insider' and who is an 'outsider'; and that they effectively define what is off-limits for insiders to discuss. As Tett puts it, 'Social silences matter. The system ends up being propped up because it seems natural to leave certain subjects ignored since these issues have become labelled as dull, taboo, obvious or impolite.'[3]

CROs who are, or aspire to be, part of the executive team are likely to adopt its mental map. This is likely to influence how CROs think and behave, particularly as regards the executive team's ambitions and as regards what is, is not and cannot be seen and talked about. Behavioural economics provides another approach to understanding the phenomenon: social norms and social proof.

### Social norms and social proof[4]

We humans like to belong, to fit. We readily detect the expectations of others and are adept at adapting to meet what we see as the expectations of those who belong to groups to which we aspire. As a result, social norms spread rapidly.

These norms range from dress codes, through the etiquette of social and business behaviour to rules of engagement in warfare. They include norms that we rarely discuss, such as who has precedence and the extent to which we may ask or pursue penetrating questions.

Social proof is a close relation. When we find ourselves in an uncertain situation and unsure how to behave, we may look at others for clues as to what is appropriate and act accordingly.

Social norms and social proof are reinforced by rapid feedback. If we conform, we are rewarded by acceptance. If we do not, we remain or become outsiders, lacking status and influence.

Whilst it is better that CROs have status, authority and expertise on the level of the executive team, their regular and close participation within the leadership team brings the risk that they may want to belong and avoid putting their membership in doubt.

You will therefore not be surprised that we have met CROs who appear reluctant, despite their high status and nominal independence, to raise subjects that might upset those whom they regard as close colleagues. Even strong, experienced CROs have told us that since they have to work with the executive team daily and could not do the job if the executive team ostracized them, there are subjects that they at least hesitate to raise.

## Downward communications failures

Failed downward communication is rather like driving a car with a steering wheel that does not steer, but with a difference: you may not discover the communications failure until it is far too late to correct it.

A topical problem concerns messages from leaders on ethos and culture. Leaders carefully craft an ethos, a set of principles, guidelines or other messages but the message doesn't get acted on by staff. Why not? At its simplest, the message may never arrive at its destination. But the risks run deeper than this. For example, staff may receive the message correctly but be:

- disbelieving because they feel the message is inconsistent with their perception of their leaders' character or what their leader really wants;
- unreceptive because their character or the existing culture makes them unable to act on it;
- unwilling to act on it because it is contrary to their personal or financial interests, for example because of how formal or informal incentives work;
- unable to believe that leaders mean what they say because of what they know about how leaders' financial incentives work;
- disbelieving because leaders do not 'walk their talk' – they do not behave as though they mean what they say.

Different risks need different mitigation, which is one reason why analysis matters.

## Communication across the organization

All organizations beyond the smallest are subdivided into multiple overlapping groups. Divisions may be temporary or permanent, functional, geographical, vertical, horizontal or between floors of an office block. They may be organized, like a board or a brass band, or informal – perhaps based on interests such as ballet, boxing or baking.

Groups readily develop identities that easily become silo-like boundaries that complicate communication with those in other groups. Even in the age of email, twitter and Instagram, it may be difficult to pass information to another group simply because you don't actually know any of its members.

This happens as much to boards as in offices, factories or villages. It even happens when people from different groups work together closely on a daily basis. As Edgar H Schein of the MIT Sloan School of Management observed of medical teams, as regards patient safety:

> *I find that the biggest problems are the communication failures between doctors, nurses, and techs – especially where you have not only the different occupational cultures of doctors and nurses, but also the additional fact that they have different status and rank in most societies.*[5]

## *Communications with the outside world*

Communication across your organization's external boundaries is likely to be more difficult. Identity differences are likely to be greater, with outsiders perceived as more 'outside' than other groups within your organization: so too with the physical barriers to communication.

These differences have multiple manifestations. There may be a reluctance to accept critical thoughts coming from without. We have heard senior people say, 'That couldn't happen in my company: we are not like that!' only to discover, in one case as a result of a series of major investigations and huge fines, that things were even worse than had been suggested. 'Not invented here' is also a well-known phenomenon.

If your organization subcontracts functions, you will wish to ensure that they are carried out in a way that does not risk your reputation. We have already discussed the problems in transmitting messages downwards. In the case of sending them to an outsider such as a subcontractor, the risks can be magnified by the added inside–outside distance. Contractual terms, particularly those to do with performance, may set up unintended incentives. Is it realistic to rely on a subcontractor to tell you bad news if it may trigger a penalty?

There is another aspect of delegating a task to an outsider. Beyond the risks of the delegation going wrong is the perception that delegation divests the delegator of responsibility. Stakeholders seem willing to accept that subcontracting some tasks is legitimate and does relieve the organization of responsibility when something goes wrong at the subcontractor. But this is an area where stakeholders have proved to take varying views.

Our conclusion is that if an organization subcontracts a function that stakeholders regard as 'core' they are unlikely to regard subcontracting as relieving the organization of any responsibility for the subcontracted functions. On the other hand, the more the function is peripheral, the greater the probability that stakeholders will not hold the organization responsible if the subcontractor is found to be inadequate.

But even here, stakeholders are becoming more exacting. Companies holding themselves out as 'ethical' are likely to find that their stakeholders expect them to contract with equally ethical suppliers. Thus underpaid cleaning staff, even though employed by outside contractors, have become a reputational issue for well-known organizations, as have unpaid interns. Issues about sources of raw materials, ranging from diamonds through fish to timber, have led their end users to espouse ethical purchasing policies to enhance their reputational capital.

## Risk blindness

Without information that flows freely within your organization, your leaders at all levels risk being blind to risks that matter.

When critical information fails to flow upwards to leaders, they will find themselves unknowingly in the dark as they develop their views on the organization

The board of Volkswagen seems to have been utterly unaware that, in order to meet targets, staff had lied about NOx emissions and planted hidden 'defeat' software that misled regulators.

Another common scenario concerns failure to join up relevant information. One part of your organization may know something important of which another part is ignorant.

Jet fuel is special stuff, designed, among other things, to be stable in contact with hot metal surfaces. The aviation industry has long been vigilant to keep the stuff away from copper in all its forms because contact with copper can make it unstable and capable of clogging the fuel supply to jet engines.

John Minton is a chemical engineer specialized in finding out why things go wrong at sea. One day he came across an unstable cargo of jet fuel produced by a major oil company and transported in its own ships.

When he investigated, he discovered a silo at work. The oil company people responsible for making the fuel and supplying it to airlines shared the aviation industry obsession with keeping copper out of the supply chain. But the same company's shipping division, which transported the fuel around the world, was putting it into standard ships' tanks fitted with hundreds of meters of copper heating coils - blissfully unaware that contact with copper coils could make the fuel unacceptable to its users, even potentially dangerous.

Groupthink is a third factor. We have already given one explanation of this, but we think anthropology suggests another perspective. Bourdieu observed that groups of people develop ways of thinking that include cultural and mental maps and ideas of what should and should not be discussed. As a result, insiders end up not discussing subjects that outsiders consider important.

At a dinner party, the consequences are likely to be conversation that an outsider sees as cliquey, frustrating and self-reinforcing, because participants' knowledge, experience and perspectives all come from the same box. Trapped inside, participants are unaware that they are in a box. Still less can they examine the beliefs and assumptions in and around the box or accept new ideas from outside.

Translated to leadership teams, the effect of what insiders see as diversity but outsiders see as homogeneity can be as predictable as it is devastating.

## Failure to learn

One of the most effective ways to learn is from mistakes: your own – including those that do not have bad consequences – and those of others. Systematically learning from errors gives you the opportunity to deal with systemic issues before they erupt as the cause of your next crisis.

Learning also helps prevent crises from tipping into reputational disasters. When it is discovered that an organization has failed to learn from its own experience, or from well-publicized experience elsewhere, its leadership is likely to face particularly severe criticism, especially if the failure meant that a subsequent crisis was not avoided.

Organizations fail to learn lessons for a variety of reasons, such as:

- The relevant facts or experience are not recognized as a problem or near miss from which lessons might be learned.
- The relevant facts or experience remain undiscovered – or covered up –for example in the case of a 'near miss' or performance failures, so that lessons cannot be learned.
- The facts come to light but the investigation fails to identify root causes.
- The facts come to light, are investigated and lessons are learned locally: but the lessons are not disseminated so that others in the organization can learn.

Even when the facts come to light, are investigated and lessons are learned locally, 'outsiders' who would benefit from them may be unable to absorb lessons from 'insiders'. The problem can be more acute when the lesson comes from outside the organization, where the force of 'that could not happen here' seems even greater.

### Questions to mull

- Compared to good news, how fast does bad news travel to the top of your organization?
- How much important bad news never reaches your leadership team?
- How confident are you that lessons are systematically learned from all mishaps, including those that do not have bad outcomes?
- What subjects fall into your board's 'social silences'?
- What, and how strong, is your evidence?

## Notes

1 Buffett (2010).
2 FRC (2014b).
3 Tett (2015), p 45.
4 Dolan *et al* (2010).
5 Schein *et al* (2015), p 110.

# Character, culture and ethos 08

## Character

In the aftermath of the 2007/08 financial crisis the Ivey Business School began to explore leadership qualities. Their paper *Leadership on Trial* highlighted the importance of character, observing, 'While competencies determine what leaders *can* do, leadership character determines what they *will* do' (emphasis in original).[1] Following discussions with hundreds of leaders, Gerard Seijts and his team concluded that whilst leaders agreed that 'character matters', 'they seldom refer to it, talk about it, or use it in recruiting, selecting or developing leaders' – only when firing them.

Exploring further, they concluded that whilst competencies and commitment are critical to leadership success, character weaknesses equally set up an organization for failure. To establish and maintain suitable cultures requires 'certain characteristics in both leaders and followers – such as courage, accountability, integrity and humility'.

Having encountered multiple meanings for the term 'character', Seijts' team developed a working model for the business world involving three overlapping aspects: virtues, personality traits and values. Some of these are innate. Others develop through childhood and education, social pressures and 'life-changing events'. They predispose an individual to behave in particular ways unless other forces, such as incentives and culture, push behaviour in other directions. They developed a diagram to illustrate desirable traits (Figure 8.1).[2]

**Figure 8.1** Character dimensions and associated elements: aspects of strengths (redrawn, with permission, from Seijts *et al*, 2015)

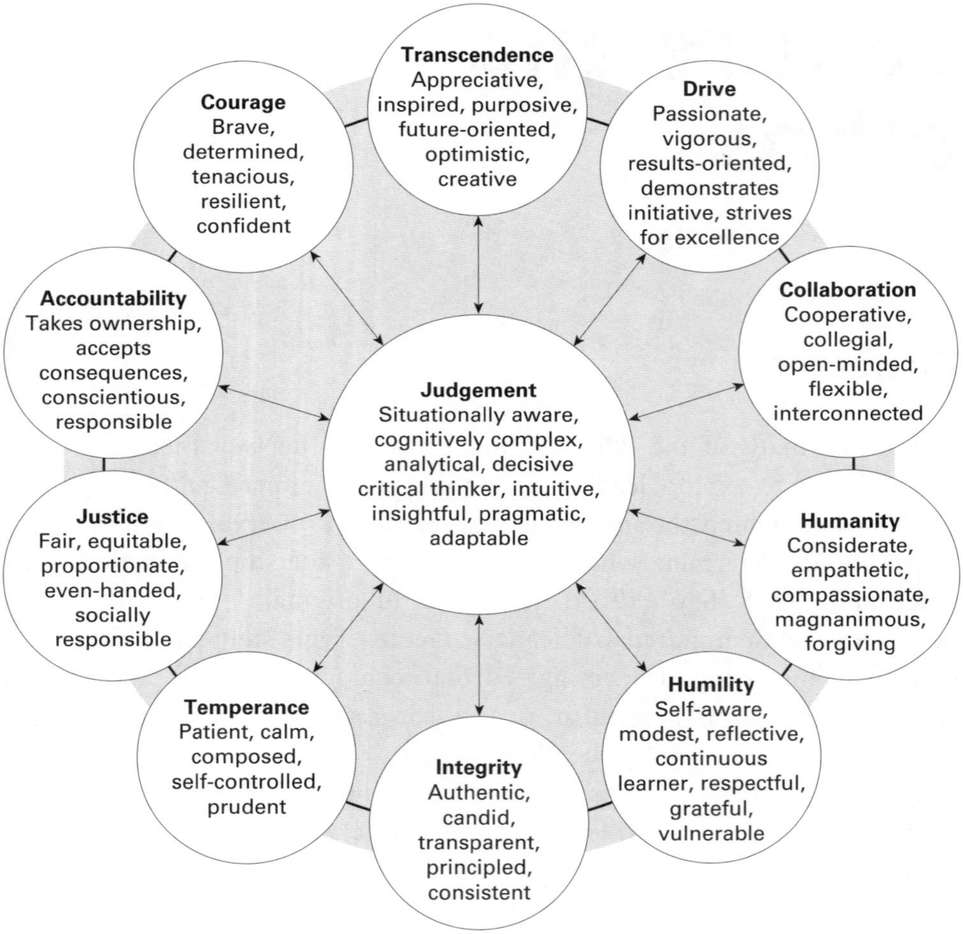


Lack of such good characteristics gives rise to risks, as does the presence of their 'opposites', such as egocentricity, impatience and greed. Building on the work of Seijts and his earlier collaboration with Mary Crossan,[3] we have used the same structure to illustrate some character weaknesses (Figure 8.2).

The interaction of such strengths and weaknesses play an important role in the effectiveness of leaders.

**Figure 8.2** Character dimensions and associated elements: aspect of weaknesses (developed by the authors from Crossan *et al*, 2013 and Seijts *et al*, 2015)

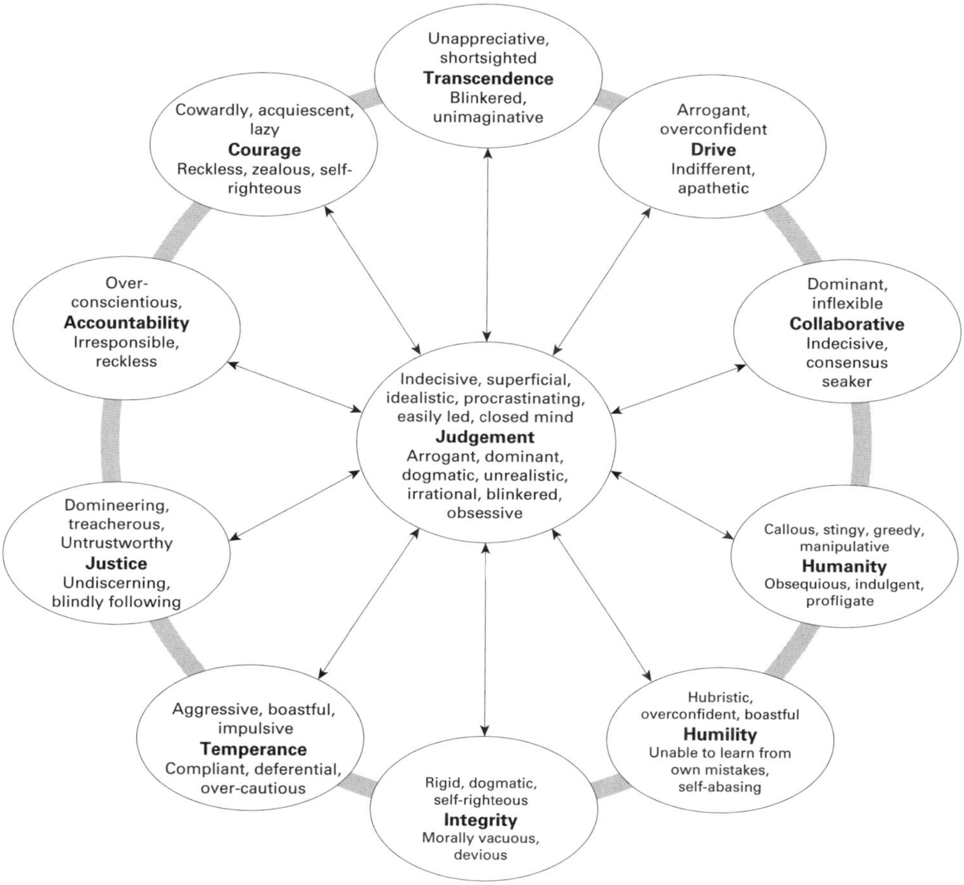


# Culture

An organization's culture is the code by which its members behave: 'the way we do things around here', as the UK's Health and Safety Executive succinctly put it.[4] This is often not the same as the culture to which leaders aspire or try to inspire. Gaps between aspiration, reality and leaders' perceptions of reality, as well as failure to recognize such gaps, represent risks, as our research has amply confirmed.

We have mentioned the perspective of anthropologists such as Bourdieu and Tett, that members of groups have mental maps and patterns that affect how they think and classify ideas, perceptions and people. These maps and patterns, typically unrecognized by users, affect the way we think and what we think; and they seem to provide a useful model that helps explain why we behave differently at home and at work – our home and work groups are not the same.

Rachel Kranton and Nobel Laureate George Akerlof looked at this from the perspective of behavioural economics, in their book *Identity Economics*. They concluded that people 'have different selves at different points in their lives'. Whilst some aspects of 'self' are close to fixed (such as race and gender), others change occasionally (for example on marriage or moving to a new country) and some change frequently. 'Some changes happen at very high frequency, such as the daily transition between home and work. The imperatives of the workplace recede at home as the imperatives of home recede at work.'[5]

So it is not surprising that many, perhaps most, people feel that they are not quite the same person at home as at work. Nor should it be any surprise that people at work behave differently at work and at home.

Anthony remembers a talented judge, now long dead, who was known to be austere, prickly and pernickety to the point of aggression when in court. Yet outside court he was known as a kind and generous teacher of young barristers and kinder still with children.

## Cultural leadership

Most leaders nowadays know that they must 'set the tone' from the top. Setting the cultural climate involves leadership by both words and behaviour and setting the choice architecture. It involves inculcating memorable principles and a desire to follow, not subvert, them. The aim is that both culture and incentives encourage people to make the choices leaders desire even when leaders are absent.

We found that leaders who failed to lead effectively on ethos and culture, and set the cultural climate, led their organizations into reputational crises. This simple observation covers a range of risk areas.

We occasionally encountered dishonest leaders.

The Independent Insurance Company was a stock market favourite. But Michael Bright, its Chief Executive, and two of his co-directors slid into dishonesty when they 'cooked' the company's books. Independent Insurance lost its reputation, gained painful regulatory attention and became insolvent. Bright, his CFO and managing director were convicted and sent to prison for fraud and conspiracy to defraud.[6]

Downright dishonesty is uncommon. At Northern Rock, a failed UK bank, staff under-reported the losses on loans that were not performing because they felt under pressure.[7] At BP, at around the time of the Texas City explosion, both safety and cost-cutting were priorities. Lack of attention to choice architecture meant that it was unclear which was to prevail. The result seems to have been a culture under which, in the absence of a clear safety threat, cost-saving prevailed.

BP illustrates another cultural problem. BP's board was keen to improve safety, but in the real world there are two contrasting aspects of 'safety'. The first is personal safety – which leads to warnings not to run down escalators and instructions to wear safety shoes. These are important measures in reducing individual accidents but they are useless in preventing system failures; and statistics on personal safety accidents are poor indicators of anything systemically wrong.

To deal with system failures, a different focus is needed: process safety. The aim is to prevent infrequent but serious, sometimes disastrous, system failures of the kind that cause refinery explosions, factory fires, nuclear meltdowns and repeated medical mishaps. These failures often have scale. If the process for starting a refinery is flawed, the refinery may blow up. If the hospital's system for learning from human mistakes is flawed, the same human error will be repeated time and again. The risks of systemic failure have to be identified and managed.

Unfortunately BP's leaders inadvertently presided over incentives that encouraged personal safety, not system or process safety. Bonuses at their Texas City refinery mainly targeted financial outcomes, with one component determined by injury data, a proxy for personal safety. There were no measures of process safety. Such a system would drive managers to focus on personal safety, not process safety. In other words, BP leaders promoted safety culture – but of the wrong kind.[8]

It is the same for every system run by humans, especially those who supervise and run systems. All of us inevitably make mistakes. The more senior we are, the more our mistakes are likely to affect the whole system; the greater their potential consequences; and the greater the risk that, unrecognized and uncorrected, our errors become systemic weaknesses.

Many organizations try to control behaviour by issuing detailed rules and guidance. The risk here is of a compliance culture where insiders see it as acceptable to wriggle around rules when outsiders, if they knew, would see insiders flying in the face of the spirit of the rules. And it is apparently common to find particular rules ignored by local custom because, found to be inappropriate in one situation, they become more widely ignored.

Cultural influences can also be driven by locality. We regularly discuss the difficulties in reconciling local cultures with the organization's stated ethos. It took courage for Kiyoshi Kurokawa, Chairman of the Japanese Diet's Inquiry into the Fukashima meltdown, to set out the problem to his fellow citizens:

> This was a disaster 'Made in Japan'. Its fundamental causes are to be found in the ingrained conventions of Japanese culture: our reflexive obedience; our reluctance to question authority; our devotion to 'sticking to the program'; our groupism; and our insularity.[9]

Every country has its own cultural strengths and weaknesses, though most will find their own weaknesses more difficult to see or accept than those of other countries.

## Failure to embed the desired culture throughout the organization

Stakeholders expect leaders to lead on the right culture and to ensure it is so embedded in the organization as to form a part of daily life. Leaders with the right intentions are not enough. The culture must permeate the organization and be adopted by all.

Identifying the appropriate culture is the first step, but there is no success until the culture is so deeply embedded that people follow its intentions even when no one is looking. Along the way, and at every intermediate level of leadership, are risks. Because people constantly observe their leaders; and they take their lead from how leaders behave, especially when they think themselves unobserved. A picture may be worth a thousand words, but a leader's behaviour is worth even more.

**Questions to mull**

- What character traits do your leaders share? Why? With what consequences?
- Which are missing?
- How would you summarize your organization's culture in no more than 100 words?
- How would you discover the extent to which people abide by it in everything they do?

# Notes

1 Gandz *et al* (2010).

2 Seijts' figure seems to go beyond the underlying research of Peterson and Seligman (2004/2016), but we think the extension is useful in the world of analysing risk, especially leadership risk. We have therefore adopted it; and have extrapolated from it in constructing Figure 8.2. See also Seligman (2015).

3 Crossan *et al* (2013).

4 Organisational culture, Health and Safety Executive http://www.hse.gov.uk/humanfactors/topics/culture.htm accessed 21/3/2016.

5 Akerlof and Kranton (2010), p 126.

6 Former Independent chief Michael Bright jailed for seven years, *Telegraph* 25/10/07 http://www.telegraph.co.uk/finance/markets/2818280/Former-Independent-chief-Michael-Bright-jailed-for-seven-years.html accessed 20/4/2016.

**7** Northern Rock former directors fined and banned by FSA, BBC News 13/4/2010 http://news.bbc.co.uk/1/hi/business/8617345.stm accessed 20/4/2016.

**8** The BP story is covered in our case studies but you will find more detailed analyses in Hopkins (2008) and Hopkins (2012).

**9** Fukashima Nuclear Accident Report (2012) Executive summary, p 9.

# Incentives 09

Incentives come in many flavours but all involve some kind of reward for desired performance or behaviour. Unfortunately, incentives often have unintended consequences. Perverse incentives, and any failure to recognize and deal with them, readily cause reputational damage when they come to light.

Financial bonuses are widespread: you hit your target and we give you money, and with it comes recognition and status. We believe the distorting influence of incentives grew in the 1990s with the advent of the bonus culture, itself probably related to the fashion for the now largely abandoned financial control model.

Incentives can be negative too: fail to meet your target and you will lose money. But what if someone you report to is a bully or reacts unpleasantly when told something unpalatable? That behaviour gives you incentives, such as to avoid the bully or to avoid passing on unwelcome news. Many incentives are of this kind.

## Financial incentives: bonuses

Many people, at all levels and in all kinds of work, receive bonuses and there is evidence that you sometimes get more of what you target, but not always.

But you must be careful what you wish for. Just as clever chimpanzees quickly work out how to extract more bananas from an experimenter, we humans use our ingenuity to achieve more rewards. Set a target of resolving all customer phone queries within five minutes and the risk is that many calls will be terminated after four minutes and 50 seconds, leaving customers seething. Set a sales target and you may find sales booked earlier than they should be. Subverted targets readily cause reputational damage when stakeholders come to realize what has been going unnoticed by leaders.

> We know of an insurance underwriter who had a bonus based on premium growth. So he grew the account with little regard to quality. In year 1 he earned 50 per cent of salary as bonus; in year 2 a further 50 per cent. In year 3 the account made a loss of £250m and he was sacked.

Small bonuses set for large numbers of people can achieve their stated aims but have disastrous consequences. Not so long ago, UK banks discovered a wonderful product to sell to their customers: payment protection insurance, known as PPI. PPI paid off your credit card debts if you fell ill, died or lost your job.

For some, it was a valuable insurance. For others it was less so; and for some it was completely useless because the terms effectively excluded the claims that they were most likely to make. But every PPI sale paid a commission and employers shared their bounty – or was it booty – with sales staff through incentive schemes.

Countless sales teams sold tens of millions of PPI policies without finding out whether they were appropriate to the buyer's needs. The result was the PPI mis-selling scandal. So far, the cost to UK banks is approaching £40 billion[1] in compensation. It added considerably to the damage to the reputation of banks; and the banks' crisis management plan, of denying responsibility, led to the growth of a new industry, the claims farmer. These entrepreneurs offer to pursue PPI (and other) claims in exchange for a large cut of the proceeds.

It does not take a large team to cause mayhem. Our AIG case study shows how incentives given to a small team can help to imperil even the largest business.

## Do large bonuses work?

Large bonuses have a different risk profile. Senior people are more influential than those below them. The bonus-driven behaviour of an individual, or even a small group of leaders, can have correspondingly large consequences.

In the aftermath of the 2008 financial crisis Professor Dan Ariely, a behavioural economist at Duke University, began to investigate how incentives work. His team couldn't afford to pay much so they set their first experiment[2] in rural India where their budget allowed them to pay generous bonuses – up to five months' spending money. Big bonuses generally led to worse performance for simple tasks involving thinking.

Why, you will ask, are these results relevant to highly educated leaders in developed countries? Ariely asked this too and went on to test two dozen MIT undergraduates. One test involved only motor skills – alternately pressing one of two keys on a computer keyboard. The second involved mental skills – identifying which two of twelve numbers (such as 4.37, 2.15 and so on) added up to ten. Bonuses were awarded according to performance. The maximum pay-out was either $30 or $300.

The results were striking. Bigger incentives led to better performance for the motor task of pressing keys; but for the cognitive task, those on larger bonuses performed much worse than those on smaller bonuses.

But these experiments still do not represent real life. We need analysis from real life: like an analysis of the actual performance of chief executives of a large cohort of large companies over a decade or two. Well, someone has done that too. Researchers Cooper, Gulen and Rau took data on CEO earnings and corporate performance for all NYSE, AMEX and NASDAQ companies from 1994 to 2011. They looked for relationships between pay and performance.[3]

The disparity of company types and sizes meant that adjustments were needed to make meaningful comparisons possible so they measured what we will summarize as 'peer group adjusted pay'.

The results are striking. For the top 10 per cent of CEOs by peer-group adjusted pay, who typically received more than 80 per cent of their pay in incentives for performance, CEOs earned negative returns of about 5 per cent over one year and 9 per cent over three years, again relative to their peers. In money terms, $21million additional generosity in CEO pay translated into a typical annual loss of $1.4billion in stock market valuation. These CEOs also led their businesses to a fall in return on assets.

Digging deeper, the research team found that, for these CEOs, what was predictive was not fixed pay but incentive pay. This was closely, and negatively, correlated with growth of stock market valuation and return on assets, with stock options being the key predictor. The team eventually discovered that CEOs who were confident enough to retain un-exercised but exercisable in-the-money stock options were more frequently involved in acquisitions than their less confident peers. And it is a well-known but dismal truth that acquisitions have been an exceptionally good incinerator of shareholder value for acquiring companies.

The researchers eventually settled on the hypothesis that 'overconfident' CEOs accept large amounts of incentive pay and then try to realize the incentives by embarking on activities that actually reduce shareholder value and their firm's future performance. Markets seem to understand this: they react more negatively to mergers announced by highly paid CEOs[4] – an impact that seems to be reputational.

The lesson for risk professionals, risk committees, remuneration committees and boards is, however, simple. Employing a CEO who demands a large pay package with big incentives may be risky to shareholders' wealth, the more so if the CEO has a history of un-exercised but exercisable in-the-money options. The CEO may have many highly attractive qualities, but the risks they present should be identified, brought into the open and actively managed.

The UK Financial Reporting Council (FRC) has recommended that the remuneration of senior executives is discussed from a risk perspective. The 2014 *Corporate Governance Code*[5] (CGC) now states that executive directors' remuneration should be designed to 'promote the long term success of the company', a change from the 2012 version, which provided that it should be designed to 'attract, retain and motivate directors of the quality required to run the company successfully'.

Having reminded boards of the conflicts of interest – we call them risks – inherent in taking views on pay from executive directors and senior managers, the CGC focuses on the design of performance-related pay. Reflecting the recommendations of Professor John Kay's *Review of Equity Markets*,[6] the CGC recommends that remuneration incentives should be compatible with risk policies and systems.

This new emphasis is echoed in the FRC's 2014 *Guidance on Risk Management*,[7] which encourages boards to consider whether the company's human resource policies and performance reward systems support the business objectives and the risk management system.

Four risk factors are missing from the FRC's guidance on the risks from remuneration packages. The first concerns remuneration consultants, whose own pay involves any element that increases as their recommended executive pay levels increase. They have a risk-riddled conflict of interest.

More insidious is the risk posed by the remuneration consultant whose firm or associates provide services for the executives whose pay they help to fix. According to the High Pay Centre, 'almost all' firms using such services bought them from a firm that also provided additional services, with half buying from audit firms.[8]

Then there is the complexity of executive remuneration packages. As we explain in Chapter 10, complexity is itself a source of risk. If the remuneration committee struggles, unaided, to understand the package and the behaviours it drives, how can it be confident that the executive's interpretation (which may not be the same as theirs) will not drive undesirable behaviour? Where pay schemes drive perverse executive behaviour, consequences are likely to be sizeable.

It has been said that the complexity of executive remuneration packages is one of the reasons why boards need to use consultants. If so, it may be that remuneration consultants are ensuring future work by devising ever more complex remuneration packages, a perverse incentive if ever there was one. Remuneration committees can reduce risks from both incentives and complexity by simplifying incentives and eschewing remuneration consultants.

The fourth risk factor has to do with how incentives really work, something that needs more research but is clearly a risk area. Andrew Smithers has argued cogently that most bonus schemes encourage the sacrifice of long-term investment in favour of more certain short-term bonuses and the use of cash piles to buy back shares rather than long-term investment.[9] We have found no serious rebuttal of his argument, which also has wider economic implications. At present, boards should mitigate the risks by keeping up to date with emerging research on how incentives actually work and taking it into account in considering incentive schemes.

## Penalties

Penalties also influence behaviour in what can be risky ways, but penalties are not a mirror image of bonuses: we feel the pain of penalties more than we feel pleasure from bonuses. Penalties are as much incentives as bonuses and they bring similar weaknesses, including perverse behaviour designed to get round the penalty.

### Loss aversion, status quo bias, endowment effect and regret aversion

Would you accept a gamble on the toss of a coin in which you lose an affordable £100 on heads and gain £150 on tails? Most would not accept the bet, and loss aversion is our ingrained response to avoid the pain of losing that which we have. Most of us will avoid risks of losses in circumstances where, in strict logic, we would be better off taking the risk.

Broadening the concept, we have status quo bias, which we exhibit when we are reluctant to change things and default to keeping them the same.

We are territorial, whether as to land, rights or mates, tending to defend our domain more vigorously than we try to extend it and giving concessions with painful reluctance. Many feel criticism and personal failure more keenly than praise and personal success. And we will demand more to give up a thing we own than we will pay to buy it – a result of the endowment effect.

We are also prone to fear that a decision we are about to take will lead us to have regrets if it turns out to be wrong. This is regret aversion and it can lead to avoiding the decision – though too few realize that avoiding or postponing a decision is functionally equivalent to making a decision to make no decision, often maintaining the status quo.

## Non-financial incentives

When we fail to listen and react constructively to someone's comments or thoughts, they will soon stop bothering to tell us what they think. By failing to listen, we do not just miss the gem currently on offer: we create an incentive not to bother next time and risk losing the benefit of what others can share of their knowledge, know-how and intelligence. Thus we sterilize one of our most valuable and versatile assets: the collective brains of our people, whom we have carefully chosen, and pay, for their skill and aptitudes.

This sterilization matters: they will still share news and develop their ideas with colleagues, but those ideas are lost to leaders. Our organization will have powerful insights within it, but, as non-listening leaders, we have denied ourselves access to them.

This is not just a loss of thinking power. It brings with it the risk that something bad happens as a result because leaders are poorly informed, the 'unknown known' problem again. When our short-comings are discovered, our reputation, and that of our organization, will suffer.

Equally, if we react badly when you bring us unwelcome news, we create an incentive for you to delay reporting bad news next time, or even hide it. If we are leaders, we risk creating systemic incentives that deny us the opportunity to deal with a latent, incubating problem before it explodes into an intractable or damaging crisis.

Undesirable incentives lead to many consequences that include communication and cultural failures that leave leaders blind to important risks; and they can be direct causes of crises. This is so at any level, but with our regular proviso: power and influence matter. The more powerful or influential are those at the source of an undesirable incentive, the greater the likelihood, other things being equal, of more severe consequences. Undesirable incentives on and from leaders have the most powerful consequences.

Dysfunctionality within, such as communication failures and inability to learn from mistakes, regularly leads to reputational damage. This is partly because dysfunctionality means that the whole is less than the sum of the parts. But it is also a sign of inadequate leadership. This is why leaders found to preside over dysfunctional organizations are particularly at risk of losing their reputations and jobs after a crisis exposes their weakness.

### Questions to mull

- List five non-financial incentives at work in your organization. What undesirable consequences might they encourage? How can you reduce the risks?
- What are the potential unintended consequences of your executive bonus system? How would you manage the risks?
- To what extent does your executive bonus scheme provide incentives that encourage leaders to put short-term reward ahead of investing for the long-term health of the business, ie after their retirement?
- If you were so inclined, how could you game the executive incentive scheme to maximize benefits? Why should your leaders not game it?

## Notes

1 Ten biggest bank scandals have cost £53bn in fines, *Financial Times* 11/4/2016 http://on.ft.com/1VgJzhI accessed 19/4/2016.
2 Ariely *et al* (2005).
3 Cooper *et al* (2014).
4 Cooper *et al* (2014).
5 Financial Reporting Council (2014a).
6 Kay (2012).
7 Financial Reporting Council (2014b).
8 High Pay Centre (2015).
9 Smithers (2013).

# Complexity 10

Whether inherited or newly created, complexity is a risk associated with leaders. If stakeholders discover that an organization is so complex that leaders cannot manage it effectively, it is a short step for them to conclude that the organization is dysfunctional. They may also treat inadequately managed or addressed complexity as a sign of leadership incompetence. Such perceptions are capable of destroying organizations, taking their leaders with them.

> The complexity of our large companies is a curse. But we have to remember that complexity is also a good thing. Companies are complex by design because it allows them to do difficult things.[1]
>
> Professor Julian Birkinshaw, London Business School

We have already mentioned the work of Charles Perrow. More recent research emphasizes how complex systems are typically unpredictable. The past affects their future. In some cases, a very small change or disturbance may cause a very large response. Complex systems may be intrinsically unstable. They may have one or more relatively stable conditions but flip, unpredictably, between them. As a consequence they may appear to be stable for long periods – until they 'flip' again.

Feedback is an important feature of systems. Some feedback promotes stability. For example, an engine controlled by a device that reduces the fuel supply as the engine speed increases will eventually settle to a steady speed. The 'device' may be you with your foot on the accelerator as you maintain a steady speed on a motorway. Cruise control works the same way. This is called negative feedback.

Now imagine that you have a microphone connected to an amplifier and loudspeaker in a room. The microphone picks up quiet sounds and amplifies them. With the volume control low all remains quiet. But when you 'turn up the volume' beyond a certain level, the amplifier transforms the quiet sound into a louder one, which the microphone picks up and the amplifier amplifies even more… and as the positive feedback continues, the result is an ear-splitting screech. This is a benign example of positive feedback. Less benign examples lead to whole systems running out of control.

Complex systems involving humans can display positive or negative feedback and they can unpredictably flip between states for no apparent reason. History matters; and the system may go through phases of apparent calm and order, which are, in truth, the products of chance or chaos and the precursor of violent instability and disorder.[2]

Meanwhile, those running or managing an apparently stable complex system may be suffering from the grand delusion that they are in control when the reality is that the system is temporarily stable for reasons that have little to do with them, until what may be a random event flips it into instability.

A regular consequence of complexity is communication failures. Information risks becoming stuck because it can't move around the system in a timely manner. But complexity has two more risky aspects.

First, complex systems, whether for operating equipment or for managing people, become progressively more difficult to predict, let alone control, as they become more complicated. By the time employee numbers reach the thousands, there will be divisional or subsidiary managers and the board becomes increasingly remote from the front line business. As this distance grows, misinformation and groupthink become increasing risks at all levels of an organization, especially at leadership levels.

Increased complexity also brings the risk of more unrecognized failure modes, some of which may be linked with positive feedback, leading to instability if triggered. This is so whether the system is a complex chemical plant or a multinational with its leaders juggling staff split between locations, cultures and functions.

This is not a new observation. The 2003 report of the Accident Investigation Board into NASA's *Columbia* disaster concisely observed, 'Complex systems almost always fail in complex ways.'[3]

One of the ultimate examples of complexity created by people is the global financial system. Before the 2007/08 crash, its leaders, regulators, economists and politicians all gloried in the system's seemingly sustained stupendous success in generating growth, money and tax revenues. So did individual bankers and financial traders. Almost no one saw the crash coming.

Things did not improve after the crash. Its consequences were complex, reflecting the system's Byzantine complexity. Just as almost no one, with the exception of a small number of 'outsiders', was able to see the crash approaching, no one was able to predict how the system would behave once it had failed. It was beyond prediction.

Perrow's conclusion was that system complexity should be reduced where possible. What regulators can do – and some are attempting this – is to encourage the reduction of complexity and potentially positive feedback loops in the system by removing cross-connections that collectively make systemic failures more likely.

It is too early to tell whether regulators are succeeding. Swathes of complexity remain and when the next financial crisis happens, regulators and politicians will discover whether they have done enough. If they have not, regulators – and perhaps this time politicians too – who are found to have failed will find their reputations in tatters.

## Questions to mull

- Write down two examples of negative feedback at work in your organization. Do they help to stabilize your organization?
- Write down two examples of positive feedback in your organization. In what circumstances might they damage your organization and its reputation? What can you do about them?
- Where might complexity be blocking the smooth flow of information around, into and out of your organization? With what potential consequences?
- What complexity outside your organization might cause damage to your organization?

## Notes

1. Birkenshaw (2015).
2. Mitleton-Kelly (2003).
3. NASA (2003), p 6.

# Board composition, skill, knowledge, experience and behaviour

11

Regulators and shareholders expect boards to be collectively competent: boards should have sufficient understanding and experience of business in general and of the special characteristics of their own business to enable them to provide oversight. Individual directors are not expected to be experts on everything. But, taken together, the board should have the skill, knowledge and experience to understand and deal with the large majority of issues that are put before it. Non-executives should share between them the full range of skill knowledge and experience so that they can challenge effectively and be able to distinguish a good response, whether from an executive or an outside consultant, from plausible bluster and vacuous blather.

Unfortunately, our research shows that this is not always the case. Lack of board skill was a contributory factor in almost 90 per cent of corporate crises analysed in *Deconstructing Failure*.[1] The question is: why?

## Insufficient understanding

There is an old saying that runs 'If you can manage one sort of business, you can manage any.' There is an element of truth in this: many principles are common to all businesses. But different types of business have their own special features which, if ignored, can cause serious damage. Some boards have not made this intellectual leap and believe that general business skills, particularly financial literacy and an interest in strategy, are all that is needed to oversee a large complex organization.

This misconception was encouraged by business schools' teaching of financial control as the best corporate model. In this, effectively a hands-off conglomerate approach, boards supported by a small corporate centre saw their main role as setting financial objectives and monitoring the performance of the business units (and subsidiaries) against them.

In the jargon of the time, business units were 'set free' from central bureaucracy and were allowed to develop their own strategies and policies. This resulted in widespread delayering, reduction of corporate central functions, little synergy and increasing remoteness of the board from the actual business.

The financial control model was very fashionable in the 1990s but its limitations in dealing with a complex market place became increasingly obvious in the new millennium. A greater degree of board involvement became necessary as regulators, pushed by their own stakeholders, began making directors more accountable for what goes on in the business.

Business schools therefore moved on,[2] and encouraged large companies to move to a strategic control model. In this the board sets the financial objectives but also provides an overall strategic direction within which the business units develop their strategies. Importantly, the board develops organization-wide policies such as risk management, compliance, governance, IT, human resources, procurement, mergers and acquisitions, outsourcing, thus re-establishing the primacy of the board.

The strategic control approach requires boards with a broader range of skills than under the old model. However, we regularly hear comments implying that many board members remain wedded to the idea that boards are essentially financial bodies and intuitively select directors accordingly.

In the early 1980s, when he ran an insurer's loss control function, Derek was asked to address the board of a disgruntled client. This medium sized pharmaceutical company had just won the contract to supply a range of drugs to a distributor in the United States.

The chairman asked Derek to explain why the insurer was 'picking' on his company by charging a 'ridiculously high' product liability premium. Derek explained that the United States had adopted a far stricter – and more expensive – liability regime than the United Kingdom, and that company's competitors would undoubtedly have factored this into their bids.

The chairman and NEDs exploded at this news and accused the executive team of deceiving them and putting the company at risk. Derek was left wondering how the board of a pharmaceutical company could be unaware of the US liability environment, a subject that newspapers had been covering for several years.

In our research paper *Deconstructing Failure* we dissected over 40 major corporate crises. Almost all had ended in reputational damage and financial losses. Leaders were regularly dismissed as a result. We discuss the findings more comprehensively in Chapter 14, but in almost every case we found that gaps in boardroom skill, knowledge and experience, coupled with a reluctance or inability of non-executive board members to challenge executives, contributed to failure. These gaps are a risk.

## Blindness from cultural maps, rules, taxonomies and social norms

As we have previously explained, anthropologists such as Bourdieu and Tett have observed that when people form coherent groups they 'create patterns of thought and classification systems' that become the basis for arranging people and ideas. Boards are one of numberless groups that do this, using what become patterns of thought to 'reinforce cultural maps, rules and taxonomies'[3] that also form part of their identity. These mental maps help differentiate insiders from outsiders, and may influence their mental picture of what makes a suitable future member. Social norms can perform a similar function.

The oft-retold tale of PwC's Ann Hopkins is an example of mental maps that reached the US Supreme Court.[4] Hopkins was a senior manager working in PwC's Washington office. She took a State Department request for proposals that others had discarded and transformed it into the largest single consulting contract PwC had ever secured. Her clients raved about her work.

Supporting her 1982 bid for partnership, her superiors wrote that securing that work was 'an outstanding performance' and one that Hopkins carried out 'virtually at the partner level', though she apparently attracted some criticism that her aggressiveness in getting work done turned to abrasiveness that she was advised to moderate. But, the only woman among 88 potential partners, she was turned down by the partnership of 662 partners, of which seven were women. Why?

Comments from partners, reported in the Supreme Court decision, included 'needs a course in charm school', 'macho', 'overcompensates for being a woman'. Partners who had 'very little contact with Hopkins' condemned her as 'universally disliked' by staff and as 'consistently annoying and irritating'. Debriefing her on the partnership decision, her supportive boss told her that she should 'walk more femininely, talk more femininely, dress more femininely, wear make-up and jewellery and have her hair styled'. The social psychologist who analysed partner behaviour from PwC records, including those of previous considerations of potential female partners, concluded that the partners were 'likely influenced by sex stereotyping'.

Sexual stereotyping is a 'group mental map' that has come to political prominence, mainly as a question of social justice but also because it deprives boards of the perspectives available from the 50 per cent of the population that is female. Sexual stereotyping is only one kind of mental map that groups may use. Stereotyping for race is another based on a visible characteristic, but these mental maps essentially define what makes 'people like us', or 'insiders' as opposed to 'people who are not like us' or 'outsiders'.

Beyond gender, groups may be self-defined by class, leisure interests (darts, golf, pinball, opera), education (school, university, subject), career (accountant, personnel specialist, lawyer, journalist, executive) and other shared factors. Indelible attributes such as these readily become unrecognized entry criteria – and bars – to groups, social and professional, including boards, invisibly limiting choice and restricting diversity.

## Diversity and skewed boards

When we analyse boards, we regularly find that birds of a feather seem to have flocked together. 'Mainly pale, male and stale' is a pejorative description that is still apt to describe some boards. But whilst gender is an important social justice issue, it masks another aspect of diversity that matters: skill, knowledge, experience and world view.

The core of the problem seems to be that existing board members cannot see that their board as a whole lacks sufficient breadth. A widespread belief seems to be that with sufficient intelligence, anyone can make up for any lack of skill knowledge and experience, if necessary by relying on experts. In a famous, almost buried, 1968 report[5] on the effectiveness of the UK Civil Service, Lord Fulton's committee criticized the phenomenon it dubbed the 'philosophy of the amateur'. Yet in 2015 *The Economist* reported that 'the cult of the gifted amateur [still] prevails' in British leadership including among political leaders.[6]

This is an important self-delusion. Filling knowledge gaps by using outside experts is risky because no one is able to see or challenge what may be a one-sided, self-interested or extreme view. Lack of breadth leads to unrecognized risks that can cause crises. When outsiders discover that the board lacked the skill, knowledge and experience that outsiders expect – bluntly that it was collectively incompetent – the organization and its leaders will suffer reputational damage.

The UK Financial Reporting Council *Corporate Governance Code* recognizes this and provides:

> The board and its committees should have the appropriate balance of skills, experience, independence and knowledge of the company to enable them to discharge their respective duties and responsibilities effectively.[7]

Despite this, most boards we have analysed are skewed, sometimes heavily when analysed by these criteria. Some are replete with current or former C-suite executives, accountants and investment bankers. Others are laden with some highly relevant background, such as geology in oil companies, engineering in engineering companies, actuarial science or economics in insurers or finance in just about any kind of company. Most board members are over 50, perhaps seen as a proxy for experience but inadequate as regards digital issues where being over 50 is more a proxy for incompetence. Despite their main role of providing challenge, few non-executives seem to exhibit the character or forensic skills associated with good lawyers, academics and journalists. Non-executives with an education in subjects such as psychology or anthropology are rare, even though every organization ultimately runs on people power. And few boards outside the insurance sector show much evidence of having a practical, broad and deep understanding of risk, let alone of the risks inherent in an economy utterly dependent on the internet not just for trade but also for the delivery of water, food and power.

So, what might be going on beneath the formal process when a board renews itself? When considering what a suitable new member would look like, System One's quick specification for the new member is likely to emerge as a description of someone with a blend of the current team's background and attributes plus any additional skills that spring to mind as relevant. System Two's ability to think differently is limited by boards' mental maps of suitability and confirmation bias, its own tendency to confirm System One's gut reaction rather than try to test it. Some of these attributes may not be articulated but can still find their way into job specifications. Shared interests and perspectives may influence who is chosen. And if the Ivey School research is correct, a commonly absent attribute among selection criteria is character.

Whilst increasing gender and ethnic diversity can bring new perspectives, skills, knowledge and experience to boards, it will only do so to the extent that boards identify the skills that an outsider can see are missing and the 'diversified' directors actually bring the missing skills. If they are, gender and ethnicity apart, 'people like us', risks from gaps in skill, knowledge and experience will remain unabated.

Much more effort – plus System Two liberated from mental maps and confirmation bias – is required to go back to basics, rigorously analyse the skills, knowledge and experience the team needs, what the team has, where the gaps are and how to eliminate attributes that are irrelevant to the choice and discourage suitable applicants. The board recruitment industry should have the expertise to advise robustly on the spread of skills needed on a board but the evidence is that few dare to tell truth to their paymasters.

Recent research on how head-hunters help recruit of chief executives[8] gives little hope from that quarter, even on well-paid roles such as C-suite recruitment. What hope, then, on a loss leader NED recruitment (or a board evaluation) assignment where there is a strong incentive to avoid upsetting the chair from whom the really lucrative project, a new CEO, is yet to come?

We once asked a leading recruitment agency how they go about selecting candidates for non-executive directorships. We were told, 'We always choose people who have been NEDs before, in case we get sued.'

We asked another why people with good forensic skills – such as lawyers, journalists and academics – were rare on boards. We were told that chairs don't like such people on their boards because they are prone to ask questions that are difficult to answer, so the agencies don't suggest such people unless specifically asked.

## Biases, heuristics, board dynamics and challenge

As we study boards, it is rare for us to encounter a NED with systematic education in how people think and behave, such as behavioural economics, sociology, anthropology or psychology. Nor do we often encounter NEDs with a career specialized in practical people management, such as an experienced human resources, personnel or people director – though we do occasionally come across both kinds.

We do not know why this is so, but we suspect a number of factors. Part of the explanation may be that psychology is taboo in many circles, making human behaviour a taboo subject for many, including boards. Some board members may believe they have the necessary skills but lack the self-awareness, or humility, to question their true extent. Others may fear the possibility of a colleague with the skill to dissect board culture or weaknesses in the route to a decision. We have been told that even now only a few business schools give as much emphasis to core skills related to ethos[9] and managing people as they do to finance, strategy and leadership.

Whatever the cause, the result appears to be that many, perhaps most, leadership and NED teams lack systematic education in behavioural economics, anthropology, psychology or sociology. The skills gap leaves them and their organizations vulnerable to risks from what is utterly normal and usually helpful human behaviour.

This know-how is germane to a family of behaviours that affect us all. It is valuable to any manager including to chairs managing boards and to NEDs in their supervisory role. Since greater influence brings greater consequences, the more senior we are, the more serious are the likely consequences if the usually helpful heuristics and cognitive biases take us in a risky direction without our noticing.

When it comes to the quality of board conversations, to make the most of the board's talents, the team also needs 'psychological safety'. This is a shared belief that the board is a safe place for personal risk-taking, leading to confidence that 'the team will not embarrass, reject or punish someone' for saying what they think.[10] Its absence risks important thoughts that are not shared.

Boards will also have biases as to what they prefer to discuss. People are most comfortable discussing the familiar. For example, many boards nowadays are heavyweight in financial, strategy and sectoral expertise but relatively lightweight in risk, people and digital know-how. Such boards are likely to be at home with finance and strategy and less comfortable discussing risk, people and internet issues.

Beyond psychology, it is worth repeating Gillian Tett's anthropological observation that groups ignore or do not discuss what they see as 'taboo, obvious, disrespectful or boring',[11] a space that contains important subjects. This insight may explain much of the reported resistance to external board evaluations – even though few leaders have any difficulty in understanding why evaluating subordinates matters.

### Questions to mull

- Describe your board's shared cultural map. How does it differ from your personal cultural map?
- What subjects does your board not discuss? Why?
- How would a sceptical outsider see your board's cultural map?
- In what respects would a sceptical outsider conclude that your board lacks skill knowledge and experience?
- To what extent has your board received systematic education in subjects that help explain how people behave, such as sociology, anthropology or psychology?

## Notes

1 Reputability (2013).
2 Goold and Campbell (1994).
3 Tett (2015), p 44.
4 Price Waterhouse v. Hopkins 490 U.S. 228 (1989), https://supreme.justia.com/cases/federal/us/490/228/case.html (accessed 2/4/2016).
5 Fulton (1968), para 15.
6 End of the accidental boss, *The Economist* 28/11/2015 http://www.economist.com/news/britain/21679215-business-gets-serious-about-running-business-end-accidental-boss accessed 28/8/2016.
7 FRC (2014a), para B.1.
8 Steuer *et al* (2016).
9 Crossan *et al* (2013).
10 Edmondson (1999).
11 Tett (2015), p 45.

# Risks from strategy and change

# 12

Strategy is a fundamental board responsibility. Failures of strategy and its implementation cost money and regularly cause leaders to lose their reputations for competence, often taking the reputation of their organization with them. This risk regularly emerges when the strategy change involves an acquisition or merger, often because insufficient effort has been put into integration and other human aspects of delivery.

## Strategy development

In our research we have read and heard many stories about how new strategy emerges and is implemented. The issues raised begin with the process of strategy development.

We have heard non-executives complain that they were excluded from strategy development until the strategy was presented to the board. They felt that at that stage, any challenge would turn into a 'back me or sack me' discussion that they wished to avoid.

Failure adequately to discuss, and if necessary challenge, strategy changes is the manifestation of behavioural risks on a grand scale. Superficially it may reflect failure to create a boardroom culture that allows timely, effective board discussions and challenge. More deeply, it can flow from factors such as inadequate board leadership, the character and behaviour of executive and non-executive board members, boardroom incentives and a reluctance to ditch sunk costs.

How can a single question challenge new strategy thoroughly without confrontation? Enter the 'pre-mortem', which can also help to reduce the risk of groupthink.

Each board member is given 15 minutes to write a concise note answering a question along these lines: 'Assume the date is a year from today and this project has failed disastrously. Please describe what went wrong and why.' Each person then reads their answer to the group before a group discussion of the answers.

As to challenging existing strategy, there is little to beat the question asked by Intel's Andy Grove of his then CEO and Chairman Gordon Moore, 'If we got kicked out and the board brought in a new CEO, what do you think he would do?'[1]

But there is also a systemic issue. Some risk teams are allowed to direct their critical faculties to strategy development and management of change. Of those that are, many will not have the training, know-how, skills and experience needed to make a thorough analysis; and few have the status to critique what may be the chief executive's current project.

The FRC has, as we have mentioned, recommended that boards ensure their risk teams have the skills, knowledge, experience, authority and support needed for them to be able to assess the risks the company faces, so boards should ensure that their risk teams are equipped, and given authority, to analyse risks from strategy and change.

## Risks from large projects and change: the planning fallacy

Mergers and acquisitions are perhaps the most extreme form of change. As we have mentioned, most acquisitions destroy value for the acquiring party. But this is not a problem confined to acquisitions: large projects also have a long track record of coming off the rails.

Daniel Kahneman recounts[2] how he became involved in a collaboration to write a textbook. His team met regularly. After a year of progress, Kahneman asked everyone to write down their personal estimate of how long it would take to complete. Answers ranged from eighteen to thirty months.

Sceptical, Kahneman asked a particularly experienced team member how similar teams had fared from this stage. Embarrassed, his colleague admitted that about 40 per cent of teams of which he was aware had failed to deliver. For those that had finished, it had taken another seven to ten years' work. Intrigued, Kahneman asked how his team compared to those that had succeeded. The answer: 'we're below average – but not by much'.

Would you have persevered or given up? Years later Kahneman wrote, 'We should have quit that day. None of us was willing to invest six more years of work in a project with a 40 per cent chance of failure.' They continued as though the discussion had never taken place. They soldiered on – for eight years. By the time the book was ready, its sponsor had lost interest.

### The planning fallacy

Kahneman described that project as 'one of the most instructive experiences' of his professional life. The first lesson was the profound distinction between two methods of forecasting that Kahneman and his colleague Amos Tversky dubbed 'the inside view' and 'the outside view'.

The second concerned the unreliability of the 'inside' view, based effectively on progress so far, some extrapolation and some margin for error. The 'inside' view's extrapolation was its weakness because it made the unrecognized assumption of plain sailing, a maintained level of commitment and no problems. Kahneman concluded that they had ignored Rumsfeld's 'unknown unknowns'.

We think they also ignored unknown knowns too – the knowledge that one of them remembered when prompted. Kahneman's penetrating question turned those unknown knowns into known knowns. Kahneman had achieved that insight by temporarily detaching someone with knowledge from their normal 'insider' perspective to obtain, rather as anthropologists do, the 'outsider' information needed to elicit three pieces of baseline information on what usually happens:

- Failure rate: 40 per cent.
- Average time? Seven to ten years.
- Our team's experience: Somewhat below average.

▶

A better approach to decision-making is to start from base rates such as these and calibrate the project's prospects relative to the base rate. And here lay Kahneman's third lesson, which he called 'irrational perseverance'.

They should have given up, but they didn't. Even when they knew it, they ignored the 'outsider' view of the project's likely failure. Kahneman came to call such behaviour 'the planning fallacy'. It explains why projects regularly overrun insiders' estimates on time and money.

What Kahneman's team did, and what we all tend to do, was to neglect base rates – what usually happens in similar situations – and build estimates from scratch. In estimating our own performance, we underestimate how things might go wrong through a mixture of biases that include: the availability heuristic – we don't have a ready list of examples of how projects go wrong; the optimistic bias – we tend to delude ourselves that bad things are less likely to happen than a realist would think; and the overconfidence bias – we are naturally an overconfident species. Groupthink readily reinforces the decision-making team's cohesion.

When the project goes wrong, someone else's money is squandered and leaders often lose their reputation for competence. Rationality regularly rules the post-mortem. If it digs sufficiently deep, everyone can see that human factors such as overconfidence, over-optimism, egotism, inertia, ignorance of history and groupthink were at work.

As Kahneman illustrated, we are less prone to these kinds of error when estimating how others will perform. That tendency is harnessed by the devil's advocate and the pre-mortem. Wise leaders will include both in their standard toolkit.

## Risks from inadequate crisis strategy, planning, practice and management

This is not a book about crisis strategy, planning or management: there is an extensive literature on these subjects. However, weakness in any of these areas is a severe reputational risk. We shall therefore discuss briefly some of the areas from a risk perspective.

Any failure to adopt a sound crisis strategy, plan thoroughly and test and practice regularly and realistically leaves the organization at risk of turning a manageable crisis into a reputational fiasco. It is like running an airport without an effective fire station trained to deal with accidents.

Good crisis strategy begins with managing the causes of crises. As we have discussed, organizations are full of systemic risks that increase as organizations grow in size and complexity. Many are foreseeable and seen by insiders who are powerless to act on their insights. More are foreseeable to outsiders, especially those given privileged access to insider knowledge. Yet too many appear to foster conditions that tend to keep leaders in the dark as to what can be catastrophic reputational risks. Failures in this area can both cause crises and tip them into reputational disasters.

Good crisis planning begins with a crisis strategy built on reality. This is a challenge. Most of us are prone to the idea that 'it couldn't happen here' and that bias is probably one of the reasons why, in our research, so many boards seem to be the last to see a crisis coming and are shocked that such a thing could happen to them.

Overcoming board risk blindness means overcoming the biases that cause it and the social norms and taboos that prevent boards from seeing, let alone talking about, weaknesses that originate in the board. Failing to find and tackle these is to leave a family of risks incubating, whilst complacency grows.

Good communication is the smoke detector for incubating crises. Someone in your organization will probably know something is going wrong well before it becomes a disaster, and others will have seen the underlying vulnerability for even longer. Unfortunately, as we have discussed, people are often reluctant to pass unwelcome news upwards. The result is that small, manageable problems become large and dangerous. Unpalatable news must be made welcome.

As we have explained, stakeholder behaviour in a crisis is crucial. Your seemingly natural advocates may become your most vocal critics and natural critics may see a crisis as an opportunity that you too would like to seize. Analysing stakeholder attitudes through the lens of crises will help you to see where you sit on the spectrum from vulnerable through resilient to antifragile – and why.

Armed with a well-tested strategy, good planning is possible. Plans should be practised and that includes every potential leader and spokesperson, however senior, going through realistic training in crisis leadership and in being interviewed aggressively under stressful conditions.

Learning to speak in a crisis is not learning to act: sincerity is essential. It is a matter of understanding, and practising dealing with, pressures and situations that are utterly unfamiliar to anyone who has not felt the heat at the heart of a crisis.

Commenting on his performance as BP's CEO and spokesman during the *Deepwater Horizon* crisis, Tony Hayward said that if he had a degree in acting from RADA (a leading drama school) rather than a degree in geology he might have done better in handling the fallout from the Gulf of Mexico oil disaster.[3]

### Questions to mull

- For how long before the board is presented with a decision to make are non-executive board members involved in developing strategy?
- To what extent is your risk team involved in developing strategy as it is formed?
- How often has your current board walked away from a strategy proposal at an early stage and at a late stage? What lessons do you draw?
- What does your board fail to discuss?

## Notes

1 Grove (1996).

2 Summarized from Kahneman (2011), pp 245–47.

3 BBC documentary 9 November 2010, quoted in the *Guardian* the same day under the headline 'Tony Hayward on BP oil crisis: "I'd have done better with an acting degree"', http://www.theguardian.com/business/2010/nov/09/bp-tony-hayward-bbc-interview accessed 28/8/2016.

# Incubation and complacency 13

We have analysed data to discover how long root cause risks incubate before they emerge to cause harm. The first data set was taken from two dozen accidents and crises analysed in *Roads to Ruin*, the Cass Business School report for Airmic[1] and our own follow-up report, *Deconstructing Failure*.[2] All involved reputational and financial damage ranging from embarrassment through severe damage to catastrophic failure.

These accidents and crises included the collapse of AIG, Enron, Arthur Andersen, Northern Rock, Independent Insurance Company and Equitable Life. Also included were the A380 prototype mismatch, rogue traders, money laundering, sanctions-busting and Libor fixing, fraud, drug company misdemeanours, the *Costa Concordia* grounding, phone hacking, child abuse scandals and aggressive tax avoidance. Almost all these events emerged between 1999 and 2012 and almost all turned out to have their origins in what we now call behavioural and organizational risks.

To these we added 12 major UK accidents analysed by Barry Turner in *Man-Made Disasters*, first published in 1979.[3] These occurred between 1966 and 1975 and included:

- the Aberfan colliery disaster, in which 116 children and 28 adults were killed as a spoil heap slid onto a primary school;
- the Coldharbour Hospital fire, in which 21 patients died;
- the Hixon Level Crossing disaster, in which 11 passengers were killed;
- the Summerland Night Club disaster, in which 50 people died as they partied;
- the 1973 London Smallpox outbreak;
- the Flixborough explosion, which killed 28.

All counted behavioural or organizational risks among their root causes and most involved reputational damage among their consequences.

Since accidents and disasters rarely have a single cause, we followed Turner's methodology. He estimated when root causes began to develop and accumulate, unrecognized by those in authority. To make the data compatible, so did we. Turner analysed incubation periods of his accidents into a series of bands ranging from 'less than one month' through 'three to eight years' to 'about 80 years'. We did likewise.

## Incubation can be surprisingly long

Figure 13.1 shows the results. We have omitted the very long tail from 20 to 80 years, so that the graph ends with 94 per cent of events having emerged after 20 years. Six per cent took even longer.

**Figure 13.1** Cumulative percentage of crises emerged by months

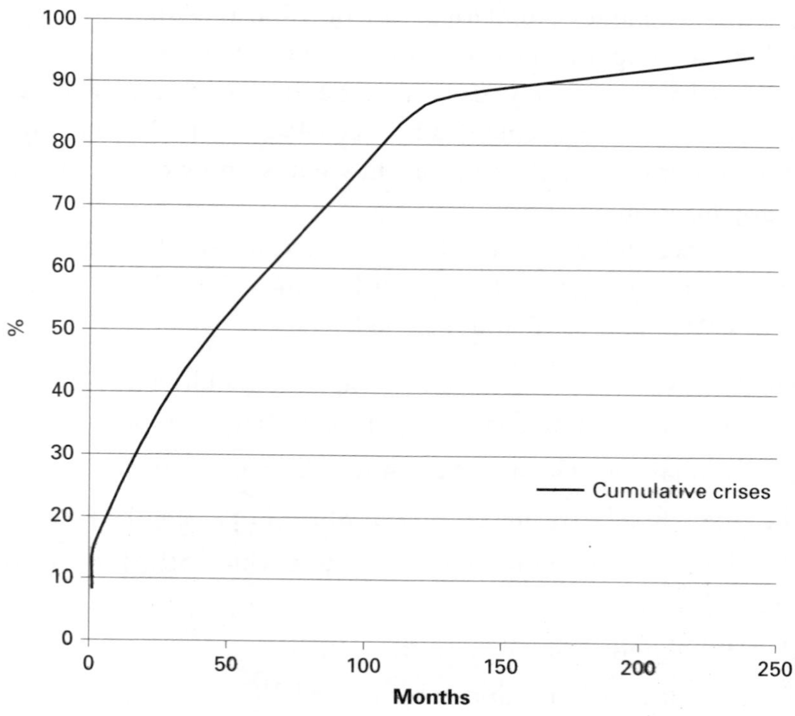

The results show that few accidents emerge quickly. Rather, most take more than three years to emerge. We believe that long incubation periods such as these have played an important part in the neglect of behavioural and organizational risks.

When a child first touches a hot object, it immediately feels the consequences – 'Ouch!' Instant – and negative – feedback means that the child learns the lesson: beware of 'hot'! Prompt feedback gives us the opportunity to learn what works and what doesn't by closely linking effects and causes. But even here our brains try to cheat us of learning: self-serving bias leads us to paint ourselves in the best possible light.

When time separates causes from effects, feedback is likely to be poor and more distorted by bias. This makes it much harder for people and organizations to learn and to identify the roots of future crises. Festering root causes can incubate and accumulate for years before emerging; so unless someone deliberately sets out to find and deal with them, they will stay that way until they materialize to cause a crisis.

Even when they emerge in a crisis, these deeper risks often remain unrecognized because, as we explained in Chapter 3, the investigation is superficial and does not dig to root causes. These only emerge when you persistently ask 'Why?' Why did they break the rules? Why did culture or incentives lead them to break them? Why was the culture the way it was? Why did that incentive encourage that undesirable behaviour? And why was that culture or incentive there in the first place?

Too often, the question 'Why?' is not pursued, so that unrecognized root causes continue to incubate. They will contribute to the next crisis when circumstances are right. Crises that follow the pattern of past crises are often far more damaging of reputations. Because subsequent crises are often investigated more thoroughly, it readily emerges that the same old root causes are still at work. Stakeholders are unforgiving when they learn that leaders failed to learn from previous mistakes, and this readily translates into seeing incompetence, a sin that is rarely forgiven and regularly leads to lost reputations and resignations.

## Complacency

Another consequence of long incubation periods is complacency. Long incubation periods allow organizations and their leaders to feel successful – and talented – for long periods, when the truth is they have been lucky that deep-rooted systemic risks have not materialized. This readily fosters the delusion that all is in fact well because nothing has gone visibly wrong – yet.

> *Gordon Brown, like every other western leader, was shockingly complacent and negligent in failing to understand what was driving the City. The British government was happy to enjoy the fruits of the boom, but it didn't ask the hard questions.*[4]
>
> Gillian Tett

We once polled about 100 company secretaries, their deputies and senior in-house lawyers who had recently completed an intense training session we had run to introduce them to behavioural and organizational risks and their reputational consequences. A cohort of this kind often knows more about internal issues than most.

We asked two pairs of questions, separating them as much as we could, which was very little. The first pair concerned the extent to which behavioural and organizational risks were understood across business generally and in their own organization (Figure 13.2). As outsiders, they saw widespread ignorance; as insiders, they thought things were less bad.

Our second pair of questions produced a similar pattern (Figure 13.3). We asked whether boards generally, and their own boards, understood behavioural and organizational risks. These answers also suggested widespread ignorance in 'other' boards and less in their own board. Both sets of answers illustrate the overconfidence effect: 'we' are better than 'them'.

In one of his BBC Reith Lectures, Atul Gawande, a surgeon interested in reducing medical mistakes, looked at analogous behaviour in the context of surgery. Soon after introducing a checklist system

**Figure 13.2** Is your organization better than others'?

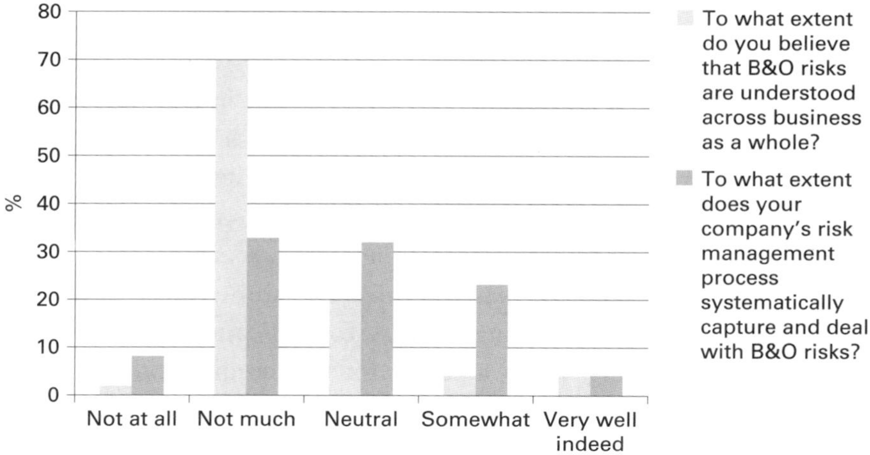


**Figure 13.3** Is your board better than others'?

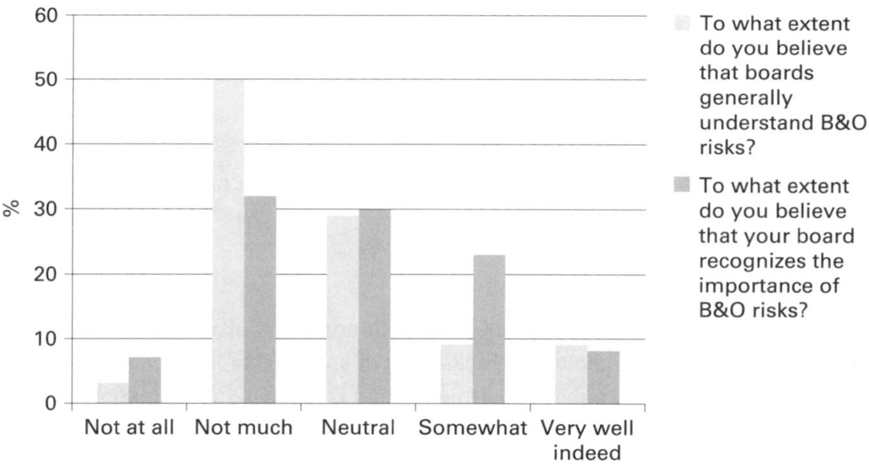


for surgeons, modelled on those used by airline pilots, he surveyed surgeon attitudes.

Most had become very happy to use checklists, but about 20 per cent really disliked them. So he asked those who really disliked them whether, if they were due to have an operation, they would want their surgeon to use such checklists. 94 per cent wanted their surgeon to use the checklists! The implication was clear: I don't need them but others do![5]

Whilst complacency is predictable, and blindingly obvious to an outsider given access to insiders' knowledge, it prevents incubating systemic risks from being recognized and treated before they cause harm.

Prolonged success and power can easily result in a leader with a strong and understandable belief that their success is based on skill. Whilst much success does involve skill, it is not always easy to ascertain the contribution of luck. And we humans are easily tempted to attribute our own success to talent alone.

As we have mentioned, Nassim Taleb has shown how easily we can be fooled into attributing success to skill and failure to bad luck – the self-serving bias – a recipe for overconfidence, especially among the successful. Daniel Kahneman has proposed a neat pair of equations connecting success, talent and luck:[6]

Success = talent + luck
Great success = a little more talent + a lot of luck

## Hubris

Hubris is an extreme form of complacency – excessive pride or self-confidence. It is a condition to which leaders, especially fêted leaders, are particularly prone.

> Lord (David) Owen, the former UK Foreign Secretary, is also a doctor with an interest in the psychological well-being of political leaders. He created a foundation to study hubris. He argues that it is 'almost an occupational hazard' for political and business leaders, feeding on 'the isolation that often surrounds such leaders'.[7]

The Ivey School's *Leadership on Trial*[8] indirectly tackles this problem by emphasizing the importance of leadership character. A good leader, they suggest, will demonstrate complementary traits: 'confident *and* humble, aggressive *and* patient, analytical *and* intuitive, principled *and* pragmatic, deliberate *and* decisive, candid *and* compassionate' (emphasis in original).[9]

Gillian Tett is more direct: 'Would-be leaders should be taught … to engage in self-reflection', she says. '[J]ust as ancient Roman generals on victory marches would task slaves to walk next to their chariots saying: "Memento mori" [remember you are mortal], we all need ways to deflate in a regular way.'[10]

**Questions to mull**

- What systemic risks lie latent in your organization?
- How can you uncover systemic risks of which you are unaware?
- Is your organization really less risky than its peers?
- To what extent are your organization's and leaders' successes due to luck?

## Notes

1. The Cass team was led by Professor Chris Parsons, and Professor Alan Punter was also a co-author.
2. Reputability (2013).
3. Turner (1997).
4. 'On the money', Gillian Tett interviewed by Laura Barton in the Guardian 30/10/2008 http://gu.com/p/22ach/stw accessed 28/8/2016.
5. http://downloads.bbc.co.uk/podcasts/radio4/reith/reith_20141202-0945b.mp3 accessed 28/8/2016.
6. Kahnemann (2011), p 177.
7. Owen (2007).
8. Gandtz *et al* (2010).
9. Gantz *et al* (2010), p 51.
10. Tett, G (2014) Hubris and the City, *Financial Times*, 3 October, http://on.ft.com/1uGI3ru accessed 19/4/2016.

# The special role – and risks – of leaders 14

In our work with colleagues at the Cass Business School on what became *Roads to Ruin*,[1] we eventually classified what we then called 'underlying weaknesses' into a series of risk areas that are potentially inherent to all organizations that are run by humans – and thus all organizations. Most of the categories of risk we have described in this book are developed from that seminal work.

## Risks from leaders

*Roads to Ruin* analysed failures whose roots were found at all levels of the organization. In *Deconstructing Failure: Insights for boards*[2] we took a different approach. Having doubled the cohort of failures studied to over 40, we focused on the role of nine board-level risk factors in failure (Figure 14.1).

We discovered that of these nine factors:

- six were present in 50 per cent or more of corporate failures;
- three were present in more than 70 per cent of failures;
- even the least frequent factors were present in about 40 per cent of failures.

All these risks play an important role in causing reputational damage if they are discovered to be present during a crisis because they damage the reputation of the organization's leadership for competence and ethicality.

**Figure 14.1** The role of leaders in failure – proportion of crisis (source: Reputability, 2013)

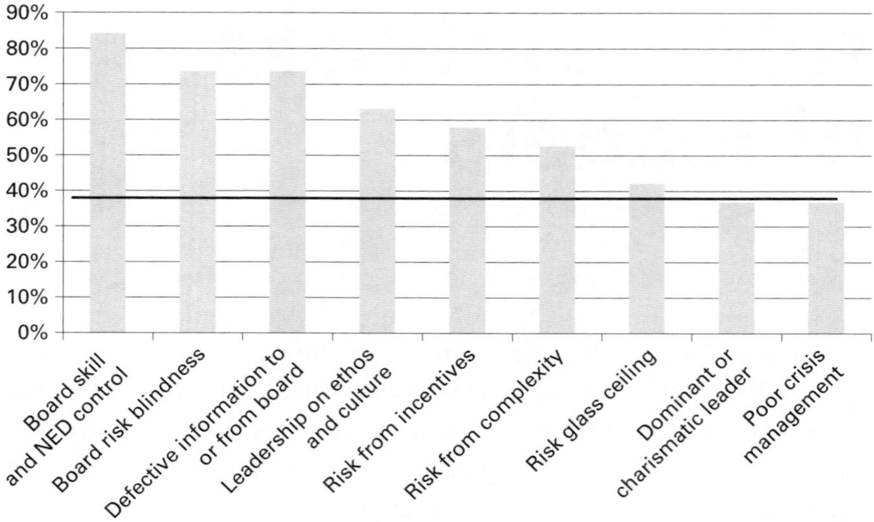


Initially we were puzzled as to why the activities of boards, which usually show high levels of intelligence and good intentions, should be such regular causes of failure. It took time to realize that there is an explanation and it is subtle. It has three elements.

Boards are usually more or less cohesive groups of people. The anthropological insight is that groups form mental maps of how their world is, how it works and this affects what can and cannot be discussed. As Gillian Tett wrote, these social silences matter because they leave some subjects 'ignored' because they are 'labelled as dull, taboo, obvious or impolite'.[3] Behavioural economists might see social silences as the result of social norms and social proof.

Whichever analysis you prefer – we think both are valuable – the result is that what an outsider would regard as important issues do not get discussed by insiders 'not because of any... plot but because ignoring these issues seems normal'.[4]

This explains why we often find that boards of failed organizations have left fundamental assumptions and attitudes unquestioned, along with senior leaders' methods, good and bad, in achieving success. They are blind to fundamental risks.

Second, board failure to explore the role of luck in success, supported by the tendency to complacency we discussed earlier, helps to keep systemic risks unidentified, unexamined, under the board's radar and unmanaged. 'Good' luck keeps latent, incubating risks hidden from the incurious.

Added to these is the question of influence. When a junior person makes a mistake or behaves inappropriately, the consequences are limited by their sphere of influence. Obviously where a junior member of staff makes the mistake that is the final trigger for a disaster the consequences may be great. Recalling Barry Turner's equation, if the junior person's role enables them to unleash a large amount of energy (such as an explosion), a disaster can result. Similarly, a junior dealer's 'fat finger' can unleash a financial calamity.

But when such an accident is deconstructed thoroughly, investigators are likely to find that its root causes lie in the failure of the system. Junior staff do not design systems: they work within them. Senior staff are responsible for system failures. Even when junior staff depart from the rules of the system, it is regularly discovered that the departure is a longstanding, well-known response to system deficiencies. It is only by persistently asking the question 'why?' that you will discover the root cause risks that were at work.

The deeper you dig, the more your questions will delve into fundamental risks from areas such as culture, incentives, communications, strategy, systems, recruitment and character. These are driven from the top. The more senior you are, the greater is your influence in these areas. Whether you discuss and decide on them or do not discuss them because your team unwittingly treats them 'off limits' or doesn't even see them, the consequences are likely to be more far-reaching. The more influence and power you have, the bigger the waves you make: for good or ill. And because these things are about the quality of leadership, they are germane to reputation.

At the top of the structure, as a board member whether executive or non-executive, you have the greatest influence of all. You hope that you will generate large, system-wide benefits. But the obverse is that what you do badly, or fail to do, can have severe systemic consequences.

Barry Turner's equation, developed in the context of physical disasters, was:

$$\text{Disaster} = \text{energy} + \text{misinformation}$$

We think there is a companion equation that sums up the role of people in reputational disasters:

$$\text{Disaster potential} = [\text{error or omission}] \times [\text{influence or power}]$$

The greater your influence and power, the more critical it is to find behavioural and organizational risks at your level, so that they can be recognized and dealt with before they cause harm. Boards and executive teams have – or should have – more of both than anyone else within an organization. They have the ability to cause more good or ill to the organization and its reputation than anyone else. This is why it is critical that risks emanating from boards are sought out and dealt with.

## Leadership charisma and dominance

There is nothing wrong with a leader being dominant or charismatic: both characteristics can bring great benefits to an organization. However, both bring with them behavioural and organizational risks that can be destructive and therefore need recognition and management.

Charismatic leaders can be powerful influences for good, but they can also lull colleagues into believing that any idea or behaviour from the leader must be right; and unintentionally undermine the self-confidence needed to challenge their ideas. The best leaders have the humility to encourage challenge and readily recognize the value of appearing on the risk register as a potential, though hopefully mitigated, risk to the organization.

Many organizations have been brought to reputational collapse and ruin by dominant leaders who have an excess of self-confidence and assertiveness over humility and other desirable qualities of character.

Dominant leaders can bring benefits through their drive and enthusiasm. But they can also present substantial risks to their organization because dominance often involves subjugation of challenge and challengers in proportion to the degree of dominance.

Such leaders may be reluctant to feature on the risk register. Risk professionals may fear to suggest they should be added. Mitigation may present practical problems – in extreme cases, it may be impossible.

Yet these are the cases in which there is the greatest need for overt recognition, and mitigation, of leadership risks.

## Who can risk-manage leaders?

Who can find board-level risks and tell boards that risks from the way they are or the way they operate, are behavioural and organizational risks to the organization and its reputation?

- Factors such as social norms, social silences, entrenched mental maps and taboos mean that board self-evaluation is unlikely to yield comprehensive or reliable results.
- External examination is likely to be ineffective or unreliable if the examiners share the social norms and silences of the board or if they have incentives to underplay what they find.
- Risk managers typically lack many or most of the skills needed to find behavioural and organizational risks at any level or risks from strategy; and most lack the status freely to raise such subjects with the board or executives.
- Raising such subjects with the board is personally dangerous even for a risk manager with the requisite status and knowledge because of the dangers inherent in bringing unpalatable perspectives to leaders.
- External board evaluation is not designed to find risks and few, if any, board evaluators have the requisite skills and know-now.

Risks emanating from leaders cannot be identified and managed effectively unless four conditions are met:

- Nothing will be achieved unless leaders explicitly make it safe for their own activities to be analysed from a risk perspective and the findings reported to leaders. This can only come from the combined authority of the chair and chief executive.
- Many of these risks are invisible to insiders. It is therefore essential to use a suitably skilled outsider, un-blinkered by leaders' social norms, to identify relevant risks before helping the board and chief

executive to assimilate what may be an unexpected inside-outsider insight. These may have effects both within the board and below the board. Risk discovery that does not cover both aspects is inadequate.

- Many risk professionals have skills gaps where individual and collective behaviour of people is concerned; and the same applies as regards strategy issues. MBA qualifications are less prevalent among risk professionals than among business leaders. This skill gap must be bridged.
- It is essential that the outsiders commissioned for this kind of work both have the character to be able to bring the most unpalatable truths to leaders; and are devoid of any perverse incentive that might discourage them.

**Questions to mull**

- Who are the most influential people on your board?
- To what extent is anyone on your board charismatic or dominant?
- What subjects does your board not discuss? Why not?
- To what extent does each member of the board welcome criticism and unwelcome news and views?
- What is the track record of each member of the board in challenging the views of others and how effective are their challenges?

## Notes

1 Atkins *et al* (2011).
2 Reputability (2013).
3 Tett (2015), p 45.
4 Tett (2015), pp 44–45.

# PART TWO
# Case studies

With the exception of the Volkswagen study, which is too recent, these studies have been based on extensive reports, books and other publicly available materials. We believe those materials to be reliable; but you should not treat these studies as final determinations of facts. Rather, if the details matter to you beyond their use as a case study, you should research the crises independently. You will find our many detailed references provide a useful starting point for study but you should not restrict yourself to them alone.

The Volkswagen study is too young for there to be enough independent reports on what happened inside Volkswagen. The study is therefore largely an analysis of public perceptions, their formation and consequences based on media reports; though, as you will read, Volkswagen has made various fundamental admissions particularly to the US authorities.

The lessons from these case studies apply to all organizations that are run, managed or led by people. When you look, you will find plenty more examples to study. They cover other kinds of organization and other parts of the world, including governments and the politicians who lead them. For example, 'Conundrum'[1] and 'The Blunders of our Governments'[2] relate and analyse a score of the most embarrassing and costly failures of UK governments of the last few decades.

Finally, we should emphasize that our studies are not about bad people. They are about honest, intelligent people behaving in what are often predictable ways. It is worth asking yourself, 'Would I have made different decisions?'

## Notes

**1** Bacon and Hope (2013)

**2** King and Crew (2013)

# BP: Texas City explosion 15

## Main risk event

Explosion at the BP refinery at Texas City

## Company involved

BP PLC

## Brief note on company

Headquartered in London and operating in 80 countries, BP is one of the world's great oil companies with a strong engineering tradition. It had its origins in 1908 in the Anglo-Persian Oil Company and traded for most of the 20th century under the name British Petroleum. Over this period it developed into a vertically integrated oil company whose activities ranged from exploration through refining and trading, to retail sales at the petrol pump. At the turn of the millennium it changed its name to BP, demonstrating its global nature after a series of US acquisitions. It also adopted the strap line 'Beyond petroleum', emphasizing its environmental credentials.

## Date of event

23 March 2005

## Background to event

Until the 1990s BP had been run on the matrix system. After becoming CEO, in 1995 John Browne reorganized the exploration and production division. In his autobiography Browne wrote,

> We devised a new decentralized organization that abandoned the matrix and gave real authority to managers who ran business units.... It was a move that would radically change the way people thought about and actually did business.[1]

Managers were given a clear sense of direction and limits, he added. They were to tell Browne what they were going to do, get it agreed and get on with it. Managers had short, simple contracts with a handful of 'meaningful' targets.[2]

Browne immediately embarked on a strategy to grow the business, something he described as 'a big gamble',[3] but the only other option he saw was for BP to be taken over – clearly a personal anathema. In the space of three years BP acquired Amoco (1998), ARCO (1999) and Burmah-Castrol (2000) to double its size to become one of the world's largest companies of any industry. He became Lord Browne in 2001 and attracted the nickname 'Sun King', as the *Financial Times* reported[4] when he had been voted the United Kingdom's most admired business leader for the third time.

BP's board included acknowledged experts in the oil business. However, one of the reports into the disaster[5] noted that John Manzoni, the board director with global responsibility for BP's refineries and their safety, had no refining experience prior to his appointment. A 2007 report[6] recommended that BP should appoint a NED with specific professional expertise in refinery operations and process safety so that safety was understood at the highest levels.

BP's acquisition of Amoco in 1998 (nominally a merger) included the Texas City Refinery. Built in 1934, it was the third largest refinery in the United States, but it had not been well maintained for many years. On acquiring Amoco, BP found a large body of functional expertise, which it 'absolutely obliterated'.[7] Both Amoco and BP had received several warnings from regulators about safety, though it is not clear that these warnings percolated through to the board.

In January 2005 an independent consultancy, Telos, reported on its safety survey at the refinery. It catalogued a litany of latent conditions such as a blame culture, inadequate resources for maintenance, leaders with skill gaps and blocks on critical news getting to leaders. It also found defective alarms, falling concrete, rusted pipes, bolts dropping from great heights and staff being overcome by fumes. Staff rated 'making money' as BP's number one priority and 'people' as its lowest, at number nine.[8] In a progress report a few weeks earlier they wrote: 'We have never seen a site where the notion "I could die today" was so real for so many [people].'[9]

## Description of event

In March 2005 an explosion and fire at Texas City occurred, killing 15 people and injuring many more.

## Post-event response

In the immediate aftermath BP reacted well. The president of BP America and Lord Browne (group CEO) were quickly on site. They promised to support the victims and their families, to cooperate with the official investigation and to run their own internal inquiry into what went wrong.

## Findings of investigations

BP's internal review, by John Mogford[10] in May 2005, found that the exploded unit's operators had failed to follow procedures, that managers failed to supervise the start-up of the unit and that when the unit over-filled and a vapour cloud formed, evacuation alarms were not sounded so that staff in nearby trailers did not have a chance to escape.

The report also found that the site working environment was characterized by a lack of trust of management, resistance to change, staff who felt powerless to suggest improvements and a culture that regularly ignored safety rules. Process safety and risk reduction targets had not been set or consistently applied. Safety lessons from other parts of BP were not learned. Staff had poor hazard awareness and accepted higher levels of risk than were acceptable at similar installations.

Changes in the already complex organization had led to a lack of clear accountabilities and poor communication, with a workforce confused as to roles, responsibilities and priorities. Poor performance management and vertical communication at the refinery meant that there were no adequate early warning systems for problems and no independent means of understanding the deteriorating standards through internal audit.

As a result of the Mogford Report, BP dismissed the plant manager and took disciplinary action against various other managers and workers. The bonuses of Browne and senior executives were cut. Tony Hayward, then Chief Executive of Exploration and Production, commented, 'We have a leadership style that is too directive and doesn't listen sufficiently well. The top of the organization doesn't listen sufficiently to what the bottom is saying.'[11]

The Mogford Report was presented to the Ethics and Environmental Assurance Committee of the board, but reportedly not to the full board.[12]

## *Baker and US Chemical Safety and Hazard Investigation Board (CSB) reports*

Following a recommendation from the CSB, BP commissioned an independent report from a panel chaired by James Baker III (a former US Secretary of State) to investigate the safety culture and management systems of BP North America.

The themes that emerged from the Baker Report[13] and the CSB's earlier Report[14] included:

- BP had given strong emphasis to personal safety (worker injury) but inadequate emphasis to and focus on process safety (ie hazard and risk analysis, system design and maintenance).

- 'Initiative overload', high levels of overtime and staff turnover helped to undermine safety.
- BP's board had been monitoring process safety based on personal injury rates presented by local management, who may just have been 'ticking boxes'. There was a gulf between the reality of process safety systems and the board's hopes and perception in London, with BP's board failing to provide effective oversight of safety culture globally.
- BP's short-term focus and decentralized management culture delegated discretion to US refinery management without clearly defining process safety expectations, responsibilities and accountabilities.
- There were numerous instances of lack of operating discipline, a toleration of deviations from safe operating practices, and complacency toward process safety.
- The CSB noted that BP had shown inadequate responses to accidents; that federal regulations were frequently ignored, and that a priority was put on production, rather than safety. It also noted that 'cost cutting, failure of investment, and production pressure from group executive managers impaired the process safety performance at Texas City', and that 'deficiencies in BP's mechanical integrity programme resulted in a "run to failure" of process equipment at Texas City'.[15]
- BP had failed to learn from the 1987 explosion and other incidents at its Grangemouth Refinery, or from the experience of the industry at large. Its safety system failed to translate high safety ideals ('no accidents, no harm to people, no harm to the environment') into measurable risk management criteria.
- The CSB recommended that BP's main board appoint an additional non-executive director with 'specific professional expertise and experience in refinery operations and process safety'.[16]

## Consequences of event

Lord Brown announced his early retirement on 12 January 2007, days before the publication of the Baker Report on 16 January 2007.[17]

Subsequent compensation settlements exceeded $1.6bn and there were various criminal penalties and fines for health and safety violations.

## Risk management lessons

### *Lesson 1: NEDs must challenge the executive*

Without being present at board meetings, one can only deduce from subsequent events the extent of challenge. If the board did ask questions about the Texas City Refinery's health and safety record and maintenance, why did it have so little impact on safety during the seven years of BP ownership prior to the explosion? Or was it kept in the dark or misled? And to what extent did Browne's apparent success, charisma and popularity in the City of London deter non-executives from challenging? It was later reported by that there were no dissenting voices in the boardroom, leaving Browne with neither self-awareness nor a sounding board. From where could honest feedback come?[18]

### *Lesson 2: Boards must be aware of the perverse outcomes of incentives*

Incentives, whether explicit or tacit, can influence behaviour; but there is a risk that they may have perverse outcomes that threaten the longer term interests of the company. The mix of management incentives appeared to favour increasing production and cutting costs. They did not actively downplay safety or risk management, but the result seems to have been vigorous cost cutting without active regard for maintenance and safety.

Another incentive flowed from the culture of blame at Texas City. If something went wrong, the reaction was to blame someone rather than to explain it by finding the root causes and fixing them, applying a just culture to those involved. Typically this results in errors being hidden where possible.

## Lesson 3: Boards must remove the risk glass ceiling

A 'risk glass ceiling' may prevent risk professionals from communicating unwelcome news to leaders either from fear of repercussions or from the difficult diplomacy needed to address risks emanating from the board itself. A risk glass ceiling at BP was identified by the CSB, which reported, 'Personnel were not encouraged to report safety problems and some feared retaliation for doing so.'[19]

## Lesson 4: Risk management needs to be coordinated at the top

A fundamental principle of enterprise risk management is that the various strands of risk management – corporate and operational together with their aggregations and accumulations – need to be coordinated at or near board level. At that time almost half of large US and UK companies had already appointed a CRO or equivalent to undertake this role. However, this level of coordination, analysis and control appears to have been lacking at BP at the time of Texas City. There was clearly little join up between process safety and people safety, with the former being neglected. Baker concluded that BP's board '[had] not provided effective process safety leadership and [had] not adequately established process safety as a core value across all its five U.S. refineries'.[20]

Top-level coordination of risk management is even more important with reputational risk as its management is complex and extends to every part of the organization.

## Lesson 5: Boards need to understand the value of the corporate reputation

There is some indication that BP had appreciated the importance of its corporate reputation in the past. It had used a licence to operate system whereby new projects had to satisfy a range of criteria, including reputational impact, prior to approval. It seems doubtful that this was applied to the US acquisitions since these were not primary natural resource extraction projects.

If the value of BP's reputation had been fully recognized by the board, 'owned' at that level and the risks to it fully understood, oversight of the refinery and the risks it presented may well have been very different.

Reputations are most readily lost when a trigger event involves what is perceived to be a core competence or involves management behaviour that is seen by stakeholders as unacceptable. In the aftermath of the Texas City explosion BP's reputational capital helped maintain investor confidence. However, as the bad news from the highly critical investigations became public, the reputational capital began to drain away. This was to prove costly when the *Deepwater Horizon* crisis arose a few years later.

## Questions to mull

- Empowerment of businesses with the reduction of the role of head offices was very fashionable in the early 2000s. To what extent might BP's decentralization have contributed to the disaster?
- What are the potential behavioural, organizational and reputational risks associated with a strategy of growth by acquisition? How might these be addressed?
- Do you think the BP board had sufficient understanding of refineries or process safety? How and why might this have come about?
- Why did the BP board not learn from the Grangemouth disaster?
- How do you rate the effectiveness of communication at BP? What blocked communication?
- Was cultural leadership by the BP board adequate?
- What were the latent systemic risks at the Texas City Refinery that contributed to the disaster? What evidence is there that the board understood them?
- How would you find, and get your board to give attention to, incubating systemic risks in your organization?

# Notes


1 Browne (2010), p 63.

2 Ibid, pp 64–5.

3 Ibid, p 67.

4 Sun King of the oil industry, *Financial Times* 12/1/2007 http://on.ft.com/1jy1I9P accessed 20/4/2016.

5 Baker Report (2007) *Report of the BP US Refineries Independent Safety Review Panel*, Appendix F: BP Post-Texas City Measures, p 33, http://news.bbc.co.uk/1/shared/bsp/hi/pdfs/16_01_07_bp_baker_report.pdf accessed 7/4/2016.

6 CSB Report (2007) U.S. Chemical Safety and Hazard Investigation Board, *Investigation Report: Refinery explosion and fire (15 killed, 180 injured)*, BP Texas City, Texas, Report No. 2005-04-I-TX, p 214, March, http://www.csb.gov/assets/1/19/CSBFinalReportBP.pdf accessed 7/4/2016.

7 Manzoni statement to Bronse, http://www.texascityexplosion.com/etc/broadcast/files/ev5/BONSE--Gower,%20Pat.pdf accessed 20/1/2016.

8 Faults at BP led to one of worst US industrial disasters, *Financial Times* 18/12/2006 http://on.ft.com/1QHiGiY accessed 20/1/2016.

9 Texas City site integrity and safety leadership, Telos 13/12/2004 slide 9 http://www.texascityexplosion.com/etc/broadcast/files/docs/0387.pdf accessed 4/2/2016.

10 Mogford Report (2005) *Fatal Accident Investigation Report, Isomerization Unit Explosion: Final report* 9/12/2005, http://cip.management.dal.ca/publications/final_report.pdf accessed 12/1/2012.

11 Hayward shares candid views on 2006, *Telegraph* 18/12/2006 http://www.telegraph.co.uk/finance/2952547/Hayward-shares-candid-views-on-2006.html accessed 7/4/2016.

12 Hopkins (2008), p 105

13 Baker Report (2007), op cit.

14 CSB Report (2007), op cit.

15 Ibid, p 25.

16 Ibid, p 214.

17 After 41 years and a fivefold rise in profits, Lord Browne makes a reluctant exit at BP, *Guardian* 12/1/2007 http://gu.com/p/dkya/stw accessed 13/6/2016.

**18** As rebellious insider, new BP chief Hayward is dismantling legacy of predecessor, *Houston Chronicle*, 14 October 2007. http://www.chron.com/business/steffy/article/As-rebellious-insider-new-BP-chief-Hayward-is-1583237.php accessed 13/10/2016.

**19** CSB Report (2007), p 26.

**20** Baker Report (2007), p xii.

# BP: *Deepwater Horizon* 16

## Main risk event

Explosion of the BP *Deepwater Horizon* oil drilling rig in the Gulf of Mexico, followed by multiple deaths and injuries, fire and substantial marine pollution.

## Company involved

BP PLC

## Brief note on company

See Texas City case study (page 145).

## Date of event

20 April 2010

## Background to event

BP's recent history had included a number of highly publicized events including:

- In 2005 there was an explosion at its Texas City Refinery (see Chapter 15), following which BP reached an settlement agreement with the US Occupational Safety and Health Administration (OSHA) to improve its safety practices at the site.

- Leaks were discovered in 2006 from the poorly maintained Prudhoe Bay oil pipeline in Alaska.
- In 2006 the OSHA fined BP about $2.4 million in relation to unsafe operations at the BP-Husky refinery in Oregon, Ohio.
- In February 2007 Tony Hayward, the incoming Chief Executive, said that BP would 'focus like a laser on safe and reliable operations'.[1]
- In 2007 BP was fined $303 million by the US Commodity Futures Trading Commission in relation to an admitted episode of 'conspiring to manipulate and corner' the propane market.[2]
- In October 2009 the OSHA proposed its 'largest ever' fine against BP in relation to 'hundreds of violations of the [Texas City settlement] agreement and hundreds of new violations' at the Texas City Refinery site.[3]

In October 2009 BP began drilling in the Macondo oilfield in the Gulf of Mexico. It used *Deepwater Horizon*, one of the most powerful semi-submersible rigs, owned and operated by Transocean. The well was in 5,000ft of water, which put the project at the cutting edge of technology. The main well and service contractor was Halliburton.

At the time of the disaster there were 126 people on board, comprising staff from each of these companies and from several other contractors involved in the project.

## Description of event

In April 2010 the well was almost complete, the cement casing was hardening, and the rig was due to move on. However, a blowout caused an explosion, killing 11 workers and igniting a fireball that could be seen 40 miles away. Efforts to block the flow using the blowout preventer, to extinguish the fire and to plug the well failed. Two days later, the rig sank, with oil gushing from the well.

The spill continued into July when it was finally capped. By then, the slick had extended to 68,000 square miles and had become the largest in the history of the petroleum industry. The well was eventually declared 'dead' two months later. But the oil slick caused enormous economic and environmental damage in the surrounding states. BP became involved in a huge three-year clean-up operation.

## Post-event response

The public were soon reminded of BP's history and Tony Hayward's promise to focus 'like a laser' on safety.

BP's crisis management improved significantly over the period of the clean-up but at the start it made a series of errors that lost the PR initiative and damaged its reputation:

- Tony Hayward initially stated that the spill 'frankly was not our accident', since another company entirely owned and operated the blowout preventer.[4] This gave the impression that BP was denying its responsibilities.
- BP backed away from this stance but were seen as playing down the environmental impact when Hayward said, 'The amount... of oil and dispersant we are putting into [the ocean] is tiny in relation to the total water volume.'[5]
- Public trust in BP fell when it was accused of having doctored pictures of its Houston crisis control room to make the room appear busier than it was – even making a poor job of the Photoshopping.[6]
- At the end of May, following persistent challenge by the media, Hayward said in an interview, 'There's no one who wants this over more than I do, I'd like my life back.'[7] This was perceived, whether fairly or not, as being selfish and uncaring about the plight of the victims and media focus on him grew.
- In June he was criticized in the United States for attending a yacht race off the Isle of Wight whilst the spill continued. President Obama's chief of staff described this as 'Another in a long line of PR gaffes.'[8]
- Hayward received a vote of confidence from the board but was replaced[9] as CEO by Bob Dudley in October 2010.
- In a speech at the Cambridge Union in November 2010, Hayward admitted that contingency plans drawn up by BP for 'the ultimate low-probability, high-impact event' were completely inadequate. In a BBC documentary he said that 'The whole industry had been lulled into a sense of false security after 20 years of drilling in deep water without a serious accident, until now' and that he 'would have needed to study drama at RADA rather than geology at Edinburgh University' if he wanted to perform better under the media spotlight.[10]

One commentator described the public mood as 'outrage'.[11] Another suggested that despite being the USA's largest producer of oil and gas, BP had become 'public enemy number one'.[12] The situation was not helped by BP's advertising slogan 'Beyond petroleum', which aimed to emphasize the company's core environmental credentials. The pressure group Greenpeace even ran a competition[13] to re-design BP's logo. The gap between promises and performance had not gone unnoticed.

There also was much media criticism of the US government's role in respect of both regulation and clean up.[14] This may have been part of the reason for a possibly diversionary PR attack by the US government on BP. President Obama repeatedly referred to the company by its old name of 'British Petroleum'[15] and on one occasion stated that Tony Hayward 'wouldn't be working for me' given Hayward's post-event statements.[16]

BP's market value fell by 39 per cent, relegating it from second to fourth largest international oil company. Analysts predicted a total financial cost of about $40 billion.[17]

BP launched an internal technical investigation. The US Senate launched a full enquiry, grilling BP, Transocean and Halliburton, who blamed each other. President Obama set up a Presidential Commission to investigate the spill and its causes.

The under-resourced Minerals Management Service (MMS), responsible for promoting oilfield leasing and revenue collection as well as safety, was accused of failing to ensure proper risk assessments. Within a month it had been abolished and its responsibilities reassigned. BP resisted making available its video footage of the spill but was eventually forced into releasing it.

BP was forced to suspend dividend payments. President Obama's scathing criticism led to BP setting up a $20 billion compensation fund modelled on the 9/11 fund.[18] Fitch downgraded BP to BBB and the share price fell to a 14-year low, 50 per cent below its pre-spill level. The price of credit default swaps on BP's debt rose from about 40 pre-crisis to 614.[19]

In July Hayward's commitment to safety was questioned. Rumours circulated that oil majors were mulling BP as a possible takeover target,[20] though no bid emerged. Staff seethed at what they saw as inept crisis communications.[21] The following month, efforts to control the spill finally succeeded and on 19 September the well was finally declared to be 'dead'. A week later the *Financial Times*' Lex column declared: 'BP is one more accident away from oblivion.'[22]

## Findings of investigations

Like all offshore drilling projects, this was a highly complex operation involving a number of firms. The trigger arose from a series of circumstances and the absence of any one might have prevented the event reaching an appalling scale. According to the various findings of the investigations mentioned below, the most likely contributory technical factors were:

- failure of the well's cement liner, allowing gas to leak into the well;
- staff misreading pressure test data;
- when dense drilling mud in the well was replaced with lighter sea water, the weight of the seawater proved insufficient to keep the gas from blowing back up the well;
- the blowout preventer failed due to a hydraulic leak and failed batteries;
- the gas flowed up the well to the rig, where it ignited, causing an explosion;
- subsequent attempts to operate the blowout preventer failed.

There were several investigations and hearings into the disaster over the next few years. The most important were BP's internal report, known as the Bly Report, published in September 2010,[23] and the report of the National Commission on the BP *Deepwater Horizon* Oil Spill and Offshore Drilling, published in January 2011.[24]

### *The Bly Report*

The Bly Report reached initial conclusions on the technical reasons for the accident, but highlighted the potential importance of analysing systemic issues beyond the report's scope.

### *Report of the National Commission on the BP* Deepwater Horizon *Oil Spill and Offshore Drilling*

Introducing the report of the National Commission, one of its co-chairs said that when he had set out, he had assumed, because of the history, that BP was 'probably... a rogue company,' though it later turned out that Halliburton and Transocean had also made 'equally unexplainable mistakes'.[25]

Digging to root causes, the report concluded that the most errors could be traced back to 'a single overarching failure... a failure of management', leading to a failure of risk management; and that this was exacerbated by a failure adequately to integrate the operations of BP, Transocean and Halliburton. Communications failures abounded.

The report concluded that the root causes were widespread outside BP and that risk management failures by BP, Transocean and Halliburton were so systemic that 'they place[d] in doubt the safety culture of the entire industry'.

Having described BP's crisis response as 'underwhelming', the report derided BP's reliance on a wildlife expert who had died some years previously and the inclusion of crisis planning for seals and walruses, neither of which are ever found in the Gulf. One link connected to a Japanese 'entertainment' site. Most of these shortcomings were found to be shared by the plans of ExxonMobil, Chevron, ConocoPhillips and Shell filed with the MMS.

The report also concluded that MMS was weak, undermined by the industry and by politicians, under-resourced, lacking in the skills needed to do its job and hopelessly conflicted as a safety regulator by its role in raising revenue from Gulf oil operations.[26]

## Consequences of event

The event affected BP's share price. The subsequent litigation, investigations and court proceedings were largely complete by June 2016.

- The *Deepwater Horizon* Oil Spill Trust was a $20 billion fund set up following BP's meeting with President Obama in June 2010. As

**Figure 16.1** BP's share price fell by about 50 per cent, with a longer term impact of about 25 per cent (data source: Yahoo)

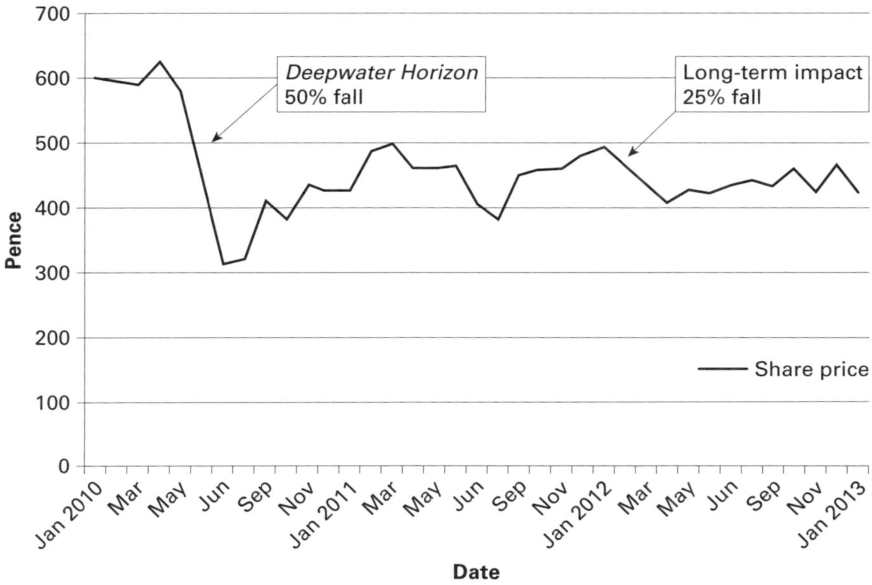


of June 2015 it was reported to be 'running low'[27] and any shortfall is to be made good from BP's flow of profits.

- US Department of Justice November 2012:[28] Federal criminal charges were settled when BP paid $4 billion and pleaded guilty to 11 counts of manslaughter, two misdemeanours and a felony count of lying to Congress. This last concerned 'manipulat[ing] internal estimates to understate the amount of oil flowing from the well and withh[olding] data that contradicted BP's public estimate of 5,000 barrels of oil per day'. BP agreed to four years of government monitoring of its ethics and safety practices.
- US District Court Litigation Settlement:[29] BP agreed to settle claims from Alabama, Florida, Louisiana, Mississippi and Texas States as well as from more than 400 local government entities. The main payments were as follows:
  - a civil penalty of $5.5 billion under the Clean Water Act, payable over 15 years;

- an additional $7.1 billion to the United States and the five Gulf states over 15 years for natural resource damages;
- $4.9 billion over 18 years in respect of economic and other claims made by the five coastal states;
- up to $1 billion to resolve claims made by more than 400 local government entities.

In July 2016 BP announced that it could now 'reliably estimate' its total liabilities at $61.6 billion.[30] Little, if any, was insured.

A Class Action was initiated in the USA by certain shareholders[31] and other lawsuits were pending. A Hollywood film released in 2016 threatened to immortalize the tragedy. BP gave it a scathing review.[32]

## Risk management lessons

At the end of 2007 the appointment of the new CEO Tony Hayward gave the investors the hope of a fresh start. However, BP's history and unresolved vulnerability to underlying risks struck again at *Deepwater Horizon*. By this time reputational capital had already been depleted, only to be further damaged by poor initial crisis management.

### *Lesson 6: Your history and track record, as perceived by outsiders, will frame stakeholders' perceptions as a crisis develops*

You may justifiably feel proud of your track record in dealing successfully with crises. But it is dangerous to believe that, in a new crisis, your stakeholders will forgive your track record of having crises just because you are good at crisis management. If your track record, taken with the new crisis, suggests that you have a better reputation than you deserve, your reputation will be adjusted – downwards.

### *Lesson 7: Boards should ensure that promises are kept*

When he took over as CEO, Tony Hayward promised to focus like a laser on safety. Much work was no doubt being done behind the scenes but BP's track record was poor and the 2009 OSHA report cast BP in a bad light. When stakeholders brought BP's track record back into focus, after the *Deepwater* disaster struck, they downgraded BP, in whom they had lost trust.

## *Lesson 8: Organizations must develop and implement a sound crisis management process*

Failure to develop a sound crisis strategy and plan and to practise its implementation is a reputational risk in its own right. Remarks made by Tony Hayward soon after his departure, and the report of the National Commission, suggest inadequate crisis planning by BP. The former also suggests that Hayward was not comfortable with operating in the public glare and raises questions as to the extent of his participation in crisis training.

### Questions to mull

- Why do you think that BP was slow to address the OSHA requirements on Texas City? To what extent did that failure influence the public attitude to the subsequent *Deepwater Horizon* disaster?
- What did the BP board not understand as regards risks to BP's reputation?
- Did outsourcing operations reduce or increase reputational risk? Why?
- Before the *Deepwater Horizon* accident, to what extent was it predictable from the outside that:
  - BP was systemically vulnerable to crisis?
  - if BP had a crisis, it was particularly likely to cause reputational damage?
- To what extent did BP recognize the risks of a weak regulator? How would you respond to weak or ineffective regulators in your sector?
- What do you think President Obama hoped to achieve by repeatedly calling BP by its old name, British Petroleum?

## Notes


1 Unlucky strike, *Financial Times* 10/2/2007, http://on.ft.com/1Rmfklt accessed 4/1/2015.

2 BP fined $373m by US government, BBC News 25/10/2007 http://news.bbc.co.uk/1/hi/business/7062669.stm accessed 30/12/2015.

3 OHSA news release 20/10/2009 https://www.osha.gov/pls/oshaweb/owadisp.show_document?p_table=NEWS_RELEASES&p_id=16674 accessed 30/12/2015.

4 BP: Stop blaming us for the leak, it wasn't our fault, *Business Insider* 10/5/2010 http://www.businessinsider.com/bp-oil-crisis-blame-2010-5?IR=T accessed 4/1/2016.

5 BP boss admits job on the line over Gulf oil spill', *Guardian* 14/5/2010 http://www.theguardian.com/business/2010/may/13/bp-boss-admits-mistakes-gulf-oil-spill accessed 4/1/2016.

6 BP photoshops picture of crisis response room to look busy, *Mediaite* 20/7/2010 http://www.mediaite.com/online/bp-fails-photoshops-picture-of-crisis-response-room-to-look-busy/ accessed 4/1/2016.

7 BP CEO Tony Hayward apologizes for his idiotic statement: 'I'd like my life back', *Business Insider* 2/6/2010 http://www.businessinsider.com/bp-ceo-tony-hayward-apologizes-for-saying-id-like-my-life-back-2010-6?IR=T accessed 4/1/2016.

8 US anger as BP oil spill chief Tony Hayward watches his yacht sail round the Isle of Wight, *Daily Telegraph* 19/6/2010 http://www.telegraph.co.uk/news/worldnews/northamerica/usa/7840720/US-anger-as-BP-oil-spill-chief-Tony-Hayward-watches-his-yacht-sail-round-the-Isle-of-Wight.html accessed 5/1/2016.

9 BP set to announce Hayward departure, *Financial Times* 26/7/2010 http://on.ft.com/1JqWt7M accessed 5/1/2016.

10 Tony Hayward: public saw us as 'fumbling and incompetent', *Guardian* 11/11/2010, http://www.theguardian.com/environment/2010/nov/11/tony-hayward-bp-oil-spill accessed 5/1/2016.

11 BP's communication response to the *Deepwater Horizon* spill, Peter M Sandman 5/5/2010 http://www.psandman.com/articles/deepwater.htm accessed 4/1/2016.

12 *Deepwater Horizon*: Frills and spills, *Financial Times* 11/6/2010 http://on.ft.com/1UCR0vk accessed 4/2/2016.

**13** Greenpeace attacks BP with competition to redesign its logo, Alex Brownsell, 20/5/2010 http://www.marketingmagazine.co.uk/article/1004622/greenpeace-attacks-bp-competition-redesign-its-logo accessed 4/1/2016.

**14** 'Political stupidity': Democrat James Carville slams Obama's Response to BP Oil Spill, ABC News 26/5/2015 http://abcnews.go.com/GMA/Politics/bp-oil-spill-political-headache-obama-democrats-slam/story?id=10746519 accessed 4/1/2016.

**15** *Deepwater Horizon*: Frills and spills, ibid.

**16** Oil spill: Barack Obama criticizes BP boss Tony Hayward, BBC News 8/6/2010 http://www.bbc.co.uk/news/10262385 accessed 4/1/2016.

**17** *Deepwater Horizon*: Frills and spills, op cit.

**18** Svanberg admits deal will annoy BP investors 17/6/2010 http://on.ft.com/1PChNIq accessed 4/2/2016.

**19** BP's shock waves, *Rolling Stone* 16/6/2010 http://www.rollingstone.com/politics/news/bps-shock-waves-20100916 accessed 5/1/2016.

**20** Inside BP: A giant wounded, *Financial Times* 15/7/2010 http://on.ft.com/14LvSw5 accessed 5/1/2015.

**21** Ibid.

**22** The troubled oil company is one more accident away from oblivion, *Deepwater Horizon*: Frills and spills, ibid. 29/9/2010 http://on.ft.com/1n2go2S accessed 5/1/2015.

**23** Bly Report 8/9/2010 http://www.bp.com/content/dam/bp/pdf/sustainability/issue-reports/Deepwater_Horizon_Accident_Investigation_Report.pdf accessed 5/1/2016.

**24** 'Deep Water: The Gulf oil disaster and the future of offshore drilling (2011) https://www.gpo.gov/fdsys/pkg/GPO-OILCOMMISSION/pdf/GPO-OILCOMMISSION.pdf accessed 5/1/2016.

**25** BBC interview with William Reilly 7/1/2011 http://news.bbc.co.uk/1/hi/programmes/world_news_america/9349780.stm accessed 5/1/2016.

**26** Ibid.

**27** Macondo spill fund running low, *Upstream*, 30/7/2015 http://www.upstreamonline.com/epaper/article1333341.ece accessed 5/1/2016.

**28** BP Exploration and Production Inc. agrees to plead guilty to felony manslaughter, environmental crimes and obstruction of Congress surrounding *Deepwater Horizon* incident, 15/11/2012 http://www.justice.gov/opa/pr/bp-exploration-and-production-inc-agrees-plead-guilty-felony-manslaughter-environmental accessed 5/1/2016.

**29** BP to pay investors $175m over Gulf spill claims, *Financial Times* 3/6/2016 http://on.ft.com/1Zixqai accessed 2/7/2016.

**30** BP estimates all remaining material *Deepwater Horizon* liabilities, BP press release 14/7/2016 http://www.bp.com/en/global/corporate/press/press-releases/bp-estimates-all-remaining-material-deepwater-horizon-liabilitie.html accessed 27/7/2016.

**31** BP faces *Deepwater Horizon* lawsuit by investors including London councils, *Guardian* 4/7/2014 http://www.theguardian.com/environment/2014/jul/04/bp-deepwater-horizon-class-action-texas accessed 5/1/2016.

**32** BP gives Deepwater Horizon disaster film a scathing review, *Financial Times*, 30 September 2016. https://www.ft.com/content/63e24752-8684-11e6-ad89-ba2f348161fb accessed 13/10/2016.

# Tesco PLC 17

We are indebted to Samantha Sultana, one of Derek's students at Cass Business School, whose MSc dissertation[1] stimulated our initial thinking for this case study.

## Main risk event

Aggressive accounting – short termism

## Company involved

Tesco PLC

## Brief note on company

Tesco PLC[2] is a multinational food and general merchandise retail group with headquarters in Cheshunt, United Kingdom. It is the second largest retailer in the world in terms of revenue. Its UK market share is approximately 28 per cent and it also operates in Ireland, Malaysia and Thailand. This scandal involved its UK operations, which are the largest in the group, employing 310,000 staff in 3,500 stores.

## Date of event

April 2012 to September 2014

## Background to event

Tesco, like several other supermarkets, had been through a period of adverse publicity that had damaged public trust in the sector. Incidents included the 'horse meat scandal' where problems in the supply chain resulted in the sale of horse meat labelled as beef.[3] There was also a dispute with the Office of Fair Trading regarding alleged price fixing of dairy products.[4] Tesco's market share in the UK grocery sector had been affected by the entry of the discount supermarkets Aldi and Lidl. As a consequence, it experienced it first decline in profits for 20 years.

In April 2014 Tesco's CFO Laurie McIlwee announced his immediate resignation from the board, offering to stay on to help until a successor was found, though later press reports suggest that 'he was not involved in the business after his resignation'.[5] In July Tesco announced that CEO Philip Clarke would step down on 1 October when Dave Lewis would join the board and become CEO; and that a new CFO, Alan Stewart, would join in December – after seven months without a CFO. On 29 August the CEO changeover was brought forward to 1 September.

On 5 September Terry Smith, a skilled analyst and investment manager, explained why he refused to invest in Tesco. He illustrated how, in 14 of the last 18 years, 'Tesco was not generating enough cash both to invest and to pay its dividend,' having 'changed its definition of return on capital employed (ROCE) eight times during those years'. Whilst earnings per share had risen steeply, ROCE, regarded by Warren Buffett as the best measure of performance (when not manipulated), had almost halved.[6] For Smith, Tesco was a flawed investment.

## Description of event

On 19 September 2014 an employee whistle-blower reported concerns about the firm's accounting practices to Tesco's legal department, who duly informed Lewis.

Lewis immediately commissioned an internal enquiry by lawyers Freshfields and accountants Deloittes. Based on initial findings, Tesco reported that there was a black hole of approximately £250m in the accounts because profits had been improperly booked. Lewis explained, 'We uncovered a serious issue and have reacted accordingly. The Board, my colleagues, our customers and I expect Tesco to operate with integrity and transparency and we will take decisive action as the results of the investigation become clear.'[7] Stewart took over as CFO the next day.

The bad news caused Tesco's share price to plunge 12 per cent, cutting £2.2bn from Tesco's market value.

Sector analysts concluded that Tesco had adopted aggressive accounting practices that artificially boosted profits, so masking the effect of deteriorating results. These involved the early booking of commercial income, which included:

- rebates that Tesco received from its suppliers when they hit certain sales targets for their products;
- payment from suppliers for preferential treatment for their products in stores.

The aggressive accounting also involved delays in recognition of costs; and there was evidence that some booked commercial income was conditional on the suppliers hitting ambitious targets that they clearly were not going to reach yet they were still expected to make payments against benefits to be received in the following financial period.

Professor Spence of Warwick Business School commented that whilst it is legitimate for businesses to 'play around' with numbers in their accounts, 'this is usually because the firm is under pressure elsewhere'. Tesco's case seemed to illustrate this pattern.[8]

The aggressive accounting resulted in the suspension of eight senior executives, four of whom subsequently left.[9] Although Chairman Sir Richard Broadbent[10] had indicated that he wanted to be a part of the solution to the problem, pressure grew on him to resign, mainly because of the time it had taken for the over-statement of profits to come to light. He therefore agreed to go as soon as a replacement was in place.

## Post-event response

Tesco's response to the whistle-blowing was rapid, decisive and transparent, no doubt helped by there being a new CEO who could have played no part in the event. Nevertheless, despite good crisis management, it could do little to stop the damage to the business in the eyes of the stakeholders. This was due to:

- the depletion of Tesco's reputational equity by previous mishaps and its first decline in profit for decades;
- the size of the mis-statement of profits.

It was neatly summed up by Kamel Ahmed, the BBC's business editor, who said, 'if you can't trust a business's accounts, there is not much left to trust'.[11] Terry Smith was blunter: company collapses are usually 'a slow-motion train wreck but investors believe the nonsense that managers spout about their success long after the warning signs are there'.[12]

On 6 October Tesco announced that Richard Cousins and Mikael Ohlsson, CEOs of Compass and IKEA, would join the board. The FT Lombard column complained, 'Neither appointment will quell complaints that Tesco's board is hampered by a lack of grocering experience.'[13]

## Findings of investigations

There were several investigations into the extent of the aggressive accounting, its causes and the potential culpability of those involved. At the time of writing, some are ongoing. The most relevant are the following:

- Deloitte: Deloittes' initial finding was that the over-statement of profits was approximately £250m. This enabled CEO David Lewis to make a rapid announcement to the City to warn investors of the problem. Deloittes was to revise the figure upwards, eventually to £263m, comprising £118m for the first six months of 2014, £70m in £2013 and £75m in 2012.[14]

- Financial Reporting Council (FRC): The FRC, which sets UK corporate governance standards, was particularly interested in the role played by PwC, which had been Tesco's external auditor for 28 years. They found that the Tesco 2013 financial accounts had been signed off several months before the over-statement of profit had become evident. PwC had noted the 'risk of manipulation' in the estimates of commercial income. Nevertheless, they apparently 'had been persuaded by the Tesco Audit Committee that the numbers stacked up'.[15]
- Financial Conduct Authority (FCA): The financial services regulator FCA gathered evidence and was sufficiently concerned to pass it to the Serious Fraud Office and discontinue its own investigation.[16]
- Serious Fraud Office (SFO): The SFO notified Tesco that it would be launching a formal criminal investigation[17] into the accounting scandal and Tesco agreed to cooperate fully. Such investigations may take several years to complete and this one is still ongoing. However, there is an unconfirmed report[18] that Tesco is seeking the UK's first plea bargain. On 1 September 2016 the SFO charged three former executives with fraud and false accounting,[19]
- Groceries Code Adjudicator: The Adjudicator found that Tesco had mistreated its suppliers,[20] not correcting erroneous records, issuing duplicate invoices and failing to make payments in some cases for years after the debt had been acknowledged. One internal email produced in evidence suggested that not paying back money owed could be used to hit a financial target.

## Consequences of event

The effect on Tesco has been serious. City AM reported[21] that the rating agencies had put Tesco on negative watch and its chart (Figure 17.1) gives some indication of the devastating effect of the scandal on the firm's share price.

Tesco's reputation has been badly damaged. Not only has this hit its net worth but it has lost a number of senior executives.

There has been some litigation by disgruntled shareholders, and one action in the United States has been settled, a class action[22] on behalf of American Depository Receipts (ADR) representing 2 per cent

**Figure 17.1** Tesco share price

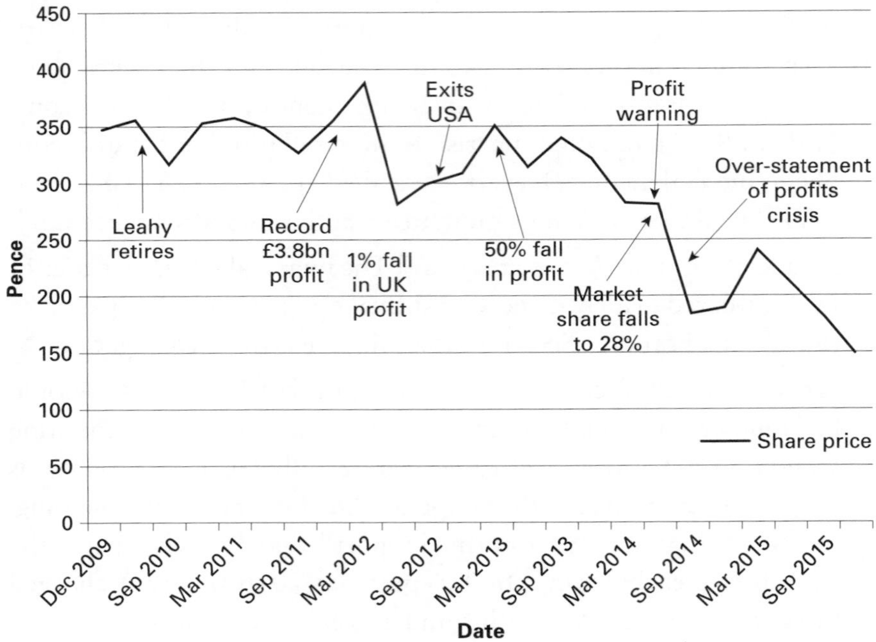


of Tesco's shares, for $12m.[23] In October 2016 a group of 60 large invertors announced a collective law suit in the UK courts.[24]

The reputational issue has clearly unsettled the Tesco management and they have recently been taking action in an attempt to remedy the situation. In January 2015 they hired advertising firm BBH and reputation consultants Blue Rubicon to advise them on turning round the firm's image. In May 2015 Tesco took on a new Brand Director, Michelle McEttrick, who had worked for Barclays Bank on drawing up a new set of values to put the bank back on course after its traders were found to have manipulated Libor interest rates.[25]

## Risk management lessons

At the time of writing the investigations and litigation are still ongoing, so more information on what really happened at Tesco may well emerge. Nevertheless, on the basis of our current understanding we can suggest the following lessons.

## *Lesson 9: Management short-termism can damage both business and reputation*

Quoted companies like Tesco are under constant pressure from investment managers, themselves driven by bonus cultures, to focus on short-term results irrespective of the damage it might do to the long-term interests of the business or its customers and suppliers.[26] If performance falls short of expectations, management will be criticized and may be undermined. This gives management incentives to respond by adopting risky policies such as aggressive accounting.

This appears to be reinforced by leading sector analyst David McCarthy, who told the BBC, 'Terry [Leahy the former CEO] built a fantastic business in Tesco... and there was a relentless focus on the consumer. But five, six, seven years ago the focus seemed to shift more towards a mantra of Tesco does not miss its numbers and in that mantra, the consumer does not feature.'[27]

## *Lesson 10: Even good crisis management may be insufficient to save the reputation*

Tesco acted well, rapidly and transparently to the crisis. This was undoubtedly made easier by having a new CEO. However, this good practice was not enough to prevent the catastrophic effect on the share price due to the enormity of the over-statement of profits and the damage done by previous scandals. Trust in Tesco's management had reached a new low point. It is no coincidence that the chairman came under pressure to resign.

## *Lesson 11: Great care must be taken on both sides of the external auditor/board relationship*

PwC had been Tesco's auditor for 28 years, something that risks an over-close relationship. This is why, after a rear-guard action by accountancy firms, corporate governance codes increasingly insist on a regular change of auditor. PwC did highlight the 'risk of manipulation' of commercial income. However, they were persuaded by the audit committee that the 'figures stacked up'. Whether PwC should have stood firm, perhaps putting their long audit relationship at risk, will be for others to decide. And the alleged defence of Tesco's accounting by the audit committee suggests an element of risk blindness on their behalf when they dealt with the auditors' questions.

**Questions to mull**

- The Tesco board appears to have put the short-term interests of large, powerful investors ahead of those of other stakeholders such as suppliers and customers, and indeed retail investors, as the ultimate owners of their shares. What do you think are the root causes of such approaches?
- What are the dangers of a longstanding audit firm relationship? How would you deal with them?
- How might lack of board-level retail expertise have played a part in this crisis?
- Why were outsiders able to see symptoms of a potential crisis at Tesco when neither the board nor the auditors, with much better information, did?
- How can you ensure that your leadership can see what outsiders would see if only they had the knowledge that insiders have?

## Notes

1 S Sultana, 'Corporate Crises – Are the underlying risks in Roads to Ruin still relevant today?' (2015) M.Sc. dissertation, Insurance and Risk Management, Cass Business School (unpublished).

2 Tesco website (2016) http://www.tescoplc.com/index.asp?pageid=282 accessed 13/1/2016.

3 Tesco shares hit by drop in sales, BBC News 5/6/2013 http://www.bbc.co.uk/news/business-22778145 accessed 13/1/2016.

4 Tesco fined £6.5m for part in dairy price-fixing, *Scotsman* 27/2/2013 http://www.scotsman.com/business/companies/retail/tesco-fined-6-5m-for-part-in-dairy-price-fixing-1-2811213 accessed 13/1/2016.

5 Tesco to pay £2m to former CEO and CFO, *Financial Times* 3/2/2015 http://on.ft.com/1CswAjb accessed 7/4/2016.

6 How investors ignored the warning signs at Tesco, Terry Smith, *Financial Times* 5/9/2015 http://on.ft.com/1oM7WxH accessed 7/4/2016.

7 Tesco RNS announcement 22/9/2014 http://www.investegate.co.uk/tesco-plc--tsco-/rns/trading-update/201409220700142186S/ accessed 7/4/2016.

8 Tesco's £250m accounting black hole is a sign of distress, Crawford Spence, 24/9/2014 http://www.wbs.ac.uk/news/tesco-s-250m-accounting-blackhole-is-a-sign-of-distress/ accessed 13/1/2016.

9 Suspended Tesco chiefs to leave next week with more to follow, *Independent* 27/11/2014 http://www.independent.co.uk/news/business/news/suspended-tesco-chiefs-to-leave-next-week-with-more-to-follow-9889103.html accessed 13/1/2016.

10 Tesco chairman resigns after accounting scandal, *Daily Mail* 23/10/2014 http://www.dailymail.co.uk/wires/ap/article-2804594/Tesco-chairman-resigns-accounting-scandal.html accessed 13/1/2016.

11 Tesco, what went wrong? BBC News 22/10/2014 http://www.bbc.co.uk/news/business-29716885 accessed 13/1/2016.

12 Hubris has set Tesco on a course into perilous seas, *Financial Times* 26/9/2014 http://on.ft.com/1Bk1cOA accessed 7/4/2016.

13 Board make-up leaves Tesco with no food for thought, *Financial Times* 6/10/2014 http://on.ft.com/1rd6bum accessed 7/4/2016.

14 Tesco in turmoil after profits overstatement, *Financial Times* 22/9/2014 http://on.ft.com/1poI9Mq accessed 7/4/2016.

15 At Tesco everyone is at fault and no one to blame, *Financial Times* 7/10/2014 http://on.ft.com/Zc9AD9 accessed 7/4/2016.

16 Tesco to be investigated by Serious Fraud Office, *Telegraph* 29/10/2014 http://www.telegraph.co.uk/finance/newsbysector/epic/tsco/11195376/Tesco-to-be-investigated-by-Serious-Fraud-Office.html accessed 7/4/2016.

17 Serious Fraud Office starts Tesco criminal investigation, BBC News 29/10/2014 http://www.bbc.co.uk/news/business-29821061 accessed 7/4/2016.

18 Tesco in talks with SFO over deal on accounting probe, *Financial Times* 6/10/15 http://on.ft.com/1hoBQeR accessed 7/4/2016.

**19** Three former Tesco executives charged with fraud, *Financial Times*, 10 September 2016. https://www.ft.com/content/7d69a61e-7682-11e6-bf48-b372cdb1043a accessed 13 October 2016

**20** Tesco knowingly delayed payments to suppliers, BBC News 26/1/2016 http://www.bbc.co.uk/news/business-35408064 accessed 7/4/2016.

**21** Tesco share price: The rise and fall of a retail empire in one chart, City AM 23/10/2014 http://www.cityam.com/1413993275/tesco-share-price-rise-and-fall-retail-empire-one-chart accessed 7/5/2016.

**22** McGuireWoods and Scott & Scott to take on Tesco in multibillion pound shareholder claim, The Lawyer 28/5/2014 http://www.thelawyer.com/mcguirewoods-and-scott-scott-to-take-on-tesco-in-multibillion-pound-shareholder-claim/ accessed 13/1/2016.

**23** Tesco pays £8m to settle US class action over accounting issues, Accountancy Live 26/11/2015 https://www.accountancylive.com/tesco-pays- per centC2 per centA38m-settle-us-class-action-over-accounting-issues accessed 7/4/2016.

**24** Tesco to be sued by 60 investors, *Financial Times*, 2 October 2016. https://www.ft.com/content/2407c3ea-8725-11e6-bbbe-2a4dcea95797 accessed 13/10/2016

**25** Tesco hires brand director to turn around scandal-plagued image, *Guardian* 24/4/2015 http://www.theguardian.com/business/2015/apr/24/tesco-hires-brand-director-to-turn-around-scandal-plagued-image accessed 7/4/2015.

**26** Tesco scandal – the perils of aggressive accounting, ACCA Global 11/8/2015 http://www.accaglobal.com/zm/en/student/sa/features/tesco-scandal.html accessed 7/4/2016.

**27** Tesco, what went wrong? BBC News, 22/9/2014 http://www.bbc.co.uk/news/business-29716885.

# American International Group (AIG)

18

## Main risk event

Aggressive corporate culture, lack of board skill, lack of control of banking subsidiary.

## Brief note on company

AIG is a major insurance and financial services group and is currently the 42nd largest company[1] in Forbes' rankings with a market capitalization of $75bn with 64,000 employees in 90 countries. Prior to the high-profile collapse of its banking subsidiary, AIG Financial Products (AIGFP), in 2007 it was ranked 20th, more than twice the size, with a market capitalization of $170bn and having 117,000 employees in more than 130 countries.[2] The group was formed in Shanghai in 1919 as American Asiatic Underwriters[3] then moved to New York in 1939 taking on the current name of AIG.

AIGFP,[4] the group's banking subsidiary, had its headquarters in Connecticut but its trading activities were based in London. It had been formed in 1987 from a team of traders from the investment bank Drexel Burnham Lambert. Over the next two decades AIGFP contributed $5bn to AIG's pre-tax income. At first AIGFP concentrated on low-risk derivative trading but in 1998 it entered the credit default swap (CDS) market which was designed to protect investors against risks from mortgage-linked securities. CDS products were unregulated and did not require the safety net of collateral. It was AIGFP's high exposure to this business during the 2007 sub-prime crisis that led to the company's downfall.

## Date of event

2007–08

## Background to event

The focus of this case study is the collapse of AIGFP in 2007/8. Nevertheless, it is helpful to understand the culture of AIG, which resulted in an earlier accounting crisis in 2005.

From 1968 to 2005 the AIG culture was dominated by the hugely successful CEO Hank Greenberg,[5] who grew the group into USA's largest life insurer and second largest commercial non-life insurer. Greenberg's business model was to drive subsidiaries to deliver 15 per cent revenue growth, 15 per cent profit growth and 15 per cent return on equity. If managers failed to achieve these targets they were removed.

In this period the board was described as 'notoriously clubby and close to Greenberg'.[6] Greenberg had hand-picked the directors and they mainly comprised friends and colleagues who had been with him for many years, plus politicians and government officials who added prestige.[7] The average age of the 15 non-executive directors was over 66.[8]

Executive directors also owed much to Greenberg. In addition to conventional share options they were able to join a lucrative Deferred Compensation Profit Participation Plan (DCPPP). Under the DCPPP they were eligible for shares in two outside companies, C.V. Star and Star International Company. These companies shared a number of directors with AIG and together owned 12 per cent of AIG's stock. Executive directors received cash payments but the real benefits of share ownership were not payable until the director reached the age of 65. If they left AIG before then they would forfeit their interest, leaving more money for those who stayed. Moreover, share participation was flexible after the event so that if the director's business had not performed well, Greenberg could reduce the director's participation in the Plan.[9] Large sums were involved in the DCPPP and most members became multi-millionaires. This was a very long-term incentive scheme whose effects deserve considerable thought.

In 2005 the appearance of ever increasing profitable growth at AIG was burst by investigations into AIG's business practices by Eliot Spitzer, the New York Attorney General. Spitzer focused on three areas:[10]

- He investigated suspected bid rigging between insurers and insurance brokers. The giant broker Marsh & McLennan, run by one of Greenberg's sons, had to pay a large fine and although AIG admitted no wrongdoing, two of its employees pleaded guilty and left the group.
- Spitzer revealed that substantial underwriting losses were being reinsured into offshore vehicles controlled by AIG. The losses were thus transformed into write-downs in the vehicles' shareholders' funds and consolidated into AIG's balance sheet, so bypassing its profit and loss account. This gave investors the false impression that AIG continued to make underwriting profits.
- He revealed that AIG had entered a seemingly sham reinsurance arrangement with General Re that had the effect of increasing AIG's claims reserves and boosting the share price.

As a result of the investigations Greenberg was forced to resign[11] at the age of 79, and AIG's auditors restated more than four years of the group's earnings. In 2006 AIG paid $1.6bn to settle charges made by Spitzer and the US Securities and Exchange Commission (SEC)[12] and subsequently provided for up to $800m to settle claims by affected investors. An AIG executive and four from General Re were convicted and imprisoned for conspiracy and fraud. Greenberg himself paid $15m to settle SEC charges that he changed AIG's accounts to improve results between 2000 and 2005.[13] Subsequently, AIG lost its coveted AAA credit rating.[14]

Martin Sullivan, who had spent 35 years in AIG's insurance business, took over as AIG CEO on Greenberg's resignation and non-executive director Frank Zarb became the new group chairman.[15] They inherited the challenge of repairing AIG's damaged reputation and changing its secretive culture. It was against this background of turmoil that the even more serious 2007/08 CDS crisis involving AIGFP was to emerge.

## Description of event

Joseph Cassano was CEO of AIGFP and said to be the highest paid employee in the AIG group with his compensation totalling about $280m over the period 2000–07. He had taken over as CEO on the retirement of mathematician Tom Savage in 2001. Savage thoroughly understood the models used by the traders but Cassano lacked the maths background. Those to whom Martin Lewis spoke in researching his *Vanity Fair* article 'The man who crashed the world' reported the of view of Cassano across AIGFP as 'a guy with a crude feel for financial risk but a real talent for bullying people who doubted him'.[16]

AIGFP shared 30–35 per cent of its profits with staff, though they had to leave half of this invested in the company. This incentivization combined with the aggressive management culture created a drive for more and more short-term profit from the business.

Initially AIGFP wrote CDS on investment grade public companies, but this book evolved to include consumer debt and sub-prime loans. As Lewis remarked, 'In the run-up to the financial crisis there were several moments when an intelligent disinterested observer might have realized that the system was behaving strangely.' Be that as it may, by 2005 AIGFP's business acquired huge volumes of sub-prime mortgage business so that it was effectively betting on the notion that US house prices would not fall. Its CDS book had a notional value of $500bn. Cassano agreed to stop that line of business in 2005; but in August 2007, he famously told the market that he struggled to envisage the company 'losing $1 on any of those transactions'.[17]

By 2007 it became evident that large numbers of more recent US sub-prime mortgage customers had defaulted. As losses on mortgage-linked securities spread to the years in which AIGFP was involved, the crisis engulfing institutions guaranteeing CDS spread to AIGFP with it huge CDS exposure. It was not the only business in that boat. In the following months the federal mortgage insurers Fannie Mae and Freddie Mac were placed in conservatorship by the US Government, Bank of America had to rescue Merrill Lynch, and the mighty Lehman Brothers filed for bankruptcy.

In Q3 2007 AIG reported a charge of $352m for net unrealized market valuation loss on AIGFP's CDS portfolio. Even so, the group stated it still believed that it would never have to make payments on the derivatives.[18] In Q4 the group announced further charges of $11.12bn, but it still wrongly believed that the valuation losses would eventually be reversed.[19] However, in 2008 the group at last began to understand the gravity the situation and AIG reported group net quarterly losses of $7.81bn, $5.36bn, $24.47bn and $61.70bn respectively. The full year net loss was an unprecedented $99.30bn.[20]

Politicians considered AIG 'too big to be allowed fail' so on 16 September 2008 the US Federal Reserve authorized an $85bn emergency loan. The US Government made three further loans resulting in the final figure of $182.50bn – the largest bailout in US history.[21]

## Post-event response

The main response to the crisis, at group level, was frequent changes in the boardroom. On 15 June 2008 Sullivan resigned as AIG CEO and was replaced by Robert Willumstead.[22] He was forced to resign by the US Government, to be replaced on 17 September by Edward Liddy as chairman and CEO.[23] In August 2009 Liddy resigned, to be replaced as CEO by Robert Benmosche with Harvey Golub as non-executive chairman.[24] In July 2010 Golub resigned as chairman following a clash with the CEO. He was replaced as chairman by Stephen Miller. Since then the corporate 'musical chairs' settled down.[25]

AIGFP was taken over by the US Federal Reserve and the decision was made to wind down the entire book of business. Cassano was forced to resign in February 2008 but was controversially kept on by AIG as a consultant at $1m per month and received a £35m bonus at the 2008 year end.[26]

In March 2009 AIG paid $165m in retention bonuses to AIGFP staff to help unwind the contracts. However, the US employees were forced to repay their bonuses by the then New York Attorney General Andre Cuomo.[27]

## Findings of investigations

There were several investigations into the crisis but perhaps the most revealing were the following:

- At a Congressional Hearing Martin Sullivan said that he was neither an accountant nor an economist – he had been an insurance man all his life. He went on to admit that he had not known the terms and risks of AIGFP's exposure to mortgage-related securities.[28]
- An investigation by PwC,[29] AIG's auditors, identified 'a material weakness in [AIG's] accounting controls and oversight relating to the fair valuation of AIGFP's CDS portfolio'.
- The SEC conducted an investigation into Cassano as to whether he had 'misled investors with overly optimistic forecasts about the extent of the firm's exposure to securities backed by risky sub-prime mortgages'. However, the inquiry was dropped without any charges being made.[30]
- The Financial Crisis Inquiry Commission Report was critical of the regulatory regime, which allowed AIG, as owners of a small savings and loan bank, to be supervised by the New York based Office of Thrift Supervision (OTS) rather than one of the major financial regulators. It stated that the OTS 'lacked the capability to supervise an institution of the size and complexity of AIG, did not recognize the risks inherent in AIG's sales of Credit Default Swaps, and did not understand its responsibility to oversee the entire company including AIG Financial Products.'[31]

## Consequences of event

The reputations of AIG and many individuals involved in the CDS crisis were wrecked. The AIG brand became so toxic that the non-life business was renamed Chartis in December 2009.[32] It was not until three years later that the management felt confident enough to revert to using AIG Property & Casualty.

**Figure 18.1** AIG share price, pre-consolidation basis (data source: Yahoo)

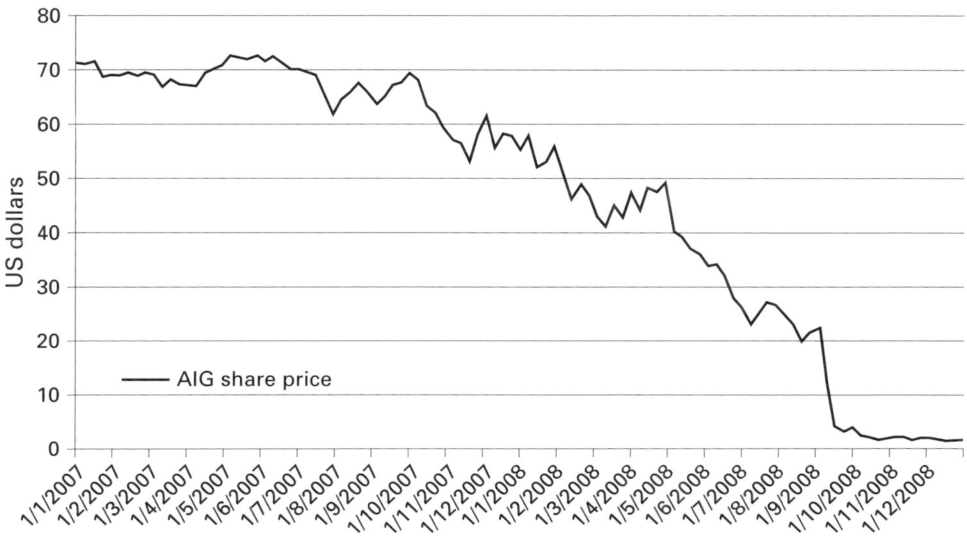


The effect of the crisis on the AIG share price was catastrophic. It fell from a high of $156.50 on 17 July 2007 to $1.25 by 16 September 2008. It recovered somewhat over the following years but has never again remotely approached the pre-crisis level.[33]

AIG's prized AAA S&P credit rating had already been downgraded to AA as a result of the 2005 accounting crisis when the agency revised its assessment of the group's management, internal controls, corporate governance and culture. In 2008, had AIG not received the bailout, it would undoubtedly have acquired junk bond status, had it survived at all. As it was, the rating was reduced to A-, a level from which it has yet to recover.[34]

AIG made paying off the bailout loan an absolute priority. It raised money through the sale of a number of subsidiaries and investments.[35] This, together with the US Treasury selling tranches of AIG shares, meant that by December 2012 the US Government's commitments were fully recovered. AIG immediately launched 'Thank you America',[36] an advertising campaign in which the Chairman and CEO publicly thanked the US Government for its help in saving their group. AIG was able to face the future as a significant global insurer, albeit less than half its pre-crisis size.

**Figure 18.2** The decline of AIG's Standard & Poor's credit rating

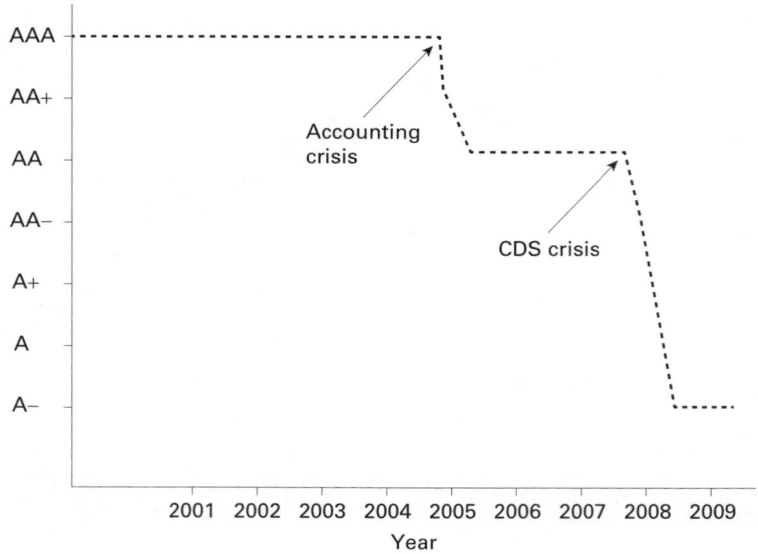


# Risk management lessons

## *Lesson 12: Dominant CEOs can produce dangerous cultures*

AIG had a dominant group CEO in Hank Greenberg and AIGFP had a dominant CEO in Joseph Cassano.

Greenberg created a culture and system of incentives where both the executive and non-executive directors had an incentive not to challenge him. Subordinates were afraid of a hostile reception and this could prevent unwelcome news moving upwards. Cassano was reportedly a bully[37] so vertical communication in the subsidiary must have been far from perfect.

Dominant CEOs can drive companies to remarkable results, certainly in the short term. However, the risks from the cultures they grow need to be recognized and managed. Workplace bullying is both unpleasant and a source of reputational risk.

## Lesson 13: Boards need appropriate skills

Boards need appropriate skills and experience if they are to appreciate the risks that the organization is exposed to and the non-executive directors need sufficient understanding, and spine, to challenge executives. Martin Sullivan was seen as 'a brilliant insurance man but [AIG] had become much more than an insurance company and he lacked a deep understanding of the financial side'.[38] However, when he replaced Greenberg as CEO he acquired responsibility for non-insurance activities.

A board whose skills included areas such as banking and credit evaluation could have been expected to raise concerns about the large AIGFP CDS portfolio in an unregulated sector without hedging. The study demonstrates the well-known banking risk of the traders' option where traders can place bets that might result in large bonuses with limited downside risk. The other evidence of lack of skill and understanding was the denial for months of the potential loss from the portfolio.

## Lesson 14: Boards need to control all of subsidiaries, core as well as non-core

PwC identified a material weakness in the Board's control of AIGFP. It was probably not subjected to the degree of board scrutiny given to the core insurance business. It has even been suggested that AIGFP was regarded more like a 'money machine' and the board did not take the precaution of hedging.[39] Clearly, boards must control core and non-core business alike

## Lesson 15: Boards need to question success as well as watching for risks

Risk management generally focuses on downside risks. However, AIG is a good example of where a board should watch closely what appears to be going well. AIGFP, and AIG under Greenberg, produced remarkable results, but why? If something might be too good to be true, you should ask whether it is!

### *Lesson 16: Regulators need the appropriate skills, resources and understanding of business to carry out their responsibilities*

AIG was regulated by the Office of Thrift Supervision, which lacked the skills and understanding to deal with such a complex and important organization. Governments should ensure regulatory competence.

> **Questions to mull**
>
> - What incentives were created by the AIG DCPPP? With what consequences?
> - When Hank Greenberg left after decades in charge, should the board have studied the prevailing culture and incentives? What would you have done?
> - What were the root causes of the AIG board's inadequate control of the AIGFP money-making machine?
> - Why did the AIG board not question AIG's apparent success?
> - How can you ensure that your own board vigorously questions the roles of luck and skill in your successes?

## Notes

1 Global 2000 leading companies, *Forbes* http://www.forbes.com/companies/american-international-group/ accessed 13/6/2016.

2 AIG 2014 annual report (PDF) AIG.com http://www.aig.com/content/dam/aig/america-canada/us/documents/investor-relations/aig-2014-annual-report-brochure.pdf accessed 13/6/2016.

3 JR Laing 8/7/1991 Are the glory years over? Much slower growth seems in the offing for AIG Barron's.

4 Atkins *et al* (2011).

5 Shelp and Ehrbar (2006).

6 http://www.bloomberg.com/bw/stories/2005-04-10/aig-what-went-wrong accessed 8/4/2016.

7 AIG highlights quest for real independence, *Financial Times* 10/4/2005 http://on.ft.com/1SUnGk6 accessed 8/4/2016.

8 *Fallen Giant*, ibid.

9 Op cit.

10 Atkins *et al* (2011).

11 http://www.bloomberg.com/bw/stories/2005-04-10/aig-what-went-wrong accessed 8/4/2016.

12 AIG settles with Spitzer, SEC for $1.6B 9/2/2006 https://secure.marketwatch.com/story/aig-pays-16b-in-settlement-with-regulators accessed 8/4/2016.

13 Greenberg pays $15m to settle SEC case, *Financial Times* 7/8/2009, http://on.ft.com/1PY1AIN accessed 8/4/2016.

14 http://www.marketwatch.com/story/aig-loses-prized-aaa-sp-ratings accessed 13/5/2016.

15 Zarb proposed as new AIG chairman, Marketwatch 23/3/2015 https://secure.marketwatch.com/story/aig-is-lobbied-to-name-frank-zarb-as-chairman accessed 8/4/2015.

16 The man who crashed the world, Michael Lewis, *Vanity Fair*, August 2009 http://www.vanityfair.com/news/2009/08/aig200908 accessed 8/4/2016.

17 Ibid.

18 AIG reports 3Q 2007 results, http://www.aig.com/financial-reports_3171_451485.html at third quarter 2007 accessed 8/4/2016.

19 AIG reports 4Q 2007 results, http://www.aig.com/Chartis/internet/US/en/Q407_Press_Release_final_tcm3171-443303.pdf accessed 8/4/2016.

20 AIG reports 1Q to 4Q 2008 and full year 2008 from relevant tabs at http://www.aig.com/financial-reports_3171_451485.html accessed 8/4/2016.

21 GAO, Federal Financial Assistance; Preliminary observations on assistance provided to AIG, GAO-09-490T, 18/3/2009, www.gao.gov/new.items/d09490t.pdf accessed 13/1/2016.

22 AIG chief Sullivan is ousted, 16/6/2008 http://www.marketwatch.com/story/aig-chief-sullivan-ousted-as-willumstad-takes-over-as-ceo accessed 8/4/2016.

23 CD&R's Liddy appointed to run AIG, Real Deals 18/8/2008 http://realdeals.eu.com/article/2008 accessed 8/4/2016.

24 AIG expected to name ex MetLife head as chief, *The Times* 3/8/2009 http://www.thetimes.co.uk/tto/business/industries/banking/article2162405.ece accessed 8/4/2016.

25 AIG Chairman Steve Miller to step down in July, Reuters 30/3/2015 http://www.reuters.com/article/us-amer-intl-group-chairman-idUSKBN0MQ22Y20150330 accessed 8/4/2016.

26 *Fallen Giant*, ibid; The man who crashed the world, ibid.

27 http://abcnews.go.com/Business/story?id=7156195 accessed 13/1/2016.

28 https://www.gpo.gov/fdsys/pkg/CHRG-110hhrg55767/html/CHRG-110hhrg55767.htm accessed 13/1/2016.

29 Revelation of losses puts heat on AIG chief, *Financial Times* 11/2/2008 http://on.ft.com/20XwTf2 accessed 13/1/2016.

30 AIG executive Cassano still faces SEC probe, Reuters 5/4/2010 http://www.reuters.com/article/cassano-probe-idUSN0518737720100405 accessed 12/6/2016; Inquiry ends on Cassano, once of AIG, *Wall Street Journal* 17/6/2010 http://online.wsj.com/article/SB10001424052748703513604575311350142446886.html accessed 13/1/2016.

31 *The Financial Crisis Inquiry Commission Report*, p 352 http://cybercemetery.unt.edu/archive/fcic/20110310173538/http://www.fcic.gov/report accessed 13/1/2016.

32 AIG UK rebrand complete, Insurance Age 1/10/2009 http://www.insuranceage.co.uk/insurance-age/news/1564207/aig-uk-rebrand-complete accessed 13/1/2016.

33 https://uk.finance.yahoo.com/q/hp?s=AIG accessed 13/1/2016.

34 Standard & Poor's revises AIG outlook to stable, *Marketwatch*, 28 May 2014. https://secure.marketwatch.com/story/standard-poors-revises-aig-outlook-to-stable-2014-05-28 accessed 13/10/2016.

35 AIG in $15.5 billion unit sale to MetLife, CNN 8/3/2010 http://money.cnn.com/2010/03/08/news/companies/AIG_sells_Alico_MetLife/ accessed 13/1/2016; AIG completes $277M sale of PineBridge, Bloomberg 29/3/2010 http://www.businessweek.com/ap/financialnews/D9EOC70G0.htm accessed 13/1/2016; American General Finance sold to Fortress Investment Group, *Evansville Courier and Press* 11/8/2010 http://www.courierpress.com/business/update-american-general-finance-sold-to-fortress-investment-group-ep-446354068-324580021.html accessed 13/1/2016; AIG to sell Star, Edison to Prudential,

Market Watch 30/9/2010 https://secure.marketwatch.com/story/aig-sells-star-edison-units-to-prudential-2010-09-30 accessed 13/1/2016.

**36** AIG: 'Thank you America' for the taxpayer-funded bailout! Huffington Post http://www.huffingtonpost.com/aig-thank-you-america_n_2395546.html accessed 8/4/2016.

**37** The man who crashed the world, ibid.

**38** Inadequate cover, *Financial Times* 6/10/2008 http://on.ft.com/1Sxh9xN accessed 12/6/2016.

**39** Why wasn't AIG hedged? Forbes 28/9/2008 http://www.forbes.com/2008/09/28/croesus-aig-credit-biz-cx_rl_0928croesus.html accessed 8/4/2016.

# EADS Airbus A380

19

## Main risk event

Complexity; supply chain problems resulting in a two-year delay in launching the A380 super jumbo airliner.

## Company involved

European Aeronautic Defence and Space Company NV (EADS)

## Brief note on company

This study involves the consortium European Aeronautic Defence and Space Company NV (EADS)[1] and its subsidiary Airbus SAS (Airbus) which was one of the two global manufacturers of commercial aircraft – the other being its fierce rival Boeing. EADS had been formed by the merger in 2000 of three aerospace companies: the French Aerospace-Matra, the German DASA and the Spanish CASA. The group was effectively majority owned by French, German and Spanish interests that were either state-owned companies or companies with close ties to the state.[2] At the time of the event EADS employed 119,500 staff.

At that time, Airbus had about 52,500 employees mainly located at its own subsidiaries in US, China, Japan and the Middle East, and in its headquarters in Toulouse. In addition, it had 150 international field service offices; a network of 1,500 suppliers stretched across 30 countries, and relied on cooperation agreements with many other companies.

## Date of event

2004–09

## Background to event

The dominating factors in influencing this crisis were:

- Airbus's determination for its new super-jumbo A380 airliner to help it to achieve market dominance over Boeing, which was developing its 787 Dreamliner;
- political issues at the European Union (EU) level and between its member states;
- and above all the complexity of the project proving beyond the abilities of the leadership and management.

In recent years Airbus had been taking market share from Boeing and it saw the launch of the A380, the largest airliner in the world, as an opportunity to consolidate its success. Boeing was developing its Dreamliner at the same time and the competition between the two companies was intense.

At the EU level the success of the A380 was regarded as important in the economic rivalry between Europe and the USA, and political interference in the consortium was evident in the management of the project. For example, project work was required to be shared between each of the EU member states having aeronautical capabilities and above all, there had to be equality of involvement by Germany and France. This led to the creation of complex organizational structures at both Airbus and its parent EADS, with the latter actually having two joint CEOs – one German and one French! Board membership at that stage appeared to be made more on nationalistic grounds rather than on relevant industry experience.

The politically influenced complexity extended to the choice of construction locations such as:

- fuselage – Hamburg, Germany;
- tailfin – Stade, Germany;

- tailplane – Getafe, Spain;
- wings – Broughton, United Kingdom;
- rudder – Porto Real, Spain;
- nose – Saint Nazare, France;
- cockpit – Meaulte, France;
- minor parts – worldwide;
- assembly – Toulouse, France.

## Description of event

The A380 completed its maiden flight in April 2005. French President Jacques Chirac had previously declaimed: 'When it takes to the skies, it will carry the colours of our Continent, and our technological ambitions, to even greater heights.'[3] So, to the outside world, the project was progressing well; but within the company serious problems were emerging.

During the previous autumn the assembly staff at Toulouse had experienced difficulties installing the 530 km of wiring in the fuselage, which comprised a complex arrangement of 98,000 individual wires and 40,000 connectors. The cabling proved to be too short, so that all the wiring had to be replaced from scratch.[4]

The Germans and French blamed each other for the fiasco, but the root of the problem was that, due to lack of overall project coordination, different – incompatible – versions of design software were in use at the various sites. This resulted in configuration management problems, as certain critical design rules for wiring were not easily transferrable between the versions of the software.[5]

## Post-event response

The wiring mismatch had been regularly reported by assembly line managers at progress meetings but it was apparently not considered significant enough by middle managers to inform senior management.

The unwelcome information did eventually work its way upward, causing Airbus's chief salesman to remark that people had been in denial about the problem.[6]

A proposal by the EADS Board that stretching the existing A330 model might provide a temporary replacement to satisfy A380 customers was soon rejected. It was not until June 2005 that Airbus came clean and formally admitted that there was a problem and notified airlines that deliveries of new aircraft would be delayed by six months.[7] This was quickly followed by an announcement of a further delivery delay of six to seven months and again in October 2006 by a third announcement effectively postponing the first delivery by two years to October 2007. This was to be followed by a mere 13 deliveries in 2008, 25 in 2009, and the full production rate of 45 aircraft per year was only to be achieved in 2010.[8]

Behind the scenes there was a political distraction involving senior management at this critical period. Reiner Hertrich, the German joint CEO of EADS was due to retire. The French head of Airbus, Noel Forgeard, with support from French President Jacques Chirac, replaced the existing French joint CEO of EADS and attempted to take sole control of what would be a simplified holding company. The Germans naturally resisted this move and replaced Hertrich by Thomas Enders, another German, as joint CEO. So, when the company should have been concentrating of the A380 crisis, the board was distracted by political infighting between Germany and France over how Airbus should be led.[9]

## Consequences of event

The third delay announcement together with a profit warning[10] that EADS earnings would be reduced by €4.8bn resulted in a 26 per cent fall in EADS share price reducing market capitalization by €5.5bn. This and the delivery delays also damaged the reputation of EADS, Airbus and their management. At the same time Boeing's share price rose by 5 per cent and orders for the Dreamliner increased. However, as we shall see later, Boeing too was beset with similar complexity issues.

The A380 crisis eventually led to the forced resignations of Noel Forgeard and his successor at Airbus, CEO Gustav Humbert, who was in turn replaced by Christian Strieff. He soon resigned, claiming he was not being given enough autonomy to do the job by EADS. He complained to the board that Airbus was not an integrated company. It didn't have a simple organization and there were shadow hierarchies left over from never-finished integrations.[11]

There were also investigations[12] of alleged insider dealing by EADS and Airbus management who had sold their shares prior to the public announcement of A380 delays. The investigations dragged on for eight years, creating uncertainty and distress for all those involved. The managers were finally cleared by a French court in March 2015.[13]

Ironically, Boeing's Dreamliner also struggled with complexity issues. It experienced a series of delays resulting in the first deliveries being made in 2011, three years behind schedule. The causes were said to be supply chain failures,[14] software issues,[15] parts problems[16] and finally a strike by employees.[17] Commenting in January 2011 on the Dreamliner delays, Boeing President and CEO Jim Albaugh stated, 'Some of the technology was not as mature as it should have been and we put a global supply chain together without thinking through some of the consequences.' He continued, 'When you put immature technology in your supply chain and don't supply adequate oversight, you have issues and that is what we had.'[18]

Now, 10 years after the start of the crisis, the reputational damage to EADS and Boeing has been repaired and both the Airbus A380 and the Boeing 787 Dreamliner are well established in the fleets of the major airlines. The legacies of the crisis are some important lessons.

## Risk management lessons

### *Lesson 17: Over-complexity can lead to disaster*

The organizational structure of EADS and Airbus was over-complex. Christian Stieff's description of the situation was damning. Such complexity often results as a left-over from previous mergers and this case was made worse by political considerations.

The A380 project itself was staggeringly complicated. Multiple locations supported by a supply chain of 1,500 companies clearly challenged the coordinating capabilities of the management. With such a complex, unwieldy system, a mix up of some kind was probably inevitable; and the subsequent poor handling of the crisis resulted in unnecessary reputational damage.

## *Lesson 18: Avoid over-reliance on immature technology*

At Airbus and Boeing, the reliance on what Boeing's Jim Albaugh described as immature technology caused delays. In the case of the A380, the problem that emerged lay in the design software. One may ask how well those on the Airbus board understood the risks associated with cutting edge technology.

## *Lesson 19: Political patronage is a double-edged sword*

This case study is an example of political interference. Patronage from politicians can be valuable but it is a double-edged sword. In the case of EADS and Airbus, politics prevented integration and provided a distraction from business decisions.

## *Lesson 20: Middle management may block unwelcome news reaching the board*

Why the bad news took so long to come to the attention of the board is not really clear. At the time the media picked up on the story that middle management had not considered significant enough to relay to the board. However, the Airbus chief salesman later said that some people just didn't want to know; and there were signs of sensitivities driven by nationality differences. Either way, it demonstrates serious communications failure.

However, even if the board had known about the problem earlier, there must be a question regarding the extent of their political distraction and also about the skills of a politically selected board to understand and deal with a technical crisis

## *Lesson 21: The law is slow and can remind the public of a crisis long after it is over*

The wheels of the law grind slowly. The investigation and prosecution of the EADS and Airbus managers suspected of insider dealing continued for eight years before being stopped. Protracted cases like this are not only unsettling for all those involved but regular progress reports in the media can keep reminding the public of the back story long after the crisis itself has subsided.

## *Lesson 22: Incomplete integration of cultures after acquisitions and mergers*

The legacy of former cultures resulting from incomplete integration at EADS, like Texas City, demonstrates the latent potential for dysfunctionality and reputational risk. Boards should remember that effective mergers and acquisitions are not just about financial objectives. They will remain troublesome until the different worlds and cultures have been integrated. Insufficient attention to this aspect leaves a potential disaster incubating.

### Questions to mull

- What should the board have done to ensure proper integration of EADS?
- Given the make-up of the EADS board, was ignorance around technical issues inevitable? How might the problem have been avoided?
- Why do you think unwelcome news was delayed in its journey to the board?
- How can you ensure that bad news flows fast upwards in your organization?

## Notes


1 www.airmic.com/sites/default/files/Roads_to_Ruin-Full_Report.pdf accessed 15/1/2016.

2 Airbus crisis deepens as France, Germany fight over job cuts, DW 20/2/2007 http://www.dw.com/en/airbus-crisis-deepens-as-france-germany-fight-over-job-cuts/a-2358356 accessed 15/1/2016.

3 Crossed wires and a multibillion-euro delay, *New York Times*, 11/12/2006 http://www.nytimes.com/2006/12/11/business/worldbusiness/11iht-airbus.3860198.html?pagewanted=all&_r=0 accessed 15/1/2016.

4 Airbus A 380, http://calleam.com/WTPF/?p=4700 accessed 15/1/2016.

5 What grounded the Airbus A380?, Catalyst 6/12/2006 http://www.cadalyst.com/management/what-grounded-airbus-a380-5955 accessed 15/1/2016.

6 Crossed wires and a multibillion-euro delay, *New York Times*, 11/12/2006 http://www.nytimes.com/2006/12/11/business/worldbusiness/11iht-airbus.3860198.html?pagewanted=all&_r=0 accessed 15/1/2016.

7 Major turbulence for EADS on A380 delay, Forbes 14/6/2006 www.forbes.com/2006/06/14/airbus-eads-boeing-614markets12.html accessed 15/1/2016.

8 Airbus confirms further A380 delay and launches company restructuring plan, Airbus press release 3/10/2006 http://www.airbus.com/presscentre/pressreleases/press-release-detail/detail/airbus-confirms-further-a380-delay-and-launches-company-restructuring-plan/ accessed 15/1/2016.

9 Atkins *et al* (2011).

10 Q&A: Airbus delays, BBC News 30/10/2006 http://news.bbc.co.uk/1/hi/business/5405524.stm accessed 8/4/2016.

11 Crossed wires and a multibillion-euro delay, ibid.

12 Airbus A380 delays not disclosed for months, NBC News 29/5/2007 www.msnbc.msn.com/id/18918869/ns/business-us_business/ accessed 12/1/2016.

13 Double jeopardy ruling grounds Airbus insider trading cases, Law 360 18/3/2015 http://www.law360.com/articles/632871/double-jeopardy-ruling-grounds-airbus-insider-trading-cases accessed 15/1/2016.

**14** Engine problem delays delivery of Boeing's Dreamliner, *New York Times* 27/8/2010 http://www.nytimes.com/2010/08/28/business/global/28boeing.html?_r=0 accessed 8/4/2016.

**15** Boeing 787 first flight delayed, Flight Global 5/9/2007 https://www.flightglobal.com/news/articles/boeing-787-first-flight-delayed-to-mid-novembermid-december-216613/ accessed 8/4/2016.

**16** Boeing finds problems with 787 fastener installation, *Seattle Times* 4/11/2008 http://www.seattletimes.com/business/boeing-finds-problems-with-787-fastener-installation/ accessed 15/1/2016.

**17** Boeing strike threat looms after tumult on 787 grounding, Bloomberg 19/2/2013 http://www.bloomberg.com/news/articles/2013-02-19/boeing-strike-threat-looms-after-tumult-of-dreamliner-grounding accessed 8/4/2016.

**18** 'Immature' technology delays new Boeing, *Sydney Morning Herald* 24/1/2011 http://www.smh.com.au/business/world-business/immature-technology-delays-new-boeing-20110123-1a1gl.html accessed 8/4/2016.

# Libor: Barclays Bank PLC 20

The rigging of the Libor interest rate damaged the reputations of the many institutions involved and adversely affected the public's already cynical view of the banking sector. This case study focuses on the role of Barclays Bank, which was the first of many banks to be dealt with by regulators.

## Main risk event

Rigging the Libor interest rate benchmark, Barclays' culture.

## Company involved

Barclays Bank PLC

## Brief note on the company

Barclays Bank PLC[1,2] is a major global financial services group with its headquarters in London. It has 130,000 employees spread across 50 countries. It is listed on the London and New York stock exchanges and, at the time of the Libor rigging crisis, it was the 7th largest bank in the world with assets totalling $2.42 trillion. The group undertakes retail banking and commercial banking together with investment banking, wealth management, and investment management.

Bob Diamond, a central figure in this case study, is a career investment banker. After working for Morgan Stanley and CS First Boston he moved to Barclays in 1996. His rise there was meteoric. Diamond was promoted to CEO of Barclays Capital (the group's investment arm) and became Barclays President in 2005, Deputy Group CEO in 2010 and Group CEO in 2011.[3,4] For some years there had been media criticism of the amount of his remuneration and perceived lack of humility – in 2010 he was the highest paid CEO in the FTSE 100. Lord Mandelson, UK Secretary of State for Business, Innovation and Skills, described him as 'the unacceptable face of banking'.[5] The public will often look for a scapegoat during a crisis and Bob Diamond, like BP's Tony Hayward, was amply set up for the role.

Barclays was established in 1690 by a Quaker family[6] whose professed values were honesty, integrity and fair dealing. The stark contrast between this culture and some of the behaviour at Barclays during the scandal was highlighted by Bob Diamond's questioners at the subsequent UK Treasury Select Committee investigation.

## Date of event

2005–09

## Background to event

### *Climate of mistrust of banks*

In the period immediately before and after the Libor scandal, the banking industry was subject to a great deal of public mistrust, from which Barclays was not immune. The banks had been blamed for the 2007/08 financial crisis, although Barclays emerged from this crisis better than some of its peers such as HBoS and RBS as it did not require a Government bailout. Nevertheless, it had to face various allegations of money laundering,[7] tax avoidance[8] and insurance mis-selling.[9] This climate of mistrust coloured attitudes towards and perceptions of Barclays and the other banks when, rightly or wrongly, people were not inclined to give them the benefit of doubt.

### *Libor*

The Libor scandal[10] involved the rigging by Barclays and some other banks of an international interest rate benchmark. The London Interbank Offered Rate (Libor) is an average interest rate calculated daily through submissions of the interest rates applied by a panel of 16 major banks in London including Barclays, JP Morgan, Swiss Bank, UBS, Royal Bank of Scotland and Deutsche Bank. Libor is regarded as the standard for institutions dealing in mortgages, loans and other financial products, and also underpins about $450 trillion in financial derivatives.

Any rigging of Libor could have enormous implications across national economies, on the interest rates paid by individuals and companies, and on investors' views of the creditworthiness of the banks themselves. At the time of the scandal, Libor was administered by the British banking trade association, the BBA. As a consequence of the crisis, the administration was taken out of London and transferred to the NYSE Euronext in 2014.

Barclays' daily interest rate submissions to BBA were made by a team of submitters in London who relied on information supplied by the Barclays derivatives traders dealing with instruments linked to Libor and to its lesser known Euro-based equivalent, Euribor.

## Description of event

The possibility that banks had been rigging Libor by supplying false information to the BBA first came to light in April 2008 in a *Wall Street Journal* article.[11] It alleged that banks were aiming to mislead the public about their financial strength in the wake of the financial crisis (as reflected in their apparent ability to borrow at lower interest rates). To achieve this they submitted fictitious rates rather than those that their traders were actually using. Since the individual banks' submissions were in the public domain, investors gained a false impression of a bank's strength.

The BBA and the International Monetary Fund[12] both challenged the *Wall Street Journal* allegations, saying that Libor remained an accurate measure of a bank's creditworthiness. However, the economists Snider and Youle[13] later confirmed that some banks' submissions were being understated, suggesting that the banks were doing this to make unfair profits on their Libor interest-linked portfolios.

It would appear that as early as 2008 central banks[14] (Bank of England (BoE) and the New York Fed) were aware that the Libor rate did not represent the rate at which banks were actually borrowing, but it was not until 2011 that regulators began formally to investigate Libor rate manipulation. The following year, the US Commodity Futures Trading Commission (CFTC), the US Department of Justice (USDJ), the UK Financial Services Authority (FSA) and the Canadian Competition Bureau announced that they were investigating collusion in the fixing of Libor rates. Barclays conducted its own internal investigation and the UK Serious Crime Office opened a criminal investigation into the actions of Barclays and a number of other banks on the London Libor panel.

To Barclays' credit it was the first bank to admit there was a problem and cooperated fully with the various investigations. As we shall see, it became evident that Barclays staff had submitted false and misleading interest rates for some years for two purposes:

1 To change the Libor rate in order to gain unfair advantage for Barclays' Libor linked portfolio. In addition, it acted in support of traders in other banks who were similarly trying to gain advantage for their own portfolios. The Barclays traders' annual bonuses reflected the total portfolio performance so there was probably a degree of perverse incentivization at work.

2 To enhance investors' perception of the bank's financial position. For certain periods management had given instructions to ensure that their submitted rates were 'in line' with other contributors, ie did not stand out from the pack. It emerged that this practice began after a discussion between the BoE and Diamond in October 2008. The BoE had mentioned a perception in 'Whitehall' that Barclays' rates were high relative to other banks (ie indicating weakness). As this was at the time when the UK Government was intervening in RBS, Bob Diamond interpreted this as a warning and informed his colleagues. Diamond later stated that he gave no specific instruction to lower Barclays' submission rates but it seems that a 'miscommunication' led to management lowering them anyway.[15]

## Post-event response

The results of these investigations began to emerge in June 2012:

- The CFTC[16] ordered Barclays to pay a $200m penalty for attempted manipulation and false reporting concerning Libor and Euribor. It had discovered in the period 2005–07 that there had been 173 separate requests for Libor fixing and 58 for Euribor. It required Barclays in future to introduce changes including:
  - making its submissions only on specified factors;
  - implementing firewalls between traders and submitters;
  - improving auditing, monitoring and training.
- Barclays entered an agreement with the USDJ[17] to pay a $160m penalty to resolve violations arising from its submissions for Libor and Euribor. Barclays admitted that between 2005 and 2007 then occasionally through 2009 its submitters were requested by its traders in London and New York via electronic messages, chat rooms, telephone conversations and in personal conversations to post false rates. The group also admitted that its traders communicated with other banks on the panel to request submissions that benefited its or its counterparts' trading positions. The size of the fine took into consideration the mitigating factors that Barclays had cooperated with the USDJ and that Barclays employees had raised concerns in 2007/8 with BBA, FSA, BoE and the New York Fed that Libor rates did not accurately reflect the market.
- The FSA[18] fined Barclays a record £59.5m for inappropriate Libor and Euribor submissions from derivatives traders and also during the financial crisis, and for ineffective systems and controls, and compliance. It said that Barclays' behaviour was 'completely unacceptable'. Bob Diamond decided to give up his bonus as a result of this fine. Politicians started calling for the board to sack him.

On 2 July Marcus Agius resigned as Barclays' Group Chairman.[19] He said:

> Last week's events – evidencing as they do unacceptable standards of behaviour within the bank – have dealt a devastating blow to

> Barclays' reputation. As Chairman, I am the ultimate guardian of the bank's reputation. Accordingly, the buck stops with me and I must acknowledge responsibility by standing aside.

The group announced that it would undertake an independent audit of the bank's business practices in an attempt to restore the bank's reputation. It would be establishing a 'zero tolerance policy' for any actions that harm Barclays' reputation.

On 3 July 2012 Bob Diamond resigned, saying that the external pressures risked the bank's franchise. Lord Turner, Chairman of the FSA, had told the regulator's annual public meeting that outrage had built up over Barclay's actions:

> The cynical greed of traders asking their colleagues to falsify their Libor submissions so that they could make bigger profits… has justifiably shocked and angered people, in particular when we are facing hard economic times provoked by the Financial Crisis.[20]

The BBC reported that both the BoE and the FSA had been unable to force Bob Diamond to resign because the FSA investigations had not shown him to be personally culpable. However, it proved impossible for the Barclays board to ignore the revealed wishes of the regulator, despite the fact that his fellow directors still supported him: Bob Diamond had to go. George Osborne, the Chancellor of the Exchequer, said that Diamond's resignation was 'the first step towards a new culture of responsibility' in banking.[21]

The same day, the group chief operating officer also resigned.[22] Barclays share price fell 16 per cent over these two days. The next day, Bob Diamond was called to give evidence to the UK House of Commons Treasury Select Committee (see below).

## Findings of investigations

Some of the findings of the investigations have already been mentioned. However, in the context of this case study, these are particularly revealing.

## *US Department of Justice, 26 June 2012*[23]

The USDJ had access to many of Barclays' internal communications on Libor and Euribor fixing. The following example is typical and clearly demonstrates that criminal activity was undeniable, premeditated, repeated and those involved knew what they were doing was wrong. Abbreviations in the exchanges below have been written in full for easier reading.

On Friday 10 March 2006 a Barclays dollar swaps trader located in London ('Trader-1') sent an email to a Barclays dollar Libor submitter ('Submitter-1'): 'Hi mate. We have an unbelievably large set on Monday. We need a really low 3-month fix; it could potentially cost a fortune. Would really appreciate any help, I'm being told by my counterparts in New York that it's extremely important. Thanks.'

Three days later, Trader-1 was back in touch with Submitter-1: 'The big day has arrived... My counterparts in New York were screaming at me about an unchanged 3-month Libor. As always, any help would be greatly appreciated. What do you think you'll go for 3-month?'

Submitter-1 responded: 'I am going [4.]90 although [4.]91 is what I should be posting.'

Trader-1 replied in part: 'I agree with you and totally understand. Remember, when I retire and write a book about this business your name will be in golden letters.'

Submitter-1 replied: 'I would prefer this not be in any books!'

Barclays's 3-month dollar Libor submission on 3 March 2006 was 4.90 per cent, which was a rate unchanged from the previous trading day and was tied for the lowest rate submitted.

## *House of Commons Treasury Select Committee 4 July 2012*[24]

Prior to the Committee hearing, the Committee Chairman, Andrew Tyrie, said 'This is the most damaging scam I can recall.' He said that Libor, which is crucial across the economy and affects millions of people, had been systematically rigged for years. Whilst it seemed that many banks were involved, Barclays was the first to own up. The reputation of the whole of Britain's financial services industry had been tarnished, eroding public trust in the banks yet further. 'Restoring reputational damage must begin immediately.'[25]

The Committee asked Bob Diamond over 300 questions about his and Barclays' role in the Libor rigging scandal. The main conclusions included:

- that not all the problems could be resolved by regulation, they required a change of culture in the banking industry;
- Barclays itself had a culture whereby behaviour in the bank was bad and in some cases criminal;
- the board didn't appear to know what was going on;
- communication in many areas was poor;
- compliance and risk management were inadequate;
- the difference between the culture of Barclays' Quaker founding fathers and that in today's bank was stark.

The hearing demonstrated, if evidence were needed just how badly Barclays' licence to operate had been eroded, damaging the reputations of other banks in the process.

## Consequences of event

At an industry level, UK regulation on Libor was tightened and manipulation was made a specific criminal offence.[26] Regulatory responsibility was placed with the Financial Conduct Authority[27] (replacing the FSA, which had been abolished following the financial crisis) and administration of the scheme was transferred from the BBA to NYSE Euronext.[28]

The poor reputation of banking and those leading it was further damaged. The media wanted a scapegoat and Bob Diamond, who rightly or wrongly had become the epitome the modern banker, felt the full force of public anger.

Barclays was heavily fined, lost its chairman, CEO, chief operating officer and a significant number of its traders. However, the main impact was on its reputation.[29] It had forfeited any remaining trust it once had in the eyes of politicians, regulators and the media. Nevertheless, customers did not appear to desert Barclays in any significant way.

The greatest challenge that faced Barclays was, and may still be, to bring about a culture change whereby bad and criminal behaviour is seen internally as unacceptable and is rooted out of the organization. Such a culture change can only be led from the top. Strong regulation has a role but, as the Treasury Select Committee observed, problems like Libor arise from a culture that is far removed from the values of Barclays' Quaker founders. Leadership culture, behaviour and incentives will have to play a part, as will a review of the character implications of decades of recruitment to and promotions at Barclays.

The magnitude of the task was highlighted as recently as May 2015 when the CFTC[30] imposed a further fine of $400m for similarly manipulating the global foreign exchange benchmark rates ISDAFIX. The CFTC imposed enforcement actions for Barclays to implement and strengthen its internal controls and procedures, including the supervision of its foreign exchange traders. What was especially disturbing was that some of this manipulation was taking place at the same time that the CFTC and other regulators were actively investigating Barclays' rigging of Libor.

## Risk management lessons

### *Lesson 23: Strong regulation can help reduce risk events but a company's culture is even more important*

Time and again those investigating the role of Barclays in this scandal made reference to the culture of the group and that of the banking industry in general. The Barclays board appeared out of touch with what was going on and allowed appalling behaviour to become an accepted norm.

## Lesson 24: In a crisis, the media will often seek a scapegoat

As BP's Tony Hayward discovered, the media is liable to look for someone to blame, even if the roots of the crisis extend far beyond the actual or perceived involvement of that person. They will not be satisfied until they force a resignation. Bob Diamond was a larger than life character who came to represent the modern 'overpaid banker'. He was an obvious target for the media and politicians. Regulators couldn't demonstrate any personal culpability but, perhaps under pressure from political and media stakeholders, wanted to remove him; so they put pressure on the board to remove him. Resisting that pressure, the chairman resigned; but when this did not satisfy, Diamond was dismissed.

There is an important lesson here for both executive and non-executive directors, especially chief executives and chairs: they should be aware that they could be singled out as scapegoats in the event of a crisis.

## Lesson 25: Have some organization become too large and complex for the leadership to control behaviour?

Most of the organizations in our case studies are huge, complex entities. Many other large and/or complex organizations have recently had reputational crises rooted in culture and behaviour such as FIFA (football),[31] the International Association of Athletics Federations (IAAF) (athletics),[32] the BBC (broadcasting),[33] News International (newspapers),[34] the Catholic[35] and Anglican[36] Churches, and Toyota (manufacturing).[37] This begs the questions: do leaders have the ability and tools to control behaviour in such leviathans; do they become too inward looking; or is there a size above which organizations are just too big for comfort?

**Questions to mull**

- Why do you think the BBA initially defended the integrity of Libor?
- Why did Barclays' board not see this coming?
- What do you think are the root causes of these problems at Barclays and other banks? What is the solution?
- Do you think that the scapegoating of Bob Diamond by politicians, regulators and the media was fair? If not, why did it happen?
- Do you think that there may be a limit to the size and complexity of an organization? If not, how would you ensure that you knew everything that you needed to know to lead it?
- What role do you think character played at Barclays in recruitment and promotion of staff? With what consequences?

## Notes


1 Barclays, *Annual Report 2014*, https://www.home.barclays/content/dam/barclayspublic/docs/InvestorRelations/AnnualReports/AR2014/Barclays_PLC_Annual_Report_%202014.pdf accessed 15/1/2016.

2 Barclays explained, 2010, http://everything.explained.today/Barclays/ accessed 15/1/2016.

3 Bob Diamond takes over as Barclays chief executive early, *Daily Telegraph* 17/12/2010 http://www.telegraph.co.uk/finance/newsbysector/epic/barc/8209352/Bob-Diamond-takes-over-as-Barclays-chief-executive-early.html accessed 15/1/2016.

4 Bob Diamond named CEO of Barclays, *Guardian* 7/9/2010 https://www.theguardian.com/business/2010/sep/07/bob-diamond-new-barclays-chief accessed 15/1/2016.

5 Lord Mandelson attacks Barclays head, BBC News 3/4/2010 http://news.bbc.co.uk/1/hi/8601512.stm; 'Barclays boss Bob Diamond resigns amid Libor scandal' BBC News http://www.bbc.co.uk/news/business-18685040 accessed 15/1/2016.

6 Barclays' Quakerism, https://www.home.barclays/about-barclays/history/our-quaker-roots.html accessed 15/1/2016.

7 Probe circles globe to find dirty money, *Wall Street Journal* 3/9/2010 http://www.wsj.com/articles/SB10001424052748703431604575468094090700862 accessed 15/1/2016.

8 Barclays gags *Guardian* over tax, *Guardian* 17/3/2009 http://www.theguardian.com/business/2009/mar/17/barclays-guardian-injunction-tax.

9 Barclays PPI, http://www.barclays.co.uk/P1242622078993 accessed 15/1/2016.

10 Libor: What is it and why does it matter? BBC News 3/8/2015 http://www.bbc.co.uk/news/business-19199683 accessed 15/1/2016.

11 Study casts doubt on key rate, *Wall Street Journal* 29/3/2008 http://www.wsj.com/articles/SB121200703762027135 accessed 15/1/2016.

12 IMF *Global Financial Stability Report* https://www.imf.org/external/pubs/ft/gfsr/ accessed 15/1/2016.

13 Snider, C (2010) 'Does the Libor reflect banks' borrowing costs?' http://www.econ.ucla.edu/people/papers/Snider/Snider506.pdf 15/1/2016.

14 Geithner made recommendations on Libor in 2008, *Wall Street Journal* 14/7/2012 http://www.wsj.com/articles/SB10001424052702303919504577524510853665528 accessed 15/1/2016.

15 Bob Diamond denies Bank of England pressure to rig rates as he admits 'reprehensible behaviour', This is Money 4/7/2012 http://www.thisismoney.co.uk/money/news/article-2168769/Bob-Diamond-denies-Bank-England-pressure-rig-rates.html#ixzz4BBFYpkqp accessed 15/1/2016.

16 US CFTC Order http://www.cftc.gov/idc/groups/public/@lrenforcementactions/documents/legalpleading/enfbarclaysorder062712.pdf accessed 15/1/2016.

17 US DoJ letter 26/6/2012 http://www.justice.gov/iso/opa/resources/337201271017335469822.pdf accessed 15/1/2016.

18 FSA final notice 27/6/2012 http://www.telegraph.co.uk/finance/9359589/Barclays-fined-59.5m-by-FSA-full-report.html accessed 20/4/2016.

19 Barclays Chairman Marcus Agius resigns over rate rigging, *Telegraph* 2/7/2012 http://www.telegraph.co.uk/finance/newsbysector/banksandfinance/9369286/Barclays-Chairman-Marcus-Agius-resigns-over-rate-rigging.html accessed 15/1/2016.

**20** Barclays boss Bob Diamond resigns amid Libor scandal, BBC News 3/7/2012 www.bbc.co.uk/news/business-18685040 accessed 15/1/2016.

**21** Ibid.

**22** Barclays executive Jerry del Missier quits over 'Libor lies', *Telegraph* 3/7/2012 http://www.telegraph.co.uk/finance/newsbysector/banksandfinance/9373154/Barclays-executive-Jerry-del-Missier-quits-over-Libor-lies.html accessed 15/1/2016.

**23** DoJ agreed statement of facts, 26/6/2012 http://www.justice.gov/iso/opa/resources/9312012710173426365941.pdf at para 13 accessed 11/4/2016.

**24** Treasury Select Committee transcript 4/7/2012 http://www.parliament.uk/documents/commons-committees/treasury/Treasury-Committee-04-July-12-Bob-Diamond.pdf accessed 20/4/2016.

**25** Treasury Committee questions Bob Diamond, http://www.parliament.uk/business/committees/committees-a-z/commons-select/treasury-committee/news/treasury-committee-calls-for-bob-diamond-and-barclays-non-execs-to-appear-next-week/ accessed 15/1/2016.

**26** EU to tighten control of benchmarks in wake of Libor scandal, DW 18/9/2013 http://www.dw.com/en/eu-to-tighten-control-of-benchmarks-in-wake-of-libor-scandal/a-17098153 accessed 15/1/2016.

**27** FCA to regulate seven additional financial benchmarks, FCA press release 22/12/2014 http://www.fca.org.uk/news/fca-to-regulate-seven-additional-financial-benchmarks accessed 15/1/2016.

**28** First day of business for new Libor administrator, UK Treasury announcement 3/2/2014 https://www.gov.uk/government/news/first-day-of-business-for-new-libor-administrator accessed 15/1/2016.

**29** Barclays' reputation takes a battering after Libor scandal, *Guardian* 10/9/2012 http://www.theguardian.com/business/2012/sep/10/barclays-reputation-battering-libor-scandal accessed 15/1/2016.

**30** US CFTC order 20/5/2015 http://www.cftc.gov/idc/groups/public/@lrenforcementactions/documents/legalpleading/enfbarclaysborder052015.pdf accessed 15/1/2016.

**31** FIFA scandal explained, Wired.com 27/5/2015 http://www.wired.com/2015/05/fifa-scandal-explained/ accessed 15/1/2016.

**32** Timeline of a scandal: How athletics was rocked by corruption claims, *Guardian* 9/11/2015 http://www.theguardian.com/sport/2015/nov/09/timeline-russia-athletics-iaaf-corruption-doping-claims accessed 15/1/2016.

**33** The sinister treatment of dissent at the BBC, *Guardian* 8/3/2015 http://www.theguardian.com/commentisfree/2015/mar/08/bbc-whistleblowers-jimmy-savile accessed 15/1/2016.

**34** *News of the World* phone-hacking scandal, BBC News 4/8/2012 http://www.bbc.co.uk/news/uk-11195407 accessed 15/1/2016.

**35** One in 50 priests is a paedophile: Pope Francis says child abuse is 'leprosy' infecting the Catholic Church, *Daily Mail* 13/7/2014 http://www.dailymail.co.uk/news/article-2690575/Pope-Francis-admits-two-cent-Roman-Catholic-priests-paedophiles-interview-Italian-newspaper.html accessed 15/1/2016.

**36** Paedophiles still view churches as 'soft touch', *Telegraph* 13/4/2015 http://www.telegraph.co.uk/news/religion/11528375/Paedophiles-still-view-churches-as-soft-touch.html accessed 15/1/2016.

**37** Timeline: Toyota from rise to recall crisis, hearings, Reuters 22/2/2010 http://www.reuters.com/article/us-toyota-timeline-idUSTRE61M0IT20100223 accessed 15/1/2016.

# Volkswagen 21

## Main risk event

It was revealed that Volkswagen (VW) had cheated on emissions testing for harmful nitrogen oxide gases in diesel vehicles in the USA, Europe and other parts of the world. The allegations relate to about 11 million cars.[1]

## Company involved

Volkswagen AG of Wolfsburg, Lower Saxony, Germany

## Brief note on company

Volkswagen AG is one of the world's largest motor manufacturers, owning the Audi, Porsche, Seat and Skoda brands in addition to the main VW brand. For such a large organization its ownership and control are very concentrated: 50.73 per cent of the shareholder voting rights are held by Porsche Automobil Holding SE of Stuttgart, with the State of Lower Saxony having 20 per cent and Qatar holding LLC 17 per cent.[2] Collectively these three shareholders own about 60 per cent of the equity, with Porsche owning a little over 30 per cent. The 'Volkswagen Law' gives Lower Saxony's 20 per cent shareholding a blocking majority against any 'important' decisions.[3]

At the time of the event the supervisory board comprised the following:[4]

| | |
|---|---|
| works council representatives | 6 |
| trades union representatives | 4 |
| Qatar representatives | 2 |
| Porsche family | 4 |
| Lower Saxony representatives | 2 |
| 'independent' | 1 |

In 2009 the *Financial Times* reported that a survey[5] of companies in the blue-chip Dax index, revealed VW had the worst governance structure, and also 'scored badly on issues such as its 'high executive pay and its non-independent supervisory board members'. It added that VW had long been criticized by investors for apparently poor governance and conflicts of interests. A series of convictions[6] in 2007–08 also revealed corrupt practices at board level.

## Date of event

2014–15

## Background to event

As early as 1973 VW was among a group of car makers caught gaming pollution emissions tests on petrol engines.[7] It was fined $120,000 but admitted no wrongdoing. Some of the vehicles tested were found to be fitted with devices that turned off the emission systems when the air-conditioning was switched on. Other cars had sensors that activated the pollution controls only at the temperature used during the tests. The present case study focuses on the later, even more damaging revelation that VW was using special software to falsify emission tests on huge numbers of diesel cars.

VW's first diesel car was the diesel VW Golf, introduced in the aftermath of the oil crises of the 1970s. Diesel technology improved over the following decades, resulting in all the major manufacturers developing mass market models able to compete with conventional petrol engine models. In the 1990s governments began actively to encourage the production of diesel cars and this eventually led to 35 per cent of cars in the EU having diesel engines.[8] The United States also adopted diesel but more slowly, reaching 4 per cent of sales by 2006.

A major advantage of diesel engines is that they emit less of the poisonous gas carbon monoxide than petrol engines. However, it gradually became evident that diesel is not as clean as governments had originally hoped. Diesel emissions were discovered to contain about 20 times more nitrogen oxides (NOx) than petrol engines and they also produce fine soot known as 'particulates'.[9] Since both NOx gases and particulates are considered to be major causes of illness and death, various governments have introduced regulations progressively to limit permissible levels of these harmful emissions. Regulations required tests to be made on diesel engines, the results of which are made public and thus favourable results are used to advertise a car's green credentials. Pollution levels permitted in the United States are much lower than those allowed under EU regulations.

The possibility that motor manufactures might attempt to 'defeat' the tests and provide favourable results is self-evident. Indeed, technology that could be adapted for this purpose is freely available. Bosch, which supplied engine management software to VW, made it clear that 'defeat' components in its software should be used only for research purposes, warning that to use it in production models would be illegal.[10]

## Description of event

In 2013 the authorities began to be concerned about the possibility of motor manufacturers cheating diesel emission tests and the EU's Joint Research Centre warned the European Commission of 'the dangers of defeat devices'.[11] The following year the US based International Council on Clean Transportation (ICCT) sponsored emissions tests on a VW Jetta, a VW Passat and a BMW X5.[12] The BMW performed well, but the VW Jetta emitted 15 to 35 times the permitted NOx emissions, and the VW Passat 5 to 20 times permitted levels.

It was subsequently revealed that an unnamed VW supplier had informed the European Commission that VW was using defeat software, but the Commission had failed to act on the information. It also emerged that in 2010 the European Commission's own scientists had warned the Commission that they 'had uncovered what researchers suspected to be a "defeat device" that could cheat emissions tests'. In 2012 their own scientists uncovered 'a clear case of "hard" cycle beating'.[13] A 2013 study by the EU's Environment Department warning of 'Increasing evidence of illegal practices [by car manufacturers] that defeat the anti-pollution systems to improve driving performance or save on the replacement of costly components.' It appears the Commission took no action to rein in the use of such devices by EU manufacturers.[14]

At about this time, the Californian Air Resources Board (CARB) began to hold discussions with VW about emissions. This led to a recall of about 500,000 vehicles in December 2014 for a software fix. Further tests by CARB showed that whilst the fix had some effect, it still left NOx emissions significantly higher than they had expected. CARB therefore carried out more sophisticated tests.

On 3 September 2015 VW admitted to CARB and EPA staff that the tested vehicles were designed and manufactured with 'a defeat device to bypass, defeat or render inoperative elements of the vehicles' emission control system'. It was explained to VW that such vehicles did not meet the relevant US standards and would be in violation of various US laws. VW was required to bring those vehicles into compliance and CARB extended their investigation to include all VW diesel cars from 2009 to 2015.[15]

On 18 September 2015 the US Environmental Protection Agency (EPA) announced the issue of a Notice of Violation to VW Group and its subsidiaries VW America and Audi.[16] The EPA spokesperson added: 'Using a defeat device in cars to evade clean air standards is illegal and a threat to public health.' The US Congress and Department of Justice also announced investigations, as did others. The media[17] compared the emerging reputational crisis with the banks' Libor scandal.

## Post-event response

On 20 September VW's CEO Martin Winterkorn issued a statement. He said that he was deeply sorry that VW had broken the trust of its

**Figure 21.1** Volkswagen's share price (data source: Yahoo)

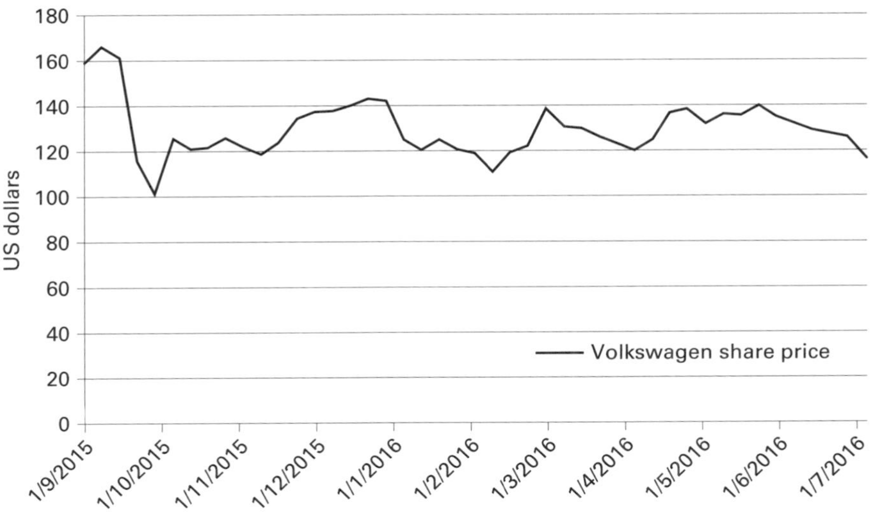


customers and the public, that he had ordered an external investigation and VW would cooperate with the authorities. He stated that VW 'do not, and will not, tolerate violations of any kind of our internal rules or of the law' and that the trust of VW's customers was its most important asset. He also revealed that the emissions problem involved 11 million vehicles worldwide, and that VW had made an initial provision of €6.5 billion.[18]

VW's share price plunged. That of other car manufacturers also fell, but not by so much.[19] Michael Horn, VW USA's Chief Executive, said that VW had 'screwed up'.[20] The following day, German prosecutors[21] announced that they were considering a criminal inquiry. Fitch[22] put VW's 'A' rating on negative watch, reflecting what it described as reputational damage to the group's brands. In the light of all this adverse publicity Martin Winterkorn's position became untenable. He resigned, emphasizing that he was not aware of any wrongdoing on his part.[23] The VW executive committee issued a statement[24] marking his resignation and praising his 'towering contributions in the past decades'. Before his resignation he was paid €16m in 2014 and he left with a pension valued at about €28.5m.[25]

Matthias Müller, former Chief Executive of Porsche, was soon appointed as VW's new CEO. He said, 'I don't think I will get down on my knees, I will be self-confident. Of course, I will apologize for things that have occurred'.[26] Reporting on Müller's appointment, the *Financial Times* said, 'Under predecessor Martin Winterkorn, decision-making at VW was highly centralized and more junior managers were frightened to speak their mind.'[27]

Berthold Huber, the former IGMetal leader who was VW's interim chair, said, 'The unlawful behaviour of engineers and technicians involved in engine development shocked Volkswagen just as much as it shocked the public.'[28] Nevertheless, various aspects of the storm continued to gain momentum on both sides of the Atlantic.

- Finance
  - It was reported[29] that €121 billion of VW's assets were debts owed on the financing of car purchases and that the European Central bank had 'suspended accepting VW asset-backed paper in its bond-buying programme'.
  - The investment arm of Nordea bank decided to put all VW investments into quarantine, allowing its fund managers to hold and sell, but not buy, VW stock and bonds.[30]
  - David Bach of the Yale School of Management compared the scandal with Enron, noting, among other points, that VW had 'endangered the health of millions' by hiding high levels of NOx from regulators. He thought the EPA fines alone could total $18 billion so that whilst VW might appear financially strong, the share price collapse was merely the first phase. 'Potentially irreparable reputational damage, a crisis of confidence and massive legal liabilities could do the company in.'[31]
- Culture
  - The Chairman of the VW Group Works Council wrote to staff: 'We need in future a climate in which problems aren't hidden but can be openly communicated to superiors... We need a culture in which it's possible and permissible to argue with your superior about the best way to go.'[32]
  - German media were reported as almost unanimous in considering that the scandal 'could affect the world's opinion of Made in Germany – the country's reputation for quality, especially in manufacturing'.[33]

- Governance
  - Financial researchers MSCI said they had been concerned for some time that VW's corporate governance score was lower than 72 per cent of companies globally. Vigeo, a French governance analyst, said that VW scored only 48 out of 100 before the crisis emerged, well below its peers, emphasizing that it reflected 'allegations of corruption over the past decade'.[34]

By the end of September commentators were concluding that since the scandal embraced so many cars over many years, it could not be the result of an undetected group of low-level engineers. Jack Nerad[35] of Kelley Blue Book, a car information service, thought it likely that the use of the defeat software reflected a 'de facto policy with regards to emissions requirements'. His views were echoed by rival manufacturers pointing out that the software would have required regular modification to fit the many models to which it was apparently applied. Nevertheless, VW continued to imply that the problem was confined to a small number of rogue staff. Indeed, on 8 October VW's USA Chief Executive Michael Horn appeared before Congress. Having apologized on behalf of Volkswagen he gave the official explanation of events, that it was apparently a couple of software engineers who incorporated the 'defeat' devices. When questioned about the official line he said 'I agree it is very hard to believe,' adding, 'This company has to bloody learn and use this opportunity in order to get their act together... people worldwide have to be managed in a different way.'[36]

On 14 October the technology magazine *Wired*[37] reported that dozens of VW people were involved in the scandal. The next day US regulators revealed that VW had admitted to 'additional suspect engineering' designed to 'help exhaust systems run cleaner during government tests'.[38]

VW began to suspend staff and announced plans to recall 8.5 million cars across Europe.[39] On 2 November the EPA announced that it had discovered cheating software on VW Touaregs, various Audis and a Porsche Cayenne all made by the Volkswagen Group.[40] VW stated that the emissions problem 'was due to the interaction of three factors:

- the misconduct and shortcomings of individual employees;
- weaknesses in some processes;

- a mindset in some areas of the company that tolerated breaches of rule.'

They added that 'deficiencies in processes have favored misconduct on the part of individuals'.[41]

As 2016 began the US Department of Justice filed a civil law suit[42] on behalf of the EPA, claiming VW violated the Clean Air Act by installing defeat software in almost 600,000 diesel vehicles in the United States. The California Air Resources Board, citing at length the serious health effects of NOx and particulates from untreated diesel engines, rejected VW's planned US recall.[43]

## Consequences of event

In October 2015 Standard and Poor's downgraded VW to A- warning that it could cut the rating by two more notches. Standard and Poor's commented: 'The downgrade reflects our assessment that VW has demonstrated material deficiencies in its management and governance and general risk management framework.'[44] VW announced its first quarterly loss, of €2.5 billion, for at least 15 years and sales fell by 5 per cent in October and 20 per cent the following month. Toyota overtook 'embattled' VW to become the world's largest car maker by sales.[45] Leonardo DiCaprio announced his intention to make a film about the emissions scandal.[46]

The European Parliament demanded an inquiry into how Brussels had handled the scandal, given that Commission officials had been aware that emissions tests were being evaded.[47] Investigations into possible criminal behaviour were initiated in France and Germany[48,49] and police raided VW offices. German motor regulators extended their investigations to include cars made by some of VW's competitors including BMW, Ford, Jaguar Land Rover, Mercedes, Nissan and Volvo.[50]

Outside shareholders began to demand that VW change its governance model.[51] Institutional investors from the United Kingdom, United States and Norway announced a lawsuit.[52] Matthias Müller announced a management shake-up,[53] having already hired a new compliance chief from Daimler to join the board.[54]

In July 2016 VW's proposed fix for 85,000 3.0L TDI cars sold in the USA was rejected,[55] but a US judge gave provisional approval to VW settling a clutch of law suits based on deceptive advertising as regards about 475,000 2.0L TDI cars sold there. VW agreed in principle to fix or buy back these cars at a cost estimated at up to $10.3bn. In addition it agreed to pay $603m to settle actual and potential state consumer protection claims; $2.7 bn into environmental remediation fund and to invest $2bn in the promotion of zero emissions vehicles.[56] VW made a provision of €16bn for the cost of fixing cars and making its first annual loss.[57] As VW suspended most sales in South Korea, an analyst raised his estimate of the cost of Dieselgate to '€25bn to €35bn'.[58]

Meanwhile, investigations by US Federal prosecutors continued.[59] A report emerged that 'some managers spotted the issues as long ago as 2014' but Winterkorn 'was so swamped with emails that he might not have read a memo written for him on the issue';[60] and New York's Attorney General alleged in a lawsuit that Műller 'was party to engineering discussions 10 years ago that led to the use of illegal defeat devices in VW group's US diesel cars'.[61]

The European Union began to demand consumer compensation similar to that offered in the United States.[62] In London, where it has been estimated that air pollution causes about 10,000 premature deaths annually and many more cases of respiratory diseases, air quality and vehicle emissions became a 2016 election issue.[63] Bereaved parents living close to one of its busiest roads sought an independent inquiry into the role of air pollution in their child's death from asthma. It was estimated that over 400 London schools are in areas where EU pollution limits are exceeded.[64] Time will tell whether this is a precursor to multiple liability claims against diesel car makers for death and ill health; liability regimes developed for asbestosis may make such claims easier to prove in congested cities.

And as we closed this study, VW agreed a $1.2 billion settlement with US dealers.[65] A VW engineer pleaded guilty to conspiracy.[66] *Handelsblatt*, the German business newspaper asked: 'Will VW ever atone for its sins? Or has it been sentenced to death by lawsuit?'[67]

## Risk management lessons

At the time of writing, investigations, criminal proceedings and litigation are still in process. It is therefore too early to judge what else might be revealed in this major scandal. Nevertheless, enormous reputational damage has been inflicted on VW even if it is largely based on public perception of what happened. The following key risk management lessons have already emerged.

### *Lesson 26: If corruption occurs within an organization, the board is in a no-win situation*

At VW, what the board knew, or ought to have known, about the cheating and at what stage has yet to be determined; but they have been challenged as either incompetently ignorant or conniving.

A similar example of this phenomenon emerged when newly appointed IAAF president Lord Coe was interviewed by Channel 4 News about his prior knowledge, as a long-standing IAAF vice-president of the covering up of doping by athletes. The interviewer asserted that as Coe had been a vice-president for some years he had either been aware of the doping problem and done nothing and so implicated in it; or if he had not been aware of it, he had been incompetent. As the interviewer put it: 'Either you were asleep on the job, or corrupt. Which is it?'[68]

The media readily simplifies issues by adopting adopts a 'black and white' view after the event, and if this analysis sticks, reputational damage, and resignations, are almost inevitable.

### *Lesson 27: Boards should learn from the mistakes of the past*

VW had been caught in the past gaming emission tests and had a track record including allegations of corruption. It seems that it had not learned from history, and that what leaders think of as 'the unthinkable' all too often happens. Repeating errors from the past is a sure way to reputational damage.

## *Lesson 28: Good corporate governance matters*

The extent to which the VW board's much criticized corporate governance actually influenced the emissions scandal is not clear at this stage. However, there were overt conflicts of interest, political influences, rivalries and evidence of driving ambition and hubris. Nor is it obvious that the supervisory board had been put together on the basis of assembling the skill, knowledge and experience needed to supervise the business.

Boards cannot afford to ignore good governance as this damages the reputations of all concerned if a crisis emerges.

## *Lesson 29: Boards need to create a culture where information can freely flow*

The statement by the works council, that VW needed a climate where it was permissible for staff to argue with their supervisors, speaks volumes about an oppressive culture that discouraged the free flow of ideas, let alone the giving of unwelcome news.

## *Lesson 30: Reputational crises are contagious*

A crisis in a sector can cause reputational damage to competitors as well as to the organization at the heart of the crisis.

If the organization is a national champion and international icon, the crisis can put the national reputation at risk. This appears to be happening with VW in Germany.

### Questions to mull

- Why do you think an inward-looking culture might have developed at VW?
- What prevented VW leaders and board from becoming aware that software was being used to cheat in emissions tests?
- How can boards ensure that their organization learns the lessons of the past?
- What can boards do to ensure that systemic risks are not incubating?
- How would you set about recognizing and dealing with leadership complacency and hubris in your own organization?

## Notes


1 Government passing the buck on air pollution, say campaigners, *Guardian* 13/9/2015 http://www.theguardian.com/environment/2015/sep/13/government-passing-the-buck-air-pollution-campaigners accessed 23/12/2015.

2 Volkswagen AG *Annual Report 2014*.

3 Germany wins EU court battle over VW law, escapes fines, Bloomberg Business, 22/10/2013 http://www.bloomberg.com/news/articles/2013-10-22/germany-wins-eu-court-fight-over-vw-law-legality-escapes-fines accessed 30/12/2015.

4 http://www.volkswagenag.com/content/vwcorp/content/en/the_group/senior_management.html accessed 22/12/2015.

5 VW governance 'worst' of German blue-chips, *Financial Times* 2/12/2009 http://on.ft.com/1CYhMtS accessed 10/4/2016.

6 Trial of VW's Hartz spotlights bribes and brothels, Forbes 17/1/2007 http://www.forbes.com/2007/01/17/volkswagen-trial-hartz-face-lead-cx_po_0117autofacescan02.html accessed 30 December 2015; Prison term in corruption case, BBC News, 22/2/2008 accessed 30/12/2015.

7 Volkswagen emissions scandal: Forty years of greenwashing – the well-travelled road taken by VW, *Independent* 24/9/2015 http://www.independent.co.uk/news/business/analysis-and-features/volkswagen-emissions-scandal-forty-years-of-greenwashing-the-well-travelled-road-taken-by-vw-10516209.html accessed 10/4/2016.

8 Critical evaluation of the European diesel car boom – global comparison, environmental effects and various national strategies, M Came and E Helmers (2013) http://www.enveurope.com/content/25/1/15 accessed 21/12/2015.

9 https://en.wikipedia.org/wiki/Diesel_exhaust accessed 22/12/2015.

10 VW dieselgate deepens – reports Bosch warning ignored, The Motor Report, http://www.themotorreport.com.au/62305/vw-dieselgate-deepens-bosch-warning-ignored accessed 20/1/2016.

11 EU warned on devices at centre of VW scandal two years ago, *Financial Times* 25/9/2015 http://on.ft.com/1KHgu54 accessed 22/12/2015.

12 EPA's notice of violation of the Clean Air Act to Volkswagen, ICCT press statement 18/9/2015 http://www.theicct.org/use-emissions-testing-light-duty-diesel-vehicles-us accessed 22/12/2015.

13 Brussels knew carmakers gamed emissions tests before VW scandal, *Financial Times*, 19 October 2016. https://www.ft.com/content/8ba08428-9554-11e6-a1dc-bdf38d484582 accessed 20/10/2016.

**14** European Commission warned of car emissions test cheating, five years before VW scandal, *Guardian* 20/6/2016 http://gu.com/p/4ydka/stw accessed 2/7/2016.

**15** Californian Air Resources board letter 18/9/2015 http://www.arb.ca.gov/newsrel/in_use_compliance_letter.htm accessed 22/12/2015.

**16** California notify Volkswagen of Clean Air Act violations / Carmaker allegedly used software that circumvents emissions testing for certain air pollutants, EPA press release 18/9/2016 http://yosemite.epa.gov/opa/admpress.nsf/bd4379a92ceceeac8525735900400c27/dfc8e33b5ab162b985257ec40057813b!OpenDocument accessed 22/12/2015.

**17** VW emissions scandal is reality's revenge, *Financial Times*, 21/9/2015 http://on.ft.com/1V8mldC accessed 10/4/2016.

**18** VW ad hoc announcement 22/9/2015 http://www.volkswagenag.com/content/vwcorp/info_center/en/news/2015/09/Ad_hoc_US.html accessed 22/12/2015.

**19** 17/9/2015 @€167; 22/9/2015 @€111 or 33 per cent https://uk.finance.yahoo.com/echarts?s=VOW.DE#symbol=VOW.DE;range=6m accessed 22/12/2015.

**20** VW emissions scandal leaves US strategy in tatters, *Financial Times* 7/1//2015 http://on.ft.com/1MZy2MF accessed 10/4/2016.

**21** German prosecutors consider inquiry into Volkswagen, *Financial Times* 23/9/2013 http://on.ft.com/1MZy2MF accessed 10/4/2016.

**22** Fitch places Volkswagen on rating watch negative, Fitch news release 23/9/2015 https://www.fitchratings.com/site/fitch-home/pressrelease?id=991188 accessed 21/1/2016.

**23** Martin Winterkorn resigns as VW boss over emissions scandal, *Financial Times* 23/9/2015 http://on.ft.com/1NLK7Xd accessed 10/4/2016.

**24** Statement from the executive committee of Volkswagen AG's supervisory board 23/9/2015 http://www.volkswagenag.com/content/vwcorp/info_center/en/news/2015/09/AR_Erklaerung.html accessed 10/4/2016.

**25** Outgoing Volkswagen CEO's exit package could top $67 million, *Washington Post* 24/9/2015 https://www.washingtonpost.com/news/on-leadership/wp/2015/09/24/outgoing-volkswagen-ceos-exit-package-could-top-67-million/ accessed 23/12/2015.

**26** Volkswagen tries to get a grip after emissions scandal, *Financial Times* 10/12/2015 http://on.ft.com/1jR3Vgf accessed 10/4/2016.

**27** Matthias Müller faces huge challenges restoring VW's credibility, *Financial Times* 27/9/2015 http://on.ft.com/1Fth1ut accessed 22/12/2015.

**28** Switzerland bans sale of VW cars with outdated emissions systems, *Financial Times* 26/9/2015 http://on.ft.com/1NRULLT accessed 11/4/2016.

**29** Volkswagen's woes risk damaging its financial services arm, *Financial Times* 28/9/2015, http://on.ft.com/1h2m3SV.

**30** Nordea press release 25/9/2015 https://www.nordea.com/en/press-and-news/news-and-press-releases/news-en/2015/2015-09-25-nordea-stops-further-investments-in-volkswagen.html accessed on 22/12/2015.

**31** Seven reasons Volkswagen is worse than Enron, David Bach, *Financial Times* 27/9/2015 http://on.ft.com/1Lelh3w accessed on 22/12/2015.

**32** Volkswagen executives describe authoritarian culture under former CEO, *Guardian* 10/1//2015 http://www.theguardian.com/business/2015/oct/10/volkswagen-executives-martin-winterkorn-company-culture accessed 11/4/2016.

**33** VW emissions scandal is personal for many Germans, *Financial Times* 24/9/2015 http://on.ft.com/1NVqQnI accessed 20/4/2016.

**34** VW investors ignored corporate governance warnings, *Financial Times* 27/9/2015 http://on.ft.com/1R9bpa6 accessed 30/12/2015.

**35** Rivals query VW's claim cheating was limited to small group, *Financial Times* 30/9/2015 http://on.ft.com/1N1A6qd accessed 22/12/2015.

**36** Volkswagen executives describe authoritarian culture under former CEO, *Guardian*, 10/10/2015 http://www.theguardian.com/business/2015/oct/10/volkswagen-executives-martin-winterkorn-company-culture accessed 22/12/2015.

**37** Dozens of managers were involved in VW's diesel scandal, Wired 14/10/2015 http://www.wired.com/2015/10/dozens-of-managers-were-involved-in-vws-diesel-scandal/ accessed 11/4/2016.

**38** Volkswagen: Secret emissions tool in 2016 cars is separate from 'defeat' cheat, *Guardian* 15/10/2015 http://www.theguardian.com/business/2015/oct/15/volkswagen-secret-emissions-tool-in-2016-cars-is-separate-from-defeat accessed 23/12/2015.

**39** VW to recall 8.5m diesel cars across Europe, *Guardian* 15/10/2015 http://www.theguardian.com/business/2015/oct/15/vw-scandal-german-authorities-reject-voluntary-recall accessed 23/12/2015.

**40** EPA news release 2/11/2015 http://yosemite.epa.gov/opa/admpress.nsf/21b8983ffa5d0e4685257dd4006b85e2/4a45a5661216e66c85257ef10061867b!OpenDocument accessed 23/12/2015.

**41** VW news release 10/12/2015 http://www.volkswagenag.com/content/vwcorp/info_center/en/news/2015/12/VW_PK.html accessed 23/12/2015.

**42** Department of Justice press release 4/1/2016 https://www.justice.gov/opa/pr/united-states-files-complaint-against-volkswagen-audi-and-porsche-alleged-clean-air-act accessed 23/12/2015.

**43** California Air Resources Board press release 12/1/2016 http://www.arb.ca.gov/newsrel/newsrelease.php?id=780 accessed 11/4/2016.

**44** S&P cuts Volkswagen's credit rating after scandal, Industry Week 12/10/2015 http://www.industryweek.com/global-economy/sp-cuts-volkswagens-credit-rating-after-scandal accessed 23/12/2015.

**45** Toyota dethrones Volkswagen as biggest car group by sales, *Financial Times* 26/10/2015 http://on.ft.com/1jKwOM5 accessed 11/4/2016.

**46** Leonardo DiCaprio to produce Volkswagen scandal film, *BBC News*, 13 October 2015. http://www.bbc.co.uk/news/entertainment-arts-34515105 accessed 13/10/2016.

**47** EU calls for investigation into Brussels' Volkswagen blunders, *Financial Times* 27/10/2015 http://on.ft.com/1KDmnPf accessed 23/12/2015.

**48** VW scandal widens as France and Italy launch deception inquiries, *Guardian* 2/10/2015 http://www.theguardian.com/business/2015/oct/02/vw-scandal-french-authorities-launch-deception-inquiry accessed 22/12/2015.

**49** German prosecutors conduct searches in VW probe, *Financial Times* 8/10/2015 http://on.ft.com/1SODYtO accessed 22/12/2015.

**50** VW diesel emissions investigation widened to include other brands, *Guardian* 11/11/2015 http://www.theguardian.com/business/2015/nov/11/vw-emissions-investigation-widened-bmw-mercedes-ford accessed 23/12/2015.

**51** VW told to rip up governance model as emissions scandal deepens, *Financial Times* 4/11/2015 http://on.ft.com/1NeFjFZ accessed 23/12/2015.

**52** Volkswagen faces shareholder claims over emissions scandal, Reuters 18/1/2016 http://www.reuters.com/article/us-volkswagen-emissions-lawsuit-idUSKCN0UW1CP accessed 11/4/2016; Norway's $850bn oil fund to sue Volkswagen, *Financial Times* 15/5/2016 http://on.ft.com/1V4cpk6 accessed 10/6/2016.

**53** Volkswagen seeks greater efficiency with new executive team, *Financial Times* 17/12/2015 http://on.ft.com/1Ze8stc accessed 23/12/2015.

**54** VW names Daimler compliance manager to help tackle scandal, Reuters 16/10/1015 http://uk.reuters.com/article/uk-volkswagen-managementchanges-daimler-KKCN0SA1QI20151016 accessed 11/4/2016.

**55** US regulator rejects VW's 3-litre car fix, *Financial Times* 14/7/2016 http://on.ft.com/29QAhan accessed 28/7/2016.

**56** VW press release 28/6/2016 http://www.volkswagenag.com/content/vwcorp/info_center/en/news/2016/06/vw_us.html accessed 28/7/2016.

**57** Volkswagen falls to biggest annual loss in its history, *Financial Times* 22/4/2016 http://on.ft.com/1Nonrin accessed 10/6/2016.

**58** Volkswagen halts sales of most vehicles in South Korea ahead of ministry review, Reuters 22/7/2016 http://uk.reuters.com/article/us-volkswagen-southkorea-idUKKCN1020K7 accessed 28/7/2016.

**59** Volkswagen still faces criminal probe after $15.3bn US settlement, *Financial Times* 28/6/2016 http://on.ft.com/299d7NH accessed 28/7/2016.

**60** VW management back in scandal spotlight, *Financial Times* 4/3/2016 http://on.ft.com/218Zv3k accessed 28/7/2016.

**61** VW boss told of emissions issue in 2006, says New York attorney general, *Financial Times* 19/7/2016 http://on.ft.com/29SCI9b accessed 28/7/2016.

**62** Brussels ups the ante in dispute with Volkswagen, *Financial Times* 7/7/2016 http://on.ft.com/29AG9Db accessed 28/7/2016; UK presses VW on compensation for British drivers, *Financial Times* 22/4/2016 http://on.ft.com/1rqfFLl accessed 10/6/2016.

**63** London pollution priorities outlined for Sadiq Khan, Air Quality News 9/5/2016 http://www.airqualitynews.com/2016/05/09/london-pollution-priorities-outlined-sadiq-khan/ accessed 28/7/2016.

**64** London: Fatal lung conditions 'more likely' in deprived boroughs, *Guardian* 6/6/2016 http://gu.com/p/4kghp/stw accessed 10/6/2016; Boris Johnson accused of burying study linking pollution and deprived schools, *Guardian* 16/5/2016 https://www.theguardian.com/environment/2016/may/16/boris-johnson-accused-of-burying-study-linking-pollution-and-deprived-schools accessed 28/7/2016; Mother wants inquiry into role of pollution in daughter's asthma death, *Guardian* 5/6/2016 http://gu.com/p/4kdqc/stw accessed 10/6/2016; Mayor promises action after 'worrying' London air pollution study, Air Quality News, 6/6/2016 https://www.airqualitynews.com/2016/06/06/mayor-promises-action-worrying-london-air-pollution-study/ accessed 2/7/2016.

**65** Volkswagen engineer pleads guilty to conspiracy in emissions scandal, *The Guardian*, 9 September 2016. https://www.theguardian.com/business/2016/sep/09/volkswagen-engineer-pleads-guilty-conspiracy-emissions-scandal- accessed 13/10/2016.

**66** Volkswagen agrees $1.2bn payment to dealers, *Financial Times*, 2 October 2016. https://www.ft.com/content/336c4db0-8874-11e6-8cb7-e7ada1d123b1 accessed 13/10/2016.

**67** Handelsblatt Global Edition Weekly Review email 22/7/2016.

**68** Jon Snow accuses Seb Coe of being 'asleep on the job or corrupt' in heated C4 interview, Huffington Post 10/11/2015 http://www.huffingtonpost.co.uk/2015/11/09/lord-coe-channel-4-news-doping-report_n_8516152.html accessed 11/4/2016.

# Mid Staffordshire NHS Foundation Trust (Stafford Hospital) 22

## Main risk event

Failure of care to patients, failure of regulation, systemic National Health Service (NHS) culture issues.

## Brief note on the organization

This patient care scandal took place at Stafford Hospital, a district general hospital run by Mid Staffordshire NHS Foundation Trust (MST) under the supervision of the West Midlands Strategic Health Authority. The latter reported to the UK Government's Department of Health, which has overall responsibility for the National Health Service (NHS)

## Date of event

January 2005 to March 2009

## Background to event

In the early part of this period MST, then an 'ordinary' hospital trust, applied to become a 'foundation trust'[1] under a scheme that would allow it to become more financially and managerially independent of external controls. It was finally awarded foundation trust status in 2008 but the tough financial decision-making and cost cutting that it undertook as part of the application process became a contributory cause of the poor care at Stafford Hospital.

As we shall see, the scandal attracted much media and political attention for several years and was subjected to five separate investigations including a full Public Inquiry. The NHS inspection regime and various individuals were heavily criticized, MST was dissolved and its services transferred to neighbouring trusts. Accident and emergency provision at Stafford Hospital was downgraded and the hospital was renamed.

## Description of event

The first public indication of poor patient care at Stafford Hospital was in 2007 when the mother of a patient set up 'Cure the NHS', a local pressure group aiming to make changes at the hospital.[2] Shortly afterwards the then NHS care regulator, the Healthcare Commission (HCC), became aware of the high death rate among those admitted there as emergencies. The HCC did not accept the hospital's explanation that these were caused by coding errors and so began a first inquiry. This was undertaken in 2008 and the report published in March 2009.[3]

The report criticized MST's management and described the appalling conditions at the hospital. It stated that it would be misleading to relate the high death rate with the poor standard of care. Indeed, the actual death rate has since been disputed as the standard methodology used could introduce bias. Nevertheless, the inadequate care at the hospital was not disputed.

## Post-event response

The Prime Minister[4] and the Secretary of State for Health[5] made public apologies to those who had suffered from the poor care at Stafford Hospital and compensation payments were made to some of the affected families.

The MST chairman resigned.[6] Its chief executive was suspended on full pay, subsequently left the trust and became CEO of Impact Alcohol and Addiction Services.[7] The chief executive of West Midlands Strategic Health Authority also left to become CEO of the Care Quality Commission, a new regulator that was set up to replace the HCC in a NHS reorganization. The UK nursing regulator suspended numerous nurses and struck off some as not fit to practise.[8]

## Findings of investigations

The MST scandal also triggered two internal NHS investigations that focused on specific aspects of how the local healthcare system operated. These were led by the Department of Health's director for emergency care and its director of primary care respectively. They reported in April 2009 and resulted in a more simplified regulatory structure at national level.[9]

As far as MST and Stafford Hospital themselves were concerned the most significant investigations were both led by Robert Francis QC. The first reported in February 2010 and made 18 local and national recommendations, including that MST should lose its foundation status. It was based on the evidence of 900 patients and families, but Francis believed that his remit should have been broader.

As a consequence, a full public inquiry was commissioned in June 2010 by the incoming government after the general election. Robert Francis was asked to lead this inquiry due to his unique knowledge of the case. The inquiry gathered a million pages of evidence and made 290 recommendations. It reported in February 2013.

## *Francis Inquiry 1 (2010)*[10]

Francis said the standard of care at Stafford Hospital was appalling and many patients had 'suffered horrific experiences that will haunt them and their loved ones for the rest of their lives'. His key observations included:

- neglect of basic elements of care;
- patients sent home too early;
- late or absent administration of pain relief;
- food and drink left out of the reach of patients;
- some patients left unwashed for up to a month;
- awful standards of hygiene;
- patients' calls for toilet assistance ignored;
- patients left in soiled sheets.

Francis said the causes of substandard care were:

- a chronic shortage of staff, particularly nursing staff;
- low morale;
- whilst many staff did their best in difficult circumstances others demonstrated a lack of compassion;
- much of the blame lay with the MST board who:
  - showed inadequate action to investigate and resolve concerns;
  - lacked an appropriate sense of urgency;
  - chose to rely on apparently favourable performance reports by outside bodies rather than effective internal assessment and feedback from staff and patients;
- the decision to save £10m in 2006–07 as part of its application for foundation status was critical. The board decided that this could only be achieved by cutting the already insufficient staffing levels.

He also drew attention to the failure of external organizations to spot the problems.

## *Francis Inquiry 2 – the public inquiry (2013)*[11]

In his damning introduction to his second report, Francis wrote that it told the story of 'appalling suffering of many patients' which was mainly caused by 'a serious failure on the part of the... Trust Board'. The board

> did not listen sufficiently to its patients and staff or ensure the correction of deficiencies brought to the Trust's attention. Above all it failed to tackle an insidious negative culture involving a tolerance of poor standards and a disengagement from management and leadership responsibilities.

One reason for this board failure was its decision to focus on meeting national accident and emergency targets, eliminating its deficit and seeking foundation status 'at the cost of delivering acceptable standards of care'.

Francis summed up the report by saying that it should be patients, not numbers, which counted.

Francis also observed that the NHS had the checks and balances necessary to prevent this sort of systemic failure. There were agencies, commissioners, regulators and professional bodies that could have been expected to detect and remedy non-compliance with acceptable care at the Trust. However, for years this had not happened and the Trust even left patients at risk for a year until the Healthcare Commission investigation was completed despite realizing there was a serious problem at Stafford Hospital.

The report included many detailed recommendations, their aims being to:

- foster a common patient-first culture;
- develop a set of easily understood standards;
- provide evidence-based means of testing compliance with these standards;
- ensure openness, transparency and candour about matters of concern;
- ensure the focus of the regulator is on policing compliance with these standards;

- make sure all those who provide care for patients are properly accountable for what they do and that the public is protected from those not fit to provide such a service;
- provide a proper degree of accountability for senior managers and leaders;
- enhance the recruitment, education, training and support of all the key contributors to the provision of healthcare – particularly those in nursing and leadership positions.

## Consequences of event

The national impact of the scandal was substantial as the satisfactory running of the NHS is constantly among the most important political issues in the public mind. The investigations were closely watched by the media as they took place either side of the 2010 general election when the Labour Party, which had originally set up the NHS, lost power to the Conservative Party.

The exposure of poor care at the hospital and failure of regulation caused severe embarrassment to politicians and resulted in a number of resignations, suspensions and sackings as well as the dissolution of the trust and the downgrading of the hospital. The regulatory regime was changed.[12] The reputations of organizations, individuals and the NHS itself were damaged.

The results of the public inquiry were well received. The King's Fund, a highly influential body that leads thinking on NHS issues, analysed the Inquiry's findings.[13] It said that it represented an important step in addressing the serious failings of care highlighted in the first Francis report. 'Patient safety is more important than party politics and what is needed now is for everyone from Parliament to the front line, to unite around delivering the culture change needed.' Specific comments included:

- The focus on making honesty and transparency the guiding principles for patient safety was welcomed.
- Implementing the change set out by government would be a long haul and require a culture change across the NHS.

- This will take place against a backdrop of severe financial pressure, with NHS organizations already facing difficult decisions about whether to prioritize patient care or balance the books.
- Realism is needed as to what can be achieved by Whitehall and regulators alone.
- Leaders within NHS organizations are best placed to foster a culture of compassionate care through motivating their teams, creating an open environment in which lessons are learned from mistakes and candour permeates from the boardroom to the ward.
- The government is right to emphasize the importance of safe staffing levels and to recognize that these should be locally determined and justified.
- Boards need to ensure that their staffing ratios are adequate, but staffing levels are only part of the answer in creating a culture of compassionate care.
- Likewise, criminal sanctions against wilful neglect provide an important legal backstop in the worst cases of poor care; but they are only part of the solution.

## Risk management lessons

### *Lesson 31: Complex organizations are prone to reputational risk*

The NHS is a highly complex organization employing over 700,000 people with a budget of over £110 bn. Coordination, control and communication in complex organizations are difficult, as is ensuring that a consistent culture is achieved throughout.

The NHS also has the complicating factor that it is regularly used as a political football with the consequence that politicians constantly play the blame game in opposition and, if in office, intervene in its running. Events such as the MST scandal with resultant reputational damage seem inevitable.

## *Lesson 32: An ethical culture needs to be led from the top*

The inquiries drew attention to a systemic culture problem in the NHS and this was particularly evident at MST. The NHS was set up to care for patients. Somehow this principle appears to have been lost on the way and in many cases has been replaced by focus on the management process and the need to balance the books.

Ethical, compassionate cultures do not happen spontaneously. They must be led from the top. In this case this should have been the MST board's role and it failed.

## *Lesson 33: Communication within an organization needs to be honest and effective*

Boards should ensure that honest and effective communication happens throughout the organization. It is clear that a substantial gulf existed between the Stafford Hospital staff and the leadership at the hospital and the trust.

The leadership did not listen to the staff and, if they did, they failed to act on the information. This problem appears to be widespread within the NHS. In 2015 the King's Fund published a survey about leadership, culture and compassionate care in the NHS. It stated:

> The most notable feature of this year's survey results was a consistent discrepancy betwen the views of executive directors and those other NHS staff, especially nurses and doctors. Executive directors tended to be much more positive about the working environment and culture within their organizations than other staff, especially nurses.[14]

## *Lesson 34: Boards should not rely on outside bodies to undertake their core duty of control*

Establishing and applying controls on the organization is a core duty of any board. Nevertheless, it would appear that this did not occur at MST. Instead the board relied more on the views of regulators such as the HCC. In practice the regulators had missed the problems.

## *Lesson 36: Regulatory bodies and other organizations applying oversight need to be joined up*

Where more than one regulator or professional body is involved in overseeing an organization and those who work in it, their approach needs to be joined up to ensure that consistent, high-quality regulation is provided.

## *Lesson 37: Avoid rewarding failure*

A number of leaders involved in these events were subsequently promoted or moved to similar positions within the sector. Irrespective of the abilities of the individuals, this action could be perceived as rewarding failure. This damages the reputation of the decision-makers who give the impression of ignoring the views of the stakeholders and protecting their peers.

On the other hand, examples occur of individuals who have made mistakes but learned from them, sometimes helping others to learn lessons. Stakeholders can often forgive such individuals and, having both recognized their failings and learned the right lessons, they may be more effective than those who have had an error-free career path.

## *Lesson 38: Risks from incentives also apply in the public sector*

It is not only those in commerce who are affected by short-termism. Politicians are affected by the electoral cycle and this can easily distort priorities and result in decisions that reflect their political cycle rather than sound management.

### Questions to mull

- To what extent did complexity contribute to this crisis?
- Why do you think that the trust leadership had become so remote from what was happening at the hospital?
- What behaviours are likely to result from politicians treating the NHS as a political football? How might these be addressed?
- To what extent do you think management incentives played a part in the scandal?
- What would you be tempted to do if you could trigger your personal incentives by taking actions that increase risks for your stakeholders? And what should you do?

## Notes

1 Foundation trusts: Questions and answers, UHB http://www.uhb.nhs.uk/foundation-q-and-a.htm accessed 15/1/2015.

2 Stafford Hospital patients 'left to scream in agony', says relative, *Telegraph* 6/2/2013 http://www.telegraph.co.uk/news/health/news/9852006/Stafford-Hospital-patients-left-to-scream-in-agony-says-relative.html accessed 15/1/2015.

3 Investigation into Mid Staffordshire NHS Foundation Trust, Healthcare Commission March 2009 http://webarchive.nationalarchives.gov.uk/20110504135228/http:/www.cqc.org.uk/_db/_documents/Investigation_into_Mid_Staffordshire_NHS_Foundation_Trust.pdf accessed 15/1/2015.

4 Brown apologises for unacceptable failings at Stafford 'Third World' hospital, *Daily Mail* 19/3/2009 http://www.dailymail.co.uk/health/article-1162552/Brown-apologises-unacceptable-failings-Stafford-Third-World-hospital.html accessed 15/1/2015.

5 Hospital condemned over deaths after 'appalling' failures in care, *Guardian* 15/3/2009 http://www.theguardian.com/society/2009/mar/17/mid-staffordshire-nhs-trust accessed 15/1/2015.

6 Stafford Hospital scandal, Everything Explained http://everything.explained.today/Stafford_Hospital_scandal accessed 15/1/2015.

**7** Stafford Hospital scandal: the bosses who escaped justice, *Telegraph* 6/1/2013 http://www.telegraph.co.uk/news/health/heal-our-hospitals/9782606/Stafford-Hospital-scandal-the-bosses-who-escaped-justice.html accessed 15/1/2015.

**8** Stafford Hospital timeline, BBC News http://www.bbc.co.uk/news/uk-england-stoke-staffordshire-20965469 accessed 15/1/2015.

**9** Mid Staffs hospital scandal: The essential guide, *Guardian* 6/2/2013 http://www.theguardian.com/society/2013/feb/06/mid-staffs-hospital-scandal-guide Accessed 15/1/2015.

**10** Francis Inquiry (2010) http://webarchive.nationalarchives.gov.uk/20130107105354/http:/www.dh.gov.uk/prod_consum_dh/groups/dh_digitalassets/@dh/@en/@ps/documents/digitalasset/dh_113447.pdf accessed 15/1/2015.

**11** Francis Inquiry (2013) http://webarchive.nationalarchives.gov.uk/20150407084003/http://www.midstaffspublicinquiry.com/sites/default/files/report/executive%20summary.pdf Accessed 15/1/2015.

**12** Press release, Care Quality Commission 6/2/2013 http://www.cqc.org.uk/content/care-quality-commission-response-francis-report accessed 15/1/2015.

**13** Our statement on the government's full response to the Francis Inquiry report, King's Fund 19/11/2013 http://www.kingsfund.org.uk/press/press-releases/our-statement-governments-full-response-francis-inquiry-report accessed 15/1/2015.

**14** Culture and leadership in the NHS – 2014, King's Fund 21/5/2014 http://www.kingsfund.org.uk/sites/files/kf/field/field_publication_file/survey-culture-leadership-nhs-may2014.pdf accessed 15/1/2015.

# PART THREE
# Practicalities

A recurrent theme in this book is that normal human behaviour is not always strictly rational and even the most able leaders may be oblivious to the potential reputational damage that they, and their influence, might trigger for their organizations and themselves.

What can be done to manage this pernicious risk? There is no 'silver bullet' but Part Three will provide a useful starting point for your own thinking, based on current best practice. Here we provide a practical guide for those who are responsible for dealing with reputational risk, whether board-level leaders, risk managers or functional specialists. We:

- provide you with brief reminders of some of the lessons from Parts One and Two;
- describe the approach taken by some leading thinkers in the field including examples from our own experience;
- outline a reputational risk management process;
- provide examples of challenges that will help you in designing and implementing a suitable process.

# The way forward 23

## Introduction

In Part One we explained:

- how, and why, respected organizations lose their reputations;
- why this often comes as a surprise to leaders and the board;
- that much vulnerability to reputational damage is predictable, though root cause risks often lie unrecognized, incubating for long periods and breeding complacency;
- that underlying root causes, usually behavioural and organizational risks, both:
  - increase the likelihood of trigger events occurring;
  - and, when such events occur, often tip into a full-blown reputational crisis;
- the limited ability of traditional risk analysis to find reputational risks and the risks that underlie them;
- the impact of inadequate preparations to deal with crises.

The case studies in Part Two illustrate our insights through stories from real life. The reputational and financial impact on companies like BP, AIG and VW, not to mention their shareholders, has been enormous, with painful personal consequences for leaders. However, the underlying root cause risks that appear time and again are likely to be absent from risk maps you have seen.

We now turn to the practical aspects of reputational risk management. What can an organization actually do systematically to find, manage and mitigate these risks? We have written Part Three with those who actually have to deal with reputational risk in mind, including:

- leaders with primary responsibility for reputation and risks to it;
- boards and non-executive directors responsible for overseeing risk management systems and reporting to shareholders and other stakeholders;
- risk managers, internal auditors and functional specialists who operate the risk system on a daily basis.

Outsiders, such as investors and regulators, will equally find our approach valuable in gauging whether organizations are intrinsically vulnerable or resilient to shocks and reputational crises.

## Implementing a reputational risk management process

When, as we recommend, you decide to bring a systematic approach to managing reputational risk, with a focus on root causes, you may meet resistance or scepticism from some of those who need to be involved. Do not be disheartened. This is a result of what we call the 'reputational risk paradox' which, whilst understandable, comes from an inadequate understanding of these risks.

### *The reputational risk paradox*

Most well-informed leaders of substantial organizations acknowledge that reputational risk is one of the most important threats they face. Some understand that these risks threaten their organization's long-term existence and are working hard to find and implement measures to address them. Sadly, our case studies suggest that many large and well-respected organizations do not approach reputational risk in a way that demonstrates an understanding of the issues or their gravity. We have heard many reasons given for avoiding this area of risk and we thought we would share some of these with you.

- 'It could not possibly happen to us: we are a well-run company so there is no point in wasting resources on a hypothetical risk.'

Self-serving bias and a failure to examine the causes of success easily leave boards complacent as to incubating existential threats. The sad truth is that whilst reputational crises are often a bolt from the blue to boards, it often emerges that others, outsiders and insiders, saw the vulnerability in advance even though they could not predict when things would go wrong, or precisely how.

- 'Reputational risk is not a risk in itself. It is merely a consequence of other corporate and operational risks. If these are managed, reputation looks after itself.'
  This view is based on the mistaken assumption that 'other' risks are comprehensively managed by the risk management system. Many trigger events that initiate a crisis, such as an explosion or accident, will probably be within the risk management system. However, the underlying, often systemic, behavioural and organizational risks are not rigorously identified, let alone managed, by classical risk systems. There will be severe reputational damage if, as the facts emerge during a crisis, stakeholders discover that the organization and its leaders have not met their expectations.
- 'Reputational risk is essentially a PR issue. If we have a crisis, the corporate communications team and its advisors will deal with any reputational damage. Crisis management is enough.'
  Crisis management matters and PR has a crucial role to play in it. But as many organizations have found to their cost, you cannot just 'spin' your way out of a major crisis. Substance matters.
  Good reputational risk management begins by seeking to prevent crises. Work should begin long before any crisis, by examining weaknesses in the foundations of your reputation. Well done, this will identify systemic weaknesses so they can be dealt with before they cause harm.
- 'We use an enterprise risk management (ERM) process. This addresses all reputational risk issues.'
  Like traditional risk management processes, ERM is based on three lines of defence. As we explained in Chapter 5, classical risk management has a gap that is critical to reputational risks: it takes inadequate account of risks emanating from human behaviour generally and from leaders in particular. In addition, classically

trained ERM professionals and internal auditors are unlikely to have the skills needed to identify, let alone manage and mitigate, behavioural and organizational risks.

- 'Reputational risk is too difficult to manage. Time is better spent on managing risks we do understand.'
  Even the Basel Committee on Banking Supervision once put these risks into the 'too difficult' box.[1] It is, however, a dereliction of duty to put risks to your organization's reputation into a box marked 'too difficult', especially since these risks are not intrinsically difficult to manage once they have been understood. With regulators and investors paying increasing attention to reputational, behavioural and organizational risks, they can no longer be ignored. Education is an important part of any solution, so you can help such people to progress by encouraging them to read this book!

## Note

1 Basel II http://www.bis.org/publ/bcbs107.pdf at Section V accessed 12/4/2016.

# System basics – getting to 'go' 24

## Process overview

Your board should assume active oversight of the risk management process for reputational risk, including systems, and controls.

There is no single right way to undertake reputational risk management. The approach we describe is designed to be integrated with your existing risk management system as much as practicable, drawing on steps taken by organizations that have given considerable thought to the subject. Figure 24.1 summarizes the structure.

## Understanding the nature of reputation and reputational risk

Most leaders understand the importance of reputation and are concerned about reputational risk, which regularly appears high in rankings of feared risks. Most probably believe they understand reputational risks; but current annual reports suggest this belief is often incorrect. We therefore believe it is currently dangerous to assume that leaders have sufficient systematic breadth and depth of knowledge as regards reputation or reputational risks.

This gap is best filled by providing authoritative education as part of the board's annual training programme. In our experience, leaders demand evidence, and we find this is best delivered by a liberal leavening of examples from real life.

**Figure 24.1** Schematic diagram of process for reputational, behavioural and organisational risk management

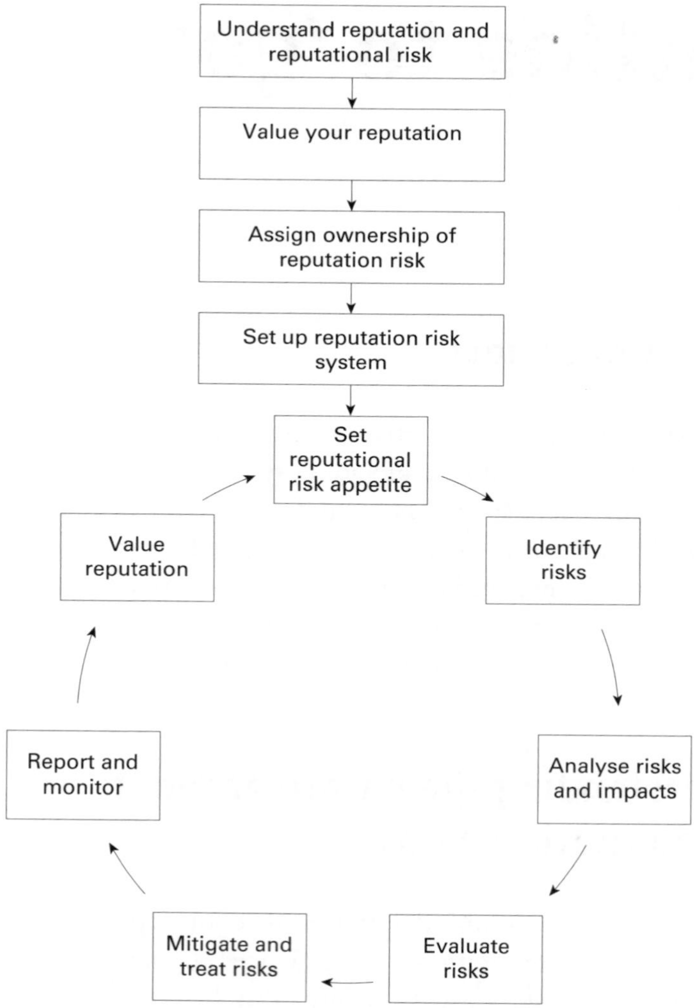


However, we have also found that a mentored dissection of a carefully chosen case study containing rather more of the story than we had space for in this book is a valuable teaching aid. It helps participants to internalize what they have learned by listening, to use the vocabulary they have learned and to practise, in safety, asking questions about unfamiliar subjects. Well led, the process can also give leaders a safe first glimpse of where their organization's weaknesses might lie.

Learning points should include:

- Why and how a good reputation is important.
- Sound practical definitions of 'reputation' and 'reputational risk' and their implications.
- An illustrated lexicon of the range of behavioural, organizational and reputational risks.
- The latent, systemic nature of many of these risks, their often long incubation periods, why complacency arises and the role of trigger events. We have illustrated some of these, and related underlying risks, in Table 24.1.

**Table 24.1** Illustrations of trigger events that caused reputational and other damage, with examples of potential underlying behavioural and organisational risks

| Type | Trigger | Examples of underlying risks commonly outside classical risk management |
|---|---|---|
| **Products and services** | **Supermarkets:** sale of horsemeat as beef<br>**VW NOx emissions:** conceal true emissions performance | Culture; incentives; complexity; internal and supplier communications failures; leadership; leaders' risk blindness; gaps in board skill, experience and knowledge |
| **Financial performance** | **AIG:** collapse due to unrecognized risks in small subsidiary | Culture; incentives; gaps in board skill, experience and knowledge; failure to question success; board risk blindness; inadequate regulators |
| **Executive and individual behaviour** | **Libor:** banks wrongdoing in mis-reporting interest rates<br>**Various rogue traders:** loss of $billions | Leadership; culture; incentives; communication failures; board risk blindness; system failures |
| **Safety and environment** | **BP Texas City explosion:** safety failures leading to fatalities<br>**BP *Deepwater Horizon*:** deaths, injuries and oil spill | Leaders' skill and knowledge; leadership; incentives; failure to integrate; ethos and culture; complexity; communication failures; board risk blindness; system failures; weak regulators; failure to learn |
| **Customer relations** | **Personal protection insurance mis-selling:** sale of inappropriate insurance products to consumers | Incentives; culture; board risk blindness; failure to question success |

**Challenges**

- To what extent do your
  - risk and internal audit team;
  - leadership team and board

have a systematic understanding of reputation, reputational risk and its behavioural and organizational risk drivers?

- To what extent are your risk, internal audit, leadership and board teams aware of any weakness you identify in these areas?
- How can you best help those who need to remedy any gaps in their knowledge?

# Valuing your reputation

## *Quantitative aspects*

One aspect of your reputation is its financial value to you. You can arrive at the financial aspect of its value using services offered by companies with methodologies designed for such valuations.

If you are a quoted company, you can compare the answer you receive with an estimate of the drop in market capital you would expect if something severely damaged your reputation. In our experience a quoted company with a good reputation should not be surprised if its market capital falls by 30 per cent to 40 per cent in a reputational crisis. The fall can be greater especially if liquidity or solvency come into question.

These measures may feel less relevant if your organization is an unquoted company with no intention of floating or a non-commercial organization such as a charity. It is nonetheless a worthwhile exercise to estimate their scale in terms of the potential financial consequences of losing your reputation. Measures such as potential loss of income may be a good starting point.

## *Qualitative aspects*

Value is not just financial. It is important that your board also achieves a rounded picture of the practical ways in which your organization's reputation affects its success, how damage might impede success and how a better reputation might help. This qualitative aspect is directly relevant to all kinds of organization. Questions to ask include:

- What advantages does our current reputation confer?
- What might be lost in a bad crisis?
- With what consequences?

It is important to compare operating with your current reputation against operating with one that has been damaged in a severe crisis. Getting to an answer will be an iterative exercise that you should revisit regularly in the light of your experience and the experiences of organizations around you, though this experience is likely to be inadequate on its own because reputational crises often repeat history but with an unexpected twist.

The process should include a realistic analysis of likely stakeholder behaviour, including in the context of a crisis. You should analyse scenarios that are considered 'unthinkable', because experience shows that such events regularly derail unprepared boards.

Thus informed, you can make an initial estimate of the resources that its protection deserves. Estimating its value will also help in setting a preliminary risk appetite for reputational damage.

This is emphatically not to say that reputation should be your leaders' guiding star. Navigating that way easily leads to a reputation that is only skin deep. Whilst it is tempting to burnish a reputation, it is dangerous to do so without building what outsiders see as solid foundations.

## *Record these values*

We recommend that you record the value, both qualitative and quantitative, of your organization's reputation on the first page of your risk register. This prominent position is justified because your reputation is likely to be one of your organization's most valuable attributes, making risks to it some of the most important risk you face.

This memorandum, at the front of your risk register, will in part be a financial amount; but we recommend you record a description of benefits enjoyed that may be lost if your reputation is harmed. This serves as a constant reminder that reputation has unquantifiable aspects.

**Challenges**

- How would you estimate the financial value of the reputation of your organization?
- What advantages and disadvantages flow from the reputation you have?
- How do these compare with those enjoyed by your most effective competitor? Which of their advantages and disadvantages do you lack?
- How would severe damage to your reputation affect your ability to operate effectively?
- How much reputational damage is your organization prepared to risk? And how much could it comfortably survive?

## Assigning ownership of reputation

Reputation is a crucial attribute. Everyone who works in an organization should be keen to preserve and contribute to improving its strength, but this does not mean that everyone can 'own' the reputation. That would be a recipe for confusion, with duplicated effort, gaps and diverging approaches taken. Distributed responsibility could easily become a source of organizational risk that would ultimately manifest itself in dysfunctionality.

A single person should take responsibility for all aspects of reputation and reputational risks and for ensuring that they are well managed. To do the job effectively, this person needs both the authority to find reputational risks and the behavioural and organizational and other risks that underlie them; and the power and authority to deal with these risks as they are found. They should have a clear incentive to maintain and grow the organization's reputation on solid foundations.

Only one person fits these criteria: the CEO. But even CEOs have a blind spot and a no-go area.

- The blind spot concerns the risks that originate with the CEO.
- The no-go area concerns the board; partly because the board sits above the CEO and partly because, in most systems of governance, the chair has primary responsibility for the running of the board and its effectiveness.

These risk areas should be the responsibility of the chair.

How these responsibilities are allocated should be a formal decision of the board and set out unambiguously in a board policy.

### Challenges

- Who takes overall responsibility for reputation and reputational risk in your organization?
- To the extent that the CEO does not, who does take responsibility? To what extent does that person have explicit authority to deal with all risks identified?
- To what extent does the chair take responsibility for reputation and reputational risk?
- Where are the gaps and overlaps in responsibility?
- How is responsibility for reputational risk delegated below board level? To what extent do those given responsibility have blind spots and no-go areas? Do they have explicit authority to deal with all risks identified?

# Setting up the reputational risk management system

25

Whilst your system for the management of reputation risks should be an integral part of your wider risk management system, extending your current risk management system to include reputational, behavioural and organizational risks will require some changes.

We are privileged to be able to share with you a good example of how a board is bringing these risks under board control. The box contains edited recommendations from an internal report shared with us by the risk manager of an anonymous medium sized international firm. He told us that the board had already had the benefit of a reputational risk awareness session as part of the annual board training programme in the previous year.

### Extract from a reputational risk report to a financial services board

#### 6.1 Recommended action for board

The following actions are recommended for the board to ensure that reputational risks are proactively identified and managed:

1 The board of directors (BOD) should undertake an exercise that will help to identify and assess important sources of behavioural, organizational and reputational risks in and around the board and enable further analysis of their potential consequences, to work out the best ways to deal with them.

▶

2 Systematic and tailored education of the board on behavioural and organizational risks and their relationship with reputational damage.

3 Enhanced reputational risk appetite should be exclusively set by the BOD. This will enable the board to set tolerances for behavioural and organizational risks, which often cause reputational damage.

4 The board should also systematically identify the behavioural and organizational risks in their midst and in the environment in which they operate, and assess the implications of what was found.

### 6.2 Recommended management actions

The company should establish a clear framework for measuring and managing reputational risk. This could include the appropriateness of the following steps:

1 Put the CEO in charge of reputational risk. The chief executive, together with the board, needs to instil and drive the risk culture within the organization and demonstrate the right behaviour by example.

2 Proactive reputational risk discussion during the executive committee (EXCO) and BOD meetings as a standing agenda.

3 Incentivize employees to guard the company's reputation. Leading companies are already making an awareness of reputational risk part of their performance management and employees can make a valuable contribution as 'eyes and ears' of the business.

4 Develop an 'outside-in' perspective on risk (guided by the belief that customer value creation, customer orientation and customer experiences are the keys to success). Apply a 'reputational lens' to key traditional risk categories to help understand how damage to reputation might result if they are not properly managed and take steps to close any gaps.

5 Value the company's reputational capital. Although methods of placing a financial value against reputation are still in their infancy, getting experts to review the impact of various reputational issues and communicating this widely across the company can certainly help drive the message home.

6 Learn from others' mistakes. Many of the major corporate reputational disasters of recent years provide textbook examples, and there are many lessons and best practices that can be adopted from their analysis.[1]

The risk manager, a senior executive immediately below the board and the executive committee, told us that although the report received the attention of the risk committee and subsequently the full board, it would probably have carried more weight had it been written by a board member.

We agree that the person putting together the plan to deal with this group of risks should be as senior as possible. But what matters most is that the plan is embraced by the full board. In practice the chair of the risk committee (if there is one) or of the audit committee are suitable board-level sponsors.

## Leadership in risk management

The causes of reputational damage often have their roots at leadership levels. It is therefore essential that the system for management of reputational, behavioural and organizational risks is led and coordinated in such a way that the risk team has real authority to analyse and report on such risks when it encounters them.

For organizations that have a chief risk officer (CRO) with direct reporting lines to a board committee, structural changes will be modest. The CRO should be given the explicit authority and duty to include these risks at all levels; and as regards such risks emanating from the board, the CRO will need an additional authority from and reporting line to the chair.

Organizations that do not have a CRO should adapt their reporting systems; for if there is one way to ensure that these risks are not comprehensively identified, let alone dealt with, it is to have the risk team reporting to a senior executive. The simplest solution is for the head of risk to have an additional direct reporting line to the chair (or audit committee chair) on reputational behavioural and organizational risks. In what follows we shall refer to CROs but you should treat that as referring to heads of risk without that designation.

To avoid perverse incentives, CROs should be rewarded and evaluated on criteria that encourage ensuring that the organization's reputation is built on enduring foundations. The design of their incentives will usually be fundamentally different from that of other executives. The timeframes in these criteria should reflect the time it takes for such risks to emerge, which can easily be up to a decade. Similar comments apply to Internal Audit.

## Risk team skills

Current risk teams are not naturally endowed in the skills needed to identify the behavioural and organizational risks that underlie reputational risks; and such risks are not a part of a typical board's vocabulary. The UK Financial Reporting Council recognized the issue in its 2014 guidance on risk management:

> *The board should consider whether it, and any committee or management group to which it delegates activities, has the necessary skills, knowledge, experience, authority and support to enable it to assess the risks the company faces and exercise its responsibilities effectively.*[2]

Andrew Bailey, formerly head of the Prudential Regulation Authority and now head of the FCA, has repeatedly emphasized[3] the importance of risk management probing governance, hubris, risk blindness, good news cultures, management effectiveness, tone from the top and how that tone is adopted below the top, concluding:

> *We seek to ensure that firms have robust governance, which includes appropriate challenge from all levels of the organization; and promote the acceptance that not all news can be good and the willingness to act on and respond promptly to bad news. We insist that remuneration is structured to ensure that individuals have skin in the game… We require that risk management and internal audit in firms are effective and act to root out poor incentives and weak controls. All of this is important and central to what we do as regulators, but let me reinforce the point that culture begins and lives, and I am afraid dies, at home, with firms.*
>
> Andrew Bailey, © Bank of England

It is vital that the detailed work on identifying and mitigating reputational risks and the underlying behavioural and organizational risks is carried out by a team that has the requisite skills. Unfortunately many, perhaps most, CROs, though exceptionally talented in many other ways, do not have great depth of knowledge and experience in the field of human and organizational behaviour and the risks that it presents. We suspect that many current risk teams also lack key skills and experience in these areas. The scope of skill gaps in these areas should be identified and addressed.

We initially thought the solution was to train risk specialists in the skills of behavioural and organizational risks, and that is likely to be the solution at senior levels of risk management where a general knowledge of all requisite skills are essential, though CROs will have exceptional depth in particular fields.

However, having researched further we have concluded that for organizations that already have a substantial human resources (HR) or personnel management team, a more cost-effective approach below CRO or head of risk level may be to train people who are already skilled in understanding and managing people to understand about behavioural and organizational risks and their reputational risk consequences.

Such specialists are to be found in some larger organizations. The professionals we have in mind will have degrees in subjects such as sociology, psychology, anthropology or organizational behaviour as well as years of relevant practical experience. It is professionals such as these with a strategic view of their organization, not those focused on areas such as employment law or benefits, that we have in mind.

We therefore recommend that organizations that already have such professionals consider selecting some for systematic training in behavioural and organizational risks and their reputational consequences. Thus trained, this cohort can work with the risk team, enriching its range of skills. In addition, these professionals will have the skills necessary for effective mitigation of behavioural and organizational risks.

Is HR really that important? Perhaps leaders do not think so, but it should be. HR can play a crucial role in identifying and mitigating behavioural, relational, organizational and reputational risk. How? By monitoring and enhancing the cultural tone of a company.

First, the HR team must ask itself if it has the necessary skills, or whether it needs to draw in experts from outside the company or to train insiders to fill gaps, for example as to risk.

Then the HR team should develop a plan of action, something like the following:

- Assessment of the current situation by a culture audit complemented by a relational audit: these are means of quantifying key aspects of a company's culture as well as the dynamics of a company's organizational relationships, internal and external.
- Analysis of the scorecards resulting from the cultural and relational audits to identify the specific improvements needed, and the organizational interventions which might be best.
- Evaluation of whether interventions should be organization-wide, or involve particular hierarchical levels or vertical divisions or units – or one or more cross-functional working groups.
- At the completion of an intervention, re-run the audit(s) in the whole (or in part) of the company to measure how much improvement has taken place.

Such audits are also useful for due diligence in mergers and acquisitions – and for post-merger integration.

To avoid what Mervyn King calls 'uninformed oversight', a company board can use these instruments, and the related training courses for board members as well as others, to ensure that the board is intelligently monitoring, mitigating and managing cultural, behavioural, relational, organizational and reputational risks.

Prabhu Guptara, Distinguished Professor of Global Management, Business and Public Policy, William Carey University, India

## A reputation committee?

Some very large organizations have established a committee to be responsible for reputation. This is an idea worth considering for the largest organizations; but the dangers are that it focuses on only part of the area, leaving gaps; and that it is tempted to focus on promoting a good reputation whilst paying insufficient attention to building it on solid foundations. We believe it is best for reputation risk management to be an integral part of risk management.

## Giving the team sufficient authority

Whilst behavioural and organizational risks are found at all levels of the organization, the root cause risks often emanate from the highest levels, for example as the consequences of board activities and decisions in areas such as structure, strategy, incentives and culture. As we have explained, this can make it difficult, and personally dangerous, for risk professionals, internal auditors and others to raise issues because to do so might be interpreted as a challenge to or criticism of a superior.

It is therefore essential that the chair, board and chief executive give the risk team explicit duty and authority to evaluate and report on behavioural and organizational risks wherever they originate from, including in and around the board. Reports reflecting such findings should be given a warm welcome. Any other reception will act as a disincentive to future frank reporting of such risks.

## Dealing with risks from board level

As we explained in Chapter 14, the power to do good goes hand in hand with the power to cause severe reputational damage.

Some risks emanating from boards may be identified by risk teams and reported to the board, and this is a valuable source of intelligence. But even the best risk teams can only see a part of the picture since they largely see particular consequences and trace their root causes.

Not all board-level risks will be visible to risk teams, who may also lack the necessary analytical skills and experience in that area. Risk-aware boards will wish to see into this blind spot; but many will question whether the risk team has the experience, skill, authority or perspective to carry out that task.

This is a valid question. Even the most experienced risk team will be unable to bring the inside-outsider view that is essential to seeing internal normality as an outsider can see it. Internal risk teams may lack the experience to identify board-level issues as such; they are likely to lack the authority needed to ensure that the board internalizes and deals with any issues highlighted and they may fear retribution if they bring unpalatable truths to power.

The best solution is periodically to use an external specialist in board-level behavioural, organizational and reputational risk to carry out an 'inside-outsider' analysis and evaluation of vulnerabilities in and around the board and executive team. We call this a 'Board Vulnerability Evaluation'.

This is not the same as a classical board effectiveness evaluation because it analyses and evaluates board attributes and activities from a risk perspective, working through from behavioural, organizational and other board risks to reputational and other consequences and beyond to mitigation. It can, however, be structured simultaneously to deliver a review of board effectiveness, thus fulfilling regulatory requirements such as those of the FRC, for external reviews of boards.

In our experience, whilst a clear strategy is needed to ensure that leaders are able to internalize the findings, an external evaluation of this kind is a highly effective way to find and deal with board-level risks. When the process is designed to capture strengths as well as weaknesses, we call the result a 'Board Resilience Evaluation'.

As to frequency, an external analysis is essential when the whole area is explored and discussed by the board for the first time. This is the most difficult phase in working on these risks.

Once the initial findings have been absorbed and acted upon, and given a CRO with authority drawn from the chair, we believe it will usually be sufficient to schedule an external board vulnerability evaluation every two or three years unless there is a particular reason to have one sooner – for example because a new chair has arrived or a crisis has occurred.

### Challenges

- How can your board ensure that the root cause risks to your organization's reputation are systematically identified and dealt with?
- Who in your organization has both the authority and power to lead the risk management process for reputational risk and the risks that underlie it, including mitigation? Do they have the necessary knowledge and skills?
- To what extent does your board have the skill and knowledge to supervise the management of reputational risks and the behavioural and organizational risks that underlie it?
- To the extent that there are gaps, how would you fill them?
- How can you ensure that those to whom reputational risk management is delegated feel safe to deal effectively with risks emanating from executives or the board?

## Notes

1 Private communication. The source wishes to remain anonymous.
2 FRC (2014b).
3 Bailey (2016).

# Operating the reputational risk management system 26

We now turn to the risk management process itself. This is essentially a cycle that repeats itself at least annually. We recommend that the system for managing behavioural, organizational and reputational risks is integrated with the existing risk management system. We have assumed that you have one and we therefore focus on the features you will need to add.

## Setting risk appetite and tolerance

Risk appetite has been defined by the UK Treasury as 'the amount of risk your organization is prepared to accept, tolerate or be exposed to at any time'.[1] Whilst this conflates risk appetite and risk tolerance, we think it is nonetheless a practical tool in thinking about acceptable levels of reputational risk.

In this area, do not be surprised if you conclude that your appetite and tolerance for reputational risk is small. Berkshire Hathaway's appetite and tolerance are zero.

*We can afford to lose money – even a lot of money. But we can't afford to lose reputation – even a shred of reputation. We must continue to measure every act against not only what is legal but also what we would be happy to have written about on the front page of a national newspaper in an article written by an unfriendly but intelligent reporter.*

Warren Buffett, biennial letter to his top managers, © Berkshire Hathaway/Warren Buffett (reproduced with permission)

## Identifying, analysing and evaluating reputational risks and their roots

Your existing risk register is likely to list trigger events that have been shown by history to pose reputational risks. If annual reports are an accurate reflection of reality, most boards currently stop here, without exploring the root causes of such crises.

This approach is fundamentally backward-looking and leaves large areas of systemic behavioural and organizational risks unidentified and therefore incubating unmanaged, waiting to deliver unpredicted shocks. The failure to recognize them over what can be years is itself a reputational risk because it amplifies the potential for reputational damage. With board encouragement and support, your risk team should therefore set out systematically to identify and analyse reputational risks and their root cause risks.

*Until recently, risk management appeared to offer security through rational mathematical models and checklist-driven review processes. Accumulated governance scandals and the widespread failure to predict financial market collapse has invited a new approach, focused more on human behaviour and qualitative data.*

Managing the people dimension of risk, Corporate Research Forum, 2010

In this section we shall very briefly recapitulate the areas of underlying risk discussed in Part One, adding challenges for you to consider. These areas are intensely interlinked, as Figure 26.1 illustrates.

**Figure 26.1** Some of the links between risk areas that drive reputational risk: they are many and complex

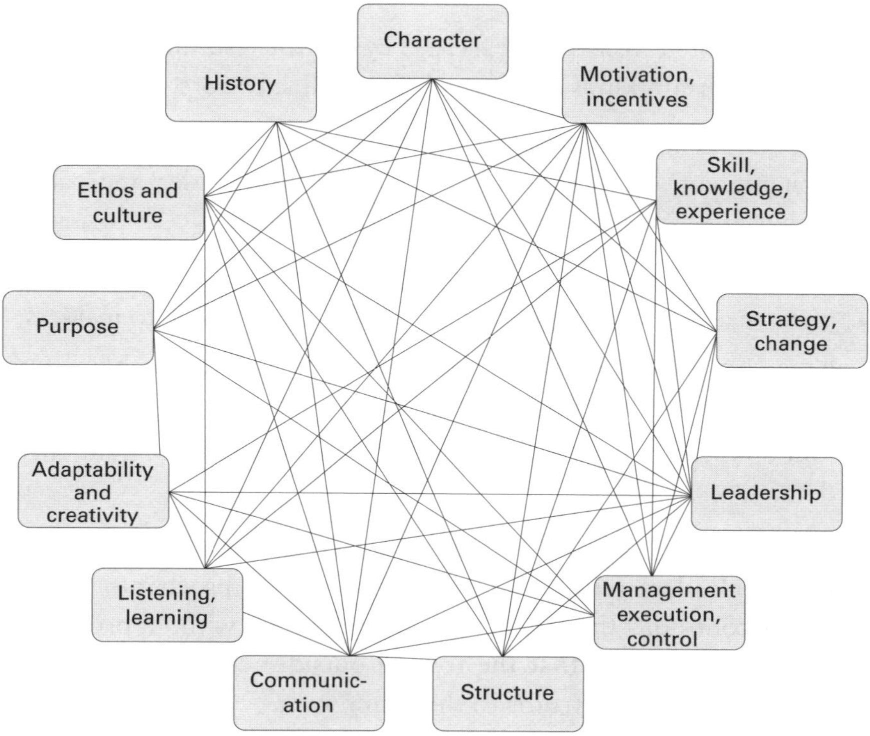


## Analysing risks and impacts

One of the greatest challenges in identifying the behavioural and organizational risks that underlie reputational risks is our inability to see ourselves as others see us. This matters because our reputation is the sum of our stakeholders' perceptions, not what we see in a mirror.

Insiders inevitably begin with insider perceptions of these risks and could attempt to explore them more thoroughly. Unfortunately, information gathered by insiders is intrinsically unreliable in this area because:

- other insiders may be reluctant to confide to an insider if they have any fear of repercussions;

- insiders' mental maps may prevent them from understanding how outsiders would react to discovering what insiders see as normal;
- the appointed insider may feel it beyond their station, or fear, to discuss, certain kinds of vulnerability with superiors.

It is essential to overcome these obstacles. In our experience, the combination of 'sceptical outsider' and the 'inside-outsider' approaches is highly effective. An outsider given confidential access to insider information can:

- observe aspects of insider normality that are invisible to insiders;
- have conversations with insiders that they would not have with other insiders for fear of repercussions;
- join up the dots to make a picture that reflects a raft of qualitative data.

With care, the well-informed 'inside-outsider' can communicate credible findings to leaders in a manner that helps them to absorb information that may contradict their mental maps and models without provoking rejection. It is critical that the trusted outsider can be relied on to bring any unpalatable truths to those in power.

In practice this means periodically using a skilled outsider trusted by insiders to discover what insiders have to tell, without disclosing sources; and to tell leaders what they discover in a manner that helps leaders internalize what they are told. We call this an 'organizational vulnerability evaluation'. It makes better use of the effort involved to capture and analyse strengths in the same operation. We call the result an ' organizational resilience evaluation'.

Vulnerability evaluations help leaders to understand how exposed the organization is both to states of affairs that might precipitate a crisis, and to an event escalating into a severe reputational crisis: and why. Resilience evaluations add to this a deeper understanding of strengths, including those that may enable the organization to benefit from certain kinds of unlooked-for crisis – Taleb's 'antifragile'.

When we began to make external analyses of organizations, we discovered just how much information about large or well-known organizations can be found in the public domain.

What is perhaps surprising is the extent to which the outside world seems to ignore that treasure trove, at least until the organization hits the headlines for the wrong reason. It may be that in normal times, confirmation bias leads people to pay more attention to information that reinforces their mental maps and models, tending to disregard that which doesn't – with the effect that these maps and models are reinforced, not questioned. We suspect that by detaching themselves from their mental maps and models, financial analysts could develop a valuable methodology to rank companies by vulnerability to reputational crises and the sudden share price falls they bring. One approach to this has been discussed, from a different perspective, by Tetlock and Gardner in their book *Superforecasting*.[2]

### Challenges: methodology

- What is the status of your risk team in your hierarchy? How might that affect its ability to report on risks from sources at or above its level?
- How can you overcome the cognitive biases that prevent insiders from seeing themselves and their organization as outsiders would see them if outsiders came to know what is really going on inside the organization?
- How can you ensure that the whole truth is told to those in power?
- How persistently do you challenge answers by asking 'What is my evidence?'

## *Stakeholder analysis and risks from stakeholders*

Any analysis of reputational risks must begin with a comprehensive analysis of stakeholders, their importance, expectations and perceptions of the organization, including the reasonableness of their expectations and perceptions. This should be carried out for stakeholders in two states: 'normal' and 'crisis' conditions.

The analysis should evaluate how their attitudes and relative importance may change in different circumstances as well as the extent to which their perceptions of the organization are well founded. It should also include how stakeholders might react to circumstances that leaders consider unthinkable. The 'unthinkable' happens all too often, demonstrating that leaders had insufficient idea of what was going on in their organization, even in their midst. Leaders will benefit from a sceptic probing to ensure that their thinking has been sufficiently stretched.

### Challenges: stakeholders

- Does your organization deserve its current reputation?
- What stakeholder perceptions are out of line with reality?
- Which stakeholder expectations are unreasonable?
- What might make which stakeholders flip their attitudes?
- How might your stakeholders' stakeholders affect stakeholder attitudes if things have gone badly wrong?
- In what respects are your regulators ineffective or incompetent? What might be the consequences?
- To what extent have you overcome your cognitive biases in answering the above questions?

## *Risks from history*

Many reputations weaken gradually. Perceptions of poor service, inadequate quality, arrogance and failure to deliver on strategy are just a few ways to increase latent stakeholder dissatisfaction. The internet makes it easy for people affected to share their experiences, frustrations, disappointments and perceptions. And if they come to realize that their perspective is typical, not an exception, your reputation will be progressively damaged.

The view of history shared by stakeholders is a powerful force in shaping reputations. And whenever bad news surfaces, you can expect stakeholders to be given a recapitulation that will frame the development of their new perceptions.

### Examples: history

- A long history of controversies, crises and poor outcomes.
- Leaders who assume that successful crisis management leaves the issues that caused a crisis forgotten.

- Promises made and expectations created, but not met.
- A history of antagonism to pressure groups and rebuffed whistle-blowers.

**Challenges: history**

- How would an intelligent but unfriendly journalist portray your history if you hit the headlines tomorrow and they learned what insiders know?
- How does this differ from the view of your leaders?
- Why are there differences, and how might they matter?
- How can you be sure that your answers reflect reality?

## *Risks from communication failures*

Communication failures leave leaders in the dark, information sitting in silos, important messages sent but not received and lessons unlearnt. They are symptomatic of a dysfunctional organization riddled with deeper behavioural and organizational risks. And whilst they are often not root cause risks, communication risks are often direct causes of reputational damage as well as symptoms of root cause risks. This is why risks from failed communication deserve particularly close attention, not only in their own right but also to discover their root causes.

### Examples: communication failures

- Bad news travels upwards more slowly than good news.
- Important information does not reach leaders, causing 'unknown knowns' and an inability to 'join up the dots'.
- Messages are not disseminated downwards or across the organization.
- Communication from the outside towards the inside, or from the inside to the outside, is ineffective.
- Superiors do not listen to what they are told by those below them or reinterpret it more favourably to themselves.
- Lessons cannot be learned from errors that do not have obvious consequences because news of the errors is suppressed.

### Challenges: communication failures

- How quickly does unwelcome news travel upwards to leaders? Is this slower than the speed at which good news travels? Why?
- How do the chair, board, CEO and other leaders each react to those who deliver unwelcome news? Why? And with what consequences?
- How effectively do managers at each level listen to those below them?
- To what extent does news get distorted as it moves through your organization? Why?
- How and to what extent do incentives affect the free flow of information in your organization? And what about the effects of culture?
- How receptive is your organization to uncomfortable ideas and criticism from outside?
- What subjects are staff members reluctant to discuss with superiors, for example because the issues are perceived as dull, taboo, obvious, impolite or downright dangerous?
- Write down a list of your blind spots. How do you know it is complete?

## *Risks from failure to learn*

A common consequence of communication failures is missed opportunities to learn from mistakes. These may be mistakes that have consequences that are widely known but are not investigated to their root causes. But for every such mistake there are likely to be scores more that are unrecognized, ignored or hidden. Lessons from these are only learned locally, if at all.

When it emerges that an organization has failed to learn lessons from errors, reputational damage is a frequent consequence.

### Examples: failure to learn

- Lessons are not learned because:
  - errors are not seen as errors;
  - errors are covered up;

- – lessons are learned only locally, if at all;
- – mishaps reported are not investigated to root causes;
- – lessons identified are not disseminated.
- Lessons are not learned from the failures of outsiders.

**Challenges: failure to learn**

- How readily, how often and how openly do you and your leaders at all levels recognize and learn from your and their own mistakes and share the learning with others? What do staff deduce about culture from what they see?
- Do those thinking of reporting mistakes feel they risk facing unpleasant consequences?
- To what extent are mistakes that lack immediate bad consequences hidden from superiors?
- What is your evidence and how reliable is it?
- To what extent are mistakes investigated to root causes and lessons disseminated?
- How does your answer change as you move from the front line to senior leaders?

## *Risks from character*

Character provides default rules of behaviour and personal ethos – such as your inbuilt concept of what is 'right' and what is not. It is a strong influence on how people behave when they believe no one is looking. Any good risk analysis will consider character: the character of leaders at all levels, the role of character selection in recruitment and promotion – and its implications.

### Examples: character

- Recruitment and remuneration policies have led to a concentration of leaders with undesirable character traits.
- Incentives, selection and promotion have led to the development and concentrations of undesirable character traits among the successful.

### Challenges: character

- What role does character play in recruitment and promotion? And in the past?
- What are the consequences of the last three decades' recruitment and promotion as regards patterns of character among staff and leaders?
- What is the effect of different backgrounds (eg educational, ethnic, geographical or religious) on the character and personal ethoses of your workforce and leadership?
- To what extent are leaders, especially at higher levels, dominant or charismatic? How are the risks of such characteristics recognized and mitigated?
- What can you deduce about character from the pay packages that executives, and other successful people, demand?

## *Risks from culture*

Culture is an important influence on people and may conflict with an individual's character. If people are affected by different cultures at home and at work, the result may be attitudes at work that would not emerge in the home environment. Culture may also distort personal standards of 'right' and 'wrong'.

To identify risks from culture, the starting point is to discover what the culture actually is. An organization's culture is difficult to identify, especially for insiders, because they may be unable to see elements of what they think of as normality. Cultural audits are a part of the human resources toolbox, but much can also be deduced from dissecting mishaps, insider stories and how people actually behaved when they found themselves facing difficult choices.

From there, risks from the organization's culture can be identified, along with risks from dissonance between the actual culture and patterns of character. Similarly risks from dissonances between reality and stakeholder perceptions and expectations should be identified. Homogeneity is unlikely, so any cultural risk evaluation needs sufficient granularity to capture important variations.

## Examples: culture

- The desired culture is:
  - inadequate or undesirable;
  - ambiguous;
  - too complicated;
  - ineffectively inculcated;
  - inconsistent with workforce character patterns;
  - poorly advocated by leaders;
  - undermined by perceptions of leaders' incentives or behaviour;
  - unacceptable to stakeholders.

### Challenges: culture

- What culture and fundamental principles does your organization wish to embrace?
  - How clear and memorable are they?
  - To what extent are they consistent with the perceived characters, behaviour and incentives of leaders at all levels including the board?
  - What are their weaknesses and ambiguities?
  - What do your stakeholders, internal and external, think of them?
- How effectively are they taught at induction, including for the board?
  - How effectively are they embedded in those who were not taught them at induction?
  - How are they affected by patterns of character among your workforce?
- To what extent does the behaviour of leaders at all levels provide a consistent and good example to be followed by subordinates?
- How does your response to departures from them affect staff attitudes?
- How often are they 'worked around' informally? What does this imply?
- What is the effect of differences in cultural background (eg educational, ethnic, geographical or religious) on the local culture in your workforce and leadership?
- How would you summarize your organization's actual culture?
- To what extent can you be confident that your perceptions reflect reality?

## *Risks from incentives*

Incentives come in many forms, but all involve some kind of reward or penalty for performance or behaviour. Even well-intentioned incentives readily risk causing undesirable behaviour that, in turn, causes reputational damage when the incentive comes to light. Similarly, incentives can distort culture and disrupt communication.

The best-known incentives are financial: you hit your target and we give you money (and recognition). They can be negative too: fail to meet your target and you will lose money (and status).

But incentives are also caused by culture and behaviour. Some behavioural incentives may have systemic consequences: for example a culture that ostracizes those who challenge the CEO may provide a strong incentive to conform. Others may be local: for example a bully whose behaviour creates an incentive not to pass on important information. This can make incentives hard to uncover even though their consequences can be severe.

Complex incentives such as those for executives may be difficult to understand; and specialists such as psychologists may predict likely undesirable behaviour that a board lacking psychology expertise may be unable to predict. Remuneration consultants' independence and incentives should be studied carefully before reliance is put upon what they advise. Anecdote suggests that some are far from incentive-free and independent.

### Examples: incentives

- Incentives that may produce unwanted or perverse consequences.
- Complex incentives that are hard to understand and whose consequences are hard to predict.
- Incentive systems that can be gamed or have unintended bad consequences; for example, performance incentives that can be met by cutting maintenance costs, thereby increasing longer term risks.
- Incentive systems that are unacceptable to stakeholders.
- Dominant or bullying behaviour at any level.
- Rewarding those who exhibit undesirable behaviour.
- Failure to welcome constructive criticism and unwelcome news may provide incentives that block information flows.

## Challenges: incentives

- To what extent do your board level remuneration consultants have incentives that conflict with the long-term health of your organization?
- To what extent does your system of financial incentives bring with it the risk of generating undesirable outcomes?
- What risks would a psychologist see in our incentive schemes? Is complexity an issue?
- Has 'gaming' incentives become a social norm or part of the culture?
- To what extent do incentives put your organization's desired culture at risk?
- List five non-financial incentives that affect:
  - you;
  - those who can reward and punish you and
  - those you can reward and punish.
- What do you learn from comparing them?

## *Risks from complexity and structure*

The official enquiries into the *Challenger* and *Deepwater Horizon* disasters shared a conclusion: 'Complex systems almost always fail in complex ways.'

Complex systems and organizational structures, whether obviously human (such as markets and large organizations) or seemingly mechanical (like space rockets and oil rigs which in fact conceal complex human systems), fail unexpectedly because complexity makes system behaviour difficult to understand and even harder to predict. Such systems can appear stable or successful for long periods – when they are in fact balanced on a knife-edge between seeming stability and instability.

When a failure eventually occurs, leaders are shocked out of the complacency into which they have been lulled. Crisis management is especially difficult because if it is hard to predict the failure of a complex system that is seemingly stable, it is far harder to predict its behaviour once it has tipped into instability.

## Examples: complexity and structure

- Feedback loops and interconnections in the system make the system intrinsically unstable and unpredictable.
- Silos lead to disrupted communication, so that important information is unavailable to decision-makers when they need it.
- Local incentives, cultures and heuristics further complicate the real-life operation of the system as designed.
- Those who preside over complex systems are misled into believing that their success is due to skill when in fact the system is, through luck, in a temporary period of stability that will end unpredictably.
- Failure modes and consequences are impossible to foresee.
- Incentive systems are too complex for their implications to be fully understood.

### Challenges: complexity and structure

- To what extent are important things known within your organization that leaders cannot find out?
- How effectively can your leaders exercise control over and predict the behaviour of the system over which they preside?
- How reliably can your leaders predict the behaviour of the external system within which they operate? How can they, and you, tell whether that seeming predictability is real, or a temporary phase of stability in an intrinsically unstable complex system?
- To what extent are activities and decision-making powers that might affect your reputation delegated to outsiders over whom you have little control, such as external counterparties or stakeholders? With what implications?
- Summarize your leadership incentive scheme and its risk implications in 200 words that would be understood by an intelligent outsider. Would a psychologist agree?

## *Risks from board composition, skill, knowledge, experience, character, culture and behaviour*

Non-executive directors will be ineffective if they lack either the ability or the strength of character to challenge executives. The ability to bring an outsiders' perspective is valuable but hard to achieve. It begins with skill, knowledge and experience. Boardroom leadership, culture, collegiality, a shared sense of identity and incentives may discourage its delivery. Directors also need personal courage to speak out.

Board analysis is the starting point. This should begin with fundamentals, independently of the nomination committee's approach, to identify the skills, knowledge, experience and character required if non-executives are to be able to understand all aspects of the organization. Gaps between NED team characteristics required and the skills actually available give rise to risks.

Whilst intelligence is essential, it is no substitute for skill, knowledge or experience. As Lord Fulton observed[3] in his devastating critique of the leadership of the UK civil service, the 'cult' of the 'gifted' 'generalist' or 'amateur' 'has the most damaging consequences' and 'is obsolete'. Yet in 2015 *The Economist* reported that 'the cult of the gifted amateur [still] prevails' in the United Kingdom.[4] The analysis should also explore the way the board actually operates. This will include analysis of risks from individual characters and from boardroom culture. These will include incentives, leadership, effectiveness and the degree to which leaders, executive and non-executive, are open to and have the strength of character to challenge. Incentives that discourage challenge, such as a fear of ostracism, of upsetting the chair or of not being reappointed, should be identified.

This risk area is likely to be out of bounds to internal risk teams. In any case, an internal review of these risk areas is likely to have little value because behavioural factors such as cognitive biases make it difficult for insider groups, including boards, reliably to see their own strengths and weaknesses. Conventional external board effectiveness reviews do not consider boards from a risk perspective.

The approach we recommend follows the principles set out in the section on methodology above. A trusted outsider experienced in board risk analysis, given confidential access to the board's inner workings, can see insider normality as an outsider and thus see risks that may not be readily apparent to, or even discoverable by, insiders. Confidential conversations with insiders can open up subjects that would not otherwise be raised for fear of embarrassment or repercussions. It is crucial that the findings are communicated to the board in a manner that helps leaders to absorb information that may contradict their mental models. Benefits are greatest if this is done in a way that also provokes a constructive reaction and a call to action.

The choice of analyst matters. Beyond competence, it is important that an analyst should have no incentive to hold back on findings. Any previous or current relationship with the firm should be analysed for risk implications; and there should be no expectation that the firm or related firms will work for the organization in the foreseeable future.

### Challenges: board composition, skill, knowledge, experience, character, culture and behaviour

- What skills, knowledge and experience would a risk-aware outsider think your board's non-executives need to share in order to understand all aspects of the business including personnel, technical and back-office issues?
  - To what extent does your non-executive team meet these needs?
- To what extent were and are character, curiosity and personal courage explicit components of the specification for NEDs?
- Does the board recruit openly? If not, how does the board prevent:
  - board recruitment agencies from recycling names already on their books and within their social circles;
  - the boardroom from becoming part of a cohesive social set vulnerable to shared mental maps and groupthink?
- What subjects does your board *not* discuss, for example because they are seen as dull, taboo, obvious, impolite or downright dangerous?
- What examples are there, in the last year, of challenge to the executive team from the board and from below?
  - How was the challenge received and with what result?
  - What risk conclusions do you draw?
- To what extent do your board and leaders believe their successes are the result of good luck?
- To what extent are strong personalities present in the board? How effectively are they recognized as risks and openly managed?

## *Risks from strategy and change*

Strategy failures regularly lead leaders to lose their reputations for competence, taking the reputation of their organization with them. History shows that a substantial proportion of mergers and acquisitions destroy shareholder value for the acquiring company.

### Examples: strategy and change

- Failure to identify and understand risks inherent in the business model.
- Insufficient board-level knowledge, experience or skill to reach sound decisions on strategy, change or their implementation.
- Insufficient attention to implementation and integration.
- The planning fallacy.
- Insufficient use of non-executive expertise in testing strategy proposals.
- Inadequate risk analysis of strategy and change.

**Challenges: strategy and change**

- To what extent do executives encourage NEDs to challenge strategy and acquisition plans as they develop?
- How does the approach to evaluating new strategy compare to the approach taken to the analysis of strategy failures?
- To what extent are your risk specialists involved in strategy development?
- To what extent do your risk specialists have the skills and authority to analyse risks involved in strategy?
- How does your board avoid groupthink and shared mental models?
- To what extent does your board fully understand the assumptions and risks inherent in the business model?
- Do you use pre-mortems, devil's advocates or other techniques to reduce the effects of groupthink?
- If your chairman and CEO were sacked and replaced tomorrow, what changes of strategy would their replacements suggest, and why?

## *Risks from latency and complacency*

Systemic risks and risks from insiders' world views can incubate for long periods before they emerge to cause severe reputational damage. The underlying states are often visible to insiders who are nonetheless unable to see the risk in what they see as normality. And they are easily lulled into complacency if they attribute success mainly to skill without assessing the role of luck.

Experienced outsiders, with a detached view of what insiders see as normality, can help insiders to develop an outsider view for themselves. Sometimes these risks are visible to and recognized by subordinates (who are outsiders vis à vis leadership teams) but they may be unwilling to communicate their concerns to leaders because they fear repercussions.

### Examples: latency and complacency

- Attribution of apparent success to skill without exploring the role of luck.
- Inadequate awareness of fundamental systemic weaknesses and dependencies.
- Inability to discover systemic weaknesses through root cause analysis of seemingly minor mishaps.
- Incentives that discourage reporting and investigation of errors, especially those without obvious consequences.
- Hubris and self-confidence unmitigated by self-doubt.

**Challenges: latency and complacency**

- How effectively does your organization's risk system uncover latent and systemic risks? How would you justify your answer to an outsider?
- To what extent do your leaders analyse and acknowledge the relative roles of luck, skill and creative reporting and accounting in apparent successes?
- To what extent are your leaders affected by hubris?
- To what extent does complacency dull your organization's risk culture and risk awareness?

## *Risks from inadequate preparation for crises*

Every organization should have a robust crisis strategy and plan for and practise crisis management. Practice should include everyone who will have any leadership role at any level of crisis management. Short of participating in real crises, there is no other way for those concerned to understand the stresses and dynamics involved in crises. Failure in this area represents an important reputational risk in itself.

This is not a book about crisis management so we shall say no more here beyond the crucial importance of drawing chairs and CEOs into crisis strategy and practice to deal with the practicalities of crisis leadership and management, decision-making under extreme uncertainty, stress and handling hostile interviews.

Boards should also bear in mind that crises regularly cause the downfall of the most illustrious chairs and chief executives. Whilst the personal reputational risk of leaders is not a matter for the organization, avoiding unexpected leadership crises and succession planning are.

The unplanned loss of a senior leader can exacerbate damage to the organization's reputation if a credible, crisis-worthy successor is not immediately available. On the other hand, if you have a crisis-worthy successor available seamlessly to continue the smooth running of the organization after loss of the CEO or chairman, it can only help your organization to recover a reputation for competence, perhaps more, in the aftermath of a reputational crisis.

### Challenges: inadequate preparation for crises

- To what extent have your crisis strategy and crisis plan been tested by exercises or live use?
- To what extent are your leaders experienced in live crisis management and do they participate regularly in crisis training?
- Will your succession plan deliver instant, well-prepared replacement leaders if you lose your CEO or chair during a crisis?

### *The reverse stress test*

Reputational risk needs to be looked at from the bottom up and from the top down. A critical question to complement the specific areas we have just covered looks through the other end of the telescope. It is based on a simple question: 'What could destroy our reputation?' This deceptively simple question can be the most difficult question for insiders to answer.

One reason is that many aspects of the answers fall into the areas of social silences: the things Gillian Tett calls 'dull, taboo, obvious or impolite'. The dull must be allowed to glow, ominously. Taboos must be broken. What seems obvious must be taken from its cupboard, dusted and examined: because what seems obvious often conceals the unacceptable, the ambiguous and the obscure. And the impolite must be discussed, always with courtesy, because it may mask important issues, such as risks from leadership, character or strategy. These are better, and more safely, aired, discussed and dealt with in private than exposed in public when things have gone badly wrong.

But there is another reason: some risks may be inconceivable, at least to leaders limited by the invisible blinkers insiders unwittingly wear. In our experience their subordinates, though they wear their own blinkers, nonetheless see from different perspectives; they have a different take on what is dull, taboo, obvious or impolite, at least when talking among themselves. One challenge is to make it safe for their truths to be heard by those in power.

This is another area where a trusted outsider can help. Not only can they be a safe conduit between subordinates and leaders; they can also persist in pursuing the two-year-old's question 'Why?' and its sibling 'Why not?' as they explore what could destroy your reputation. It is an exploration that is essential even though it can be uncomfortable.

## Evaluating risks and impacts

Few reputational crises have a single root cause; most have multiple causes combined with a trigger and a history that makes things worse. The final challenge for risk professionals is to join up, see and present leaders with a coherent, meaningful picture of reputational risk and its roots. Reputational risks and their largely behavioural, organizational and historical risk origins are generally qualitative, unquantifiable and interdependent. Combinations of factors can amplify or dilute potential consequences; and strengths may create opportunities in crises. A picture can only be sketched with words, which requires a shared risk vocabulary. The ability to interpret it depends on a repertoire of other pictures and histories with which comparisons can be made.

Some reputational weaknesses emerge as predictable in shape, occasionally even as to imminence and consequences. More often, when we join up the dots and evoke a verbal picture of what we have found, it emerges that an organization has a combination of vulnerabilities that, without mitigation, seem set to enable a future crisis at a time that cannot be predicted, but of a shape that is at least dimly apparent and whose likely reputational magnitude can be estimated on a scale running from manageable to monstrous. When strengths are added to the picture, it becomes possible to gain a feel for where the organization sits on a scale that begins with vulnerability and, through resilience, ends with Taleb's antifragility.

But most important of all is the opportunity to address vulnerabilities before they cause harm. Our research shows that there is often, perhaps usually, time to remedy weaknesses found before they cause damage. This is an opportunity that leaders disdain at their peril.

## Mitigating vulnerabilities

### *Board-level vulnerabilities*

The chair will usually have responsibility for dealing with vulnerabilities identified within the board. Remedying some kinds of vulnerabilities will fall within their skill and experience. Others will not, and in such circumstances the chair should seek specialist advice.

In some cases an exceptionally experienced HR director might have the technical skills to provide at least preliminary assistance on some kinds of vulnerability, but as a fellow board member they should, unless newly arrived, be considered a part of the matrix in which the vulnerability has arisen. Rather the chair should employ a suitably skilled external adviser or mentor, preferably with no other connection to the organization.

### *Vulnerabilities below board level*

Vulnerabilities below board level are a different matter. Most of these will be behavioural, organizational or operational in nature and well within the experience of the best HR or personnel specialists, such as those with degrees in sociology, psychology, anthropology or organizational behaviour as well as years of relevant practical experience who have also received risk training. The mode of treatment will depend on the risk concerned.

## Reporting and monitoring

Analysis, mitigation and internal reporting should carry on constantly, along with continuous monitoring and annual peaks of activity associated with external reporting.

The extent of mandatory monitoring and reporting requirements depends on the regulatory regime. To provide a working example, we shall briefly describe core elements of the UK regime including the Financial Reporting Council's (FRC) guidance for publicly quoted companies. This reflects substantial insights into the causes of corporate failure derived from a variety of sources including analysis of the 2007/08 financial crisis and reports to which we contributed.

UK company law requires all but small UK companies to describe the principal risks they face in their annual report. The FRC's 2014 *Guidance on the Strategic Report*[5] expands on this by requiring boards of quoted companies to report annually on 'principal risks and uncertainties', whether they have their origins in 'strategic decisions, operations, organization or behaviour, or from external factors over which the board may have little or no direct control'.[6] Many of these risk areas are at the heart of this book.

When reporting, the board's description of these risks is to be sufficiently specific that 'a shareholder can understand why they are material to the entity'. In addition to describing the risks' origins and potential impact, companies are expected to explain how they are managed or mitigated.[7]

This represents a challenge to boards whose current risk maps systematically include neither risks from organization or behaviour nor the full range of reputational risks and their sources. But it is not acceptable to opt out or defer action. The FRC's 2014 *Guidance on Risk Management, Internal Control and Related Financial and Business Reporting*[8] provides that board responsibilities for risk include 'financial, operational, reputational, behavioural, organizational, third party, or external risks, such as market or regulatory risk, over which the board may have little or no direct control.'[9]

Recognizing that board and risk team skills in these areas may be missing, the risk guidance recommends that the board should consider whether it and those to whom it delegates risk responsibilities – typically the risk or audit committee and the risk team – have 'the necessary skills, knowledge, experience, authority and support to enable it to assess the risks the company faces and exercise its responsibilities effectively'. It goes on specifically to recommend that boards should assess their own capabilities in this area as a part of regular board effectiveness reviews before turning to the use of experts: boards are expected to satisfy themselves that experts they consult 'have sufficient authority, independence and expertise to enable them to provide objective advice and information to the board'.[10]

## Challenges: reporting and monitoring

- How do you ensure that your risk experts, whether internal or external, have sufficient independence, authority and expertise?
- How do you ensure that your board has sufficiently comprehensive risk expertise to discharge its functions and supervise its risk team effectively?
- What are the requirements of your legislators and regulators as regards monitoring and reporting risks to reputation and from behaviour and organization?

# Notes

1 *The Orange Book – Management of Risk: Principles and Concepts* (2004) HM Treasury, https://www.gov.uk/government/uploads/system/uploads/attachment_data/file/220647/orange_book.pdf accessed 29/8/2016.

2 Tetlock and Gardner (2015).

3 Fulton (1968), para 15.

4 'End of the accidental boss' *The Economist*, 28/11/2015.

5 Financial Reporting Council (2014c).

6 Ibid, 7.25.

7 Ibid, 7.26.

8 Financial Reporting Council (2014b).

9 Ibid, para 33.

10 Ibid, para 27.

# CODA

When we first started writing this book with Kogan Page, we all agreed that reputational risk needed to be rethought. They were aware that, despite the advent of enterprise risk management, major reputational debacles continue to occur with depressing regularity. Something must be wrong.

Using the insights we have developed through research, case studies, discussion with thought leaders and numerous meeting with board members, we believe we have achieved a better understanding of this killer risk.

Our most important message has been eloquently summarized in the foreword by Anthony Hilton. As he explains, too much traditional risk management and regulation is driven by an unexplored assumption that organizations are quasi-mechanical and that decision-making essentially rational. The implication is that you can set rules and risks will disappear.

In reality, organizations consist of people who exhibit the range of normal human emotions and behaviours; and it is those who lack these emotions who are out of the ordinary, not those who exhibit them. This means that mistakes are to be expected from even the most intelligent and respected business leaders.

Such errors are perfectly normal and their causes would come as no surprise to those in other disciplines such as sociology, psychology, anthropology or organizational behaviour.

Rethinking reputational risk involves bringing some of the wisdom from these disciplines into the vocabulary of risk management. If we have sown the seeds of this change then we feel we will have been successful. And recognizing that we are as human as our readers, we shall welcome all constructive suggestions for the improvement of this book.

# GLOSSARY

**affect heuristic** Sometimes we use our feelings, rather than research or decent statistics (which may not be available), to evaluate something. Using our feelings as a short cut for a more difficult evaluation is what behavioural economists call the affect heuristic.

**antifragile** Nassim Nicholas Taleb observed that we do not have a word that extends the spectrum from fragile through robust and resilient towards things that 'benefit from shocks' or 'thrive when exposed to volatility, randomness, disorder and stressors and love adventure, risk and uncertainty'. He coined the term 'antifragile' to describe such a characteristic.

**biases, cognitive** We are brought up to think of ourselves as logical beings, and those of us who studied classical economics had the notion reinforced by the idea of 'homo economicus' with rational, profit-maximizing tendencies. A cognitive bias is a systematic, often predictable, departure from strict logic in the way we think and make decisions.

**CGC** UK Corporate Governance Code.

**choice architecture** Structuring choices so as to encourage the choice of particular options – a subject popularized by 'Nudge'.[1]

**confirmation bias** Our fast, unconscious and frugal System One tries to make sense of what it learns and believe it if it can. Given time and energy, System Two will test System One's answer. System Two tends to seek evidence that confirms what System One believes rather than evidence to disprove it. This is confirmation bias.

**CRO** Chief Risk Officer.

**endowment effect** Our aversion to losses brings with it an aversion to giving up that which we have. Most of us will demand more to give up something we have than we are prepared to pay to buy the same object. Our aversion is known as the endowment effect.

**FCA** Financial Conduct Authority.

**FRC** Financial Reporting Council.

**good news culture** A culture in which it is believed that leaders only want to hear good news and do not welcome bad news.

**groupthink** Groupthink is a mode of group thinking and decision-making in which participants in a group allow their wish for consensus or unanimity to prevail over their will to consider alternatives.

**heuristics** Heuristics are mental short cuts that we all use to simplify decision-making. Daniel Kahneman described them as a 'mental shotgun' that we use to 'generate quick answers to difficult questions' without making System Two work too hard.

**incentives, financial and non-financial** Financial incentives are any incentive involving a monetary reward or penalty used to encourage or discourage a particular outcome or behaviour. All other incentives are non-financial. Non-financial incentives may come from social pressure, a bully and innumerable other causes.

**incubation and latency** Some risks, particularly systemic risks, can be present for many years without triggering serious harm. Unrecognized and therefore unmanaged, these risks will remain latent and continue to incubate until the wrong circumstances occur, when they will operate.

**inside-outsider perspective** A perspective on the inner workings of a group gained by an outsider given privileged inside access to the group.

**loss aversion** Loss aversion is the psychological response ingrained in System One to avoid the pain of losing that which we have.

**mental models** We summarize the way we believe things work into mental models and use them to make predictions and simulations.

**NED** A non-executive director. We use the term to include non-executive directors of all kinds including those on supervisory boards.

**optimistic bias** Most of us tend to delude ourselves that bad events are less likely to happen than good ones. This is the optimistic bias, which, unsurprisingly, is more prevalent among optimists.

**outrage** According to Professor Art Markman, outrage is 'an emotion that has three components. First, it has negative affect. That is, it is a bad feeling. Second, it has high arousal. That is, it is a strong and powerful emotion. Third, it occurs when people experience a violation of a moral boundary.'[2]

**overconfidence** We are overconfident when our own belief in our abilities is greater than an objective evaluation would conclude.

**planning fallacy** Professor Douglas Hofstadter is an American cognitive psychologist who coined Hofstadter's Law: 'It always takes longer than you expect, even when you take into account Hofstadter's Law.'[3] Daniel Kahneman reached a similar conclusion summarized as the planning fallacy.

**PRA** Prudential Regulation Authority, part of the Bank of England.

**principal risk** A risk or combination of risks that could seriously affect the performance, future prospects or reputation of the entity.

**recognition heuristic** There is some evidence that where we recognize one of a number of choices but have no better information, we are likely to put a lower store on the option we do not recognize.

**regret aversion** We are all prone to fear that a decision we are about to take will lead us to have regrets if it turns out to be wrong. This is regret aversion.

**reputational capital and reputational equity** When an organization benefits from its stakeholders sharing a settled trust-based feeling of warmth toward it, we say that the organization has 'reputational capital'. Some include consequent effects on share price as a component of reputational capital, but we prefer the separate term 'reputational equity' for the share price effect.

**risk glass ceiling** A barrier, often caused by culture, incentives or social behaviours norms, that prevents risk information from reaching the top of the organization, causing what we call the 'unknown known' problem.

**self-serving bias** Our innate tendency to attribute positive events to our own achievement and adverse events to outside forces or bad luck.

**SFO** UK Serious Fraud Office.

**social norms** We humans like to belong, to fit. We are adept at adapting to meet what we perceive to be the behavioural expectations of those who belong to groups to which we aspire or belong. We are good at detecting the expectations of others, and as a result they spread rapidly. These contagious expectations are social norms.

**social proof** When we find ourselves in an uncertain situation and unsure how to behave, we may look to those around us for clues for clues as to what is appropriate. This is social proof.

**social silences** Established groups of people may systematically ignore subjects because they are regarded as what Gillian Tett has called 'dull, taboo, obvious or impolite'.[4]

**stakeholders** 'Stakeholder' is a term coined at the Stanford Research Institute in 1963 to describe 'Those groups without whose support the organization would cease to exist'.[5]

**status quo bias** We exhibit the status quo bias when we are reluctant to change things and readily default to keeping them the same.

**Systems One and Two** The model of human behaviour developed by Professor Daniel Kahneman consists of two systems: System One and System Two. System One makes fast, unconscious and frugal decisions. It is impulsive, automatic and effort-free and it does not stop to ponder whether the decision is right or wrong. System Two is slow, conscious and logical. It is capable of checking conclusions reached by System One: but using it needs mental effort so we do not always use it. System Two is, however, what underlies classical economists' relentlessly rational model of human behaviour known as 'homo economicus'.

**Turner's equation** '*Disaster = energy + misinformation*'.

**unknown known** There are things that are known, sometimes widely known within organizations, that are unknown to its leaders. These are 'unknown knowns'.

## Notes


1. Thaler, R and Sunstein, C (2008) *Nudge*, Yale University Press.
2. Markman, A (2008) The psychology of outrage in the political world, https://www.psychologytoday.com/blog/ulterior-motives/200807/the-psychology-outrage-in-the-political-world accessed 15/3/2016.
3. Hofstadter, D (1979) *Gödel, Escher, Bach: An Eternal Golden Braid*, Basic Books.
4. Tett, G (2015) *The Silo Effect*, Little Brown.
5. Taken from Freeman (1983), p 31, explained at greater length in endnote 1, p 49. Echoed in Freeman and Reed (1983), p 89.

# REFERENCES


Akerlof, G and Kranton, R (2010) *Identity Economics*, Princeton University Press

Ariely, D (2008) *Predictably Irrational*, Harper Collins

Ariely, D, Gneezy, U, Loewenstein, G and Mazar, N (2005) *Large Stakes and Big Mistakes*, Federal Reserve Bank of Boston

Atkins, D, Fitzsimmons, A, Parsons, C and Punter, A (2011) *Roads to Ruin*, Cass Business School for Airmic

Ayton, P (2000) Do the birds and bees need cognitive reform? *Behavioural and Brain Sciences*, **23** (5), pp. 666–67

Bacon, R and Hope, C (2013) *Conundrum – Why Every Government Gets Things Wrong – and What We Can Do About It*, Biteback Publishing

Bailey, A (2016) Culture in financial services – a regulator's perspective, Bank of England, http://www.bankofengland.co.uk/publications/Documents/speeches/2016/speech901.pdf accessed 5/6/2016

Birkenshaw, J (2015) Are you managing complexity? https://www.london.edu/faculty-and-research/lbsr/are-you-managing-complexity accessed 20/4/2016

Boeing (2014) *Statistical Summary of Commercial Jet Airplane Accidents*, http://www.boeing.com/resources/boeingdotcom/company/about_bca/pdf/statsum.pdf (accessed 2/4/2016

Bourdieu, P (1977) *Outline of a Theory of Practice*, Cambridge University Press

Browne, J (2010) *Beyond Business*, Wiedenfield & Nicholson

Buffett, W (2010) Letter to shareholders, http://www.berkshirehathaway.com/letters/2010ltr.pdf accessed 5/4/2016

Cooper, M, Gulen, H and Raghavendra Rau, P (2014) Performance for pay? http://papers.ssrn.com/sol3/papers.cfm?abstract_id=1572085 accessed 2/4/2016

Cooper, A, Woo, CY and Dunkelberg, WC (1988) Entrepreneurs' perceived chances for success, http://www.sciencedirect.com/science/article/pii/0883902688900201 accessed 2/4/2016

Crossan, M, Mazutis, D Seijts, G and Gandz, J (2013) Developing leadership character in business programs, http://amle.aom.org/content/12/2/285.abstract accessed 7/6/2016

Dolan, P, Hallsworth, M, Halpern, D, King, D and Vlaev, I (2010) *Mindspace: Influencing Behaviour Through Public Policy*, Institute for Government, http://www.instituteforgovernment.org.uk/sites/default/files/publications/MINDSPACE.pdf accessed 23/8/2016

Dunbar, R, Lycett, J and Barratt, L (2005) *Evolutionary Psychology*, Oneworld Publications

Eaglesham, D (2015) *The Brain*, Canongate Books

Edelman (2015) *Trust Barometer 2015*, http://www.edelman.com/insights/intellectual-property/2015-edelman-trust-barometer/trust-and-innovation-edelman-trust-barometer/executive-summary/ accessed 19/4/2016

Edelman (2016) *Trust Barometer 2016*, http://www.edelman.com/insights/intellectual-property/2016-edelman-trust-barometer/ accessed 27/8/2016

Edmondson, A (1999) Psychological safety and learning behavior in work teams, http://asq.sagepub.com/content/44/2/350.abstract accessed 22/3/2016

Environment Agency (2002) The social amplification of risk, https://www.gov.uk/government/uploads/system/uploads/attachment_data/file/290303/se2-023-ts-e-e.pdf accessed 6/9/2016

Feynman, R (1974) *Cargo Cult Science*, http://calteches.library.caltech.edu/51/02/CargoCult.pdf accessed 14/3/2016

Financial Reporting Council (2014a) *The UK Corporate Governance Code*, https://www.frc.org.uk/Our-Work/Publications/Corporate-Governance/UK-Corporate-Governance-Code-2014.pdf accessed 6/9/2016

Financial Reporting Council (2014b) *Guidance on Risk Management, Internal Control and Related Financial and Business Reporting*, https://www.frc.org.uk/Our-Work/Publications/Corporate-Governance/Guidance-on-Risk-Management,-Internal-Control-and.pdf accessed 6/9/2016

Financial Reporting Council (2014c) *Guidance on the Strategic Report*, https://www.frc.org.uk/Our-Work/Publications/Accounting-and-Reporting-Policy/Guidance-on-the-Strategic-Report.pdf accessed 6/9/2016

Freeman, R (1983) *Strategic Management: A stakeholder approach*, Pitman/USA

Freeman, R and Reed, D (1983) Stakeholders and stockholders: A new perspective on corporate governance, *California Management Review*, **XXV** (3) http://cmr.berkeley.edu/search/articleDetail.aspx?article=4983 (accessed 6/9/2016

Friedman, M (1970) The social responsibility of business is to increase its profits, *New York Times*, http://www.colorado.edu/studentgroups/libertarians/issues/friedman-soc-resp-business.html accessed 10/4/2016

Fulton, Lord (1968) *The Civil Service*, HMSO, Cmnd 3638

Gandz, J, Crossan, M, Seijts, G and Stephenson, C (2010) *Leadership on Trial*, Richard Ivey School of Business

Gigerenzer, G, Todd, PM and ABC Research Group (1999) *Simple Heuristics That Make Us Smart*, Oxford University Press

Goold, M and Campbell, A (1994) *Corporate Level Strategy*, John Wiley

Grove, A (1996) *Only the Paranoid Survive*, Harper Collins

High Pay Centre (2015) *Are Remuneration Consultants Independent?* http://highpaycentre.org/files/remuneration_consultants_-_FINAL.pdf accessed 4/4/2016

Hofstadter, D (1979) *Gödel, Escher, Bach: An Eternal Golden Braid*, Basic Books

Hooghiemstra, R. (2008) *Cultural Differences in Self-Serving Behaviour*, http://www.apira2013.org/past/apira2001/papers/Hooghiemstra56.pdf accessed 23/8/2016

Hopkins, A (2008) *Failure to Learn*, CCH Australia Ltd

Hopkins, A (2012) *Disastrous Decisions*, CCH Australia Ltd

Kahneman, D (2011) *Thinking Fast and Slow*, Allen Lane

Kay, J (2012) *Review of Equity Markets and Long Term Decision Making*, https://www.gov.uk/government/uploads/system/uploads/attachment_data/file/253454/bis-12-917-kay-review-of-equity-markets-final-report.pdf (accessed 17/3/2016

Kay, J (2015) It is financial crashes we should fear, not those in aeroplanes, *Financial Times*, http://on.ft.com/1C3a8r0 accessed 9/6/2016

King, A and Crewe, I (2013) *The Blunders of our Governments*, Oneworld Books

Kruglanski, AW and Gigerenzer, G (2011) Intuitive and deliberate judgments are based on common principles, *Psychological Review*, **118** (1), pp 97–109

Loewenstein, GF, Weber, EU, Hsee, CK and Welch, ES (2001) Risk as feelings, *Psychological Bulletin*, **127**, pp 267–86

Markman, A (2008) The psychology of outrage in the political world, https://www.psychologytoday.com/blog/ulterior-motives/200807/the-psychology-outrage-in-the-political-world accessed 15/3/2016

McDonnell, W (2002) *Managing Risk: Practical lessons from recent 'failures' of EU insurers*, Financial Services Authority OP20

Mill, JS (1836) On the definition of political economy, and on the method of investigation proper to it, *London and Westminster Review*, October

Mill, JS (1874) *Essays on Some Unsettled Questions of Political Economy*, 2nd ed, Longmans, Green, Reader & Dyer

Mills, S (2016) Internal Audit and supervisory expectations – building on progress, www.bankofengland.co.uk/publications/Documents/speeches/2016/speech879.pdf accessed 7/6/2016

Mitleton-Kelly, E (2003) *Complex Systems and Evolutionary Perspectives on Organisations: The application of complexity theory to organisations*, Elsevier

NASA (2003) *Report of the Columbia Accident Investigation Board*, https://www.nasa.gov/columbia/home/CAIB_Vol1.html accessed 6/9/2016

Owen, D (2007) *The Hubris Syndrome*, Methuen

Parliamentary Commission on Banking Standards (2013) *Changing Banking for Good: Final report*, http://www.publications.parliament.uk/pa/jt201314/jtselect/jtpcbs/27/27.pdf accessed 10/4/2016

Perrow, C (1984) *Normal Accidents*, Princeton University Press

Peterson, C and Seligman, M (2004/2016) *The VIA Classification of Character Strengths*. The 2004 version used by Seijts seems no longer available but we found the current version at http://www.viacharacter.org/www/Character-Strengths/VIA-Classification

Reason, J (1990) *Human Error*, Cambridge University Press

Reputability (2013) *Deconstructing Failure: Insights for boards*, http://www.reputability.co.uk/files/press/Deconstructing-failure.pdf accessed 2/4/2016

Roscoe, S (1980) *Aviation Psychology*, Iowa State University Press

Rozenzweig, P (2014) *The Halo Effect*, Simon & Schuster

Rumsfeld, D (2002) NATO press conference, http://www.nato.int/docu/speech/2002/s020606g.htm accessed 23/8/2016

Schein, E *et al* (2015) All about culture, *Journal of Business Anthropology*, http://rauli.cbs.dk/index.php/jba/article/view/4792/5223 accessed 20/4/2016

Seijts, GH, Gandz, J, Crossan, M and Reno, M (2015) Character matters: Character dimensions' impact on leader performance and outcomes, *Organizational Dynamics*, **44**, pp 65–74

Seligman, M (2015) Chris Peterson's unfinished masterwork: The real mental illnesses. *Journal of Positive Psychology: Special issue in memory of Chris Peterson*, 10(1), 3–6. doi:10.1080/17439760.2014.888582

Shelp, R and Ehrbar, A (2006) *Fallen Giant: The amazing story of Hank Greenberg and the history of AIG*, Wiley

Smith, A (1776) On the division of labour, *The Wealth of Nations*, Books I–III

Smithers, A (2013) *The Road to Recovery: How and why economic policy must change*, John Wiley

Steuer, M, Abell, P and Wynn, H (2016) Head-hunter methods for CEO selection, http://www.braybrooke.co.uk/tabid/99/Default.aspx?articleId=1283 accessed 22 March 2016

Svenson, O (1981) Are we all less risky than our fellow drivers? http://heatherlench.com/wp-content/uploads/2008/07/svenson.pdf accessed 16/3/2016

Swiss Re (1990) *Human Error in the Cockpit*

Taleb, NN (2004) *Fooled by Randomness*, Penguin

Taleb, NN (2012) *Antifragile*, Allen Lane

Tetlock, P and Gardner, D (2015) *Superforecasting*, Random House

Tett, G (2015) *The Silo Effect*, Little Brown

Thaler, R and Sunstein, C (2008) *Nudge*, Yale University Press

Turner, B (1997) *Man-Made Disasters*, 2nd ed with Nick Pidgeon, Butterworth-Heinmann

Walker, D (2009) *A Review of Corporate Governance in UK Banks and other Financial Industry Entities: Final recommendations* (The Walker Review), http://webarchive.nationalarchives.gov.uk/+/http:/www.hm-treasury.gov.uk/d/walker_review_261109.pdf accessed 6/4/2016

# ACKNOWLEDGEMENTS

This book emerged from many years' collaboration within our consultancy Reputability. Particular thanks are due to our colleague (Professor) Peter Ayton, who provided a raft of penetrating questions, comments and insight on the first draft of Part One. We are equally grateful to our Reputability partners Mike Bell, John Tyce, Jane Howard and Rob Haslam for many discussions, challenges and insights over the years as well as for comments on drafts.

We discussed ideas, and received inspiration, constructive criticism and hard-to-get documents from a variety of people including David Abrahams, Marios Argyrou, Ian Bates, Richard Bacon, Duncan Boyle, Mehran Eftekhar, Andrew Featherstone, Julia Graham, Eman Ali Hafedh, Gary Honey, Felix Horber, Rick Hudson, John Hurrell, Kevin Murray, Chris Parsons, Alan Punter, Duncan Rogers, Gerard Seijts, Mufid Sukkar, Samantha Sultana, Diane Walker, Robin Wilson, Åsa Boholm, Tijo Salverda and Joy Hendry. We also thank those not already mentioned who commented on drafts at various stages including Alexandra and Rachel Fitzsimmons, not to mention the external readers arranged by our publishers. We found all their comments most helpful, though any remaining errors are of course our own.

We are especially grateful to Anthony Hilton for writing the Foreword. We are equally grateful to those who have graciously given permission to use words or diagrams they had crafted: Andrew Bailey, Warren Buffett, Prabhu Guptara, John Minton and Gerard Seijts.

We enjoyed working with our editorial team at Kogan Page: Jenni Hall, who commissioned our book and Amy Minshull, David Crosby, Stefan Leszczuk and Alison Elks who brought it to fruition.

And finally we must thank our beloved wives, Diana and Kristina, for their endless patience and support. To them we dedicate this book.

# THE AUTHORS

**Anthony Fitzsimmons** MA (Hons) Cantab is Chairman of Reputability LLP and an authority and leading thinker on reputational risk and the propensity of behavioural and organizational risks to cause reputational damage. Having graduated as an engineer, he qualified as a barrister and solicitor before spending 30 years, 20 as a partner, in a City law firm with ringside and inside views of crises as they unfolded and were investigated. Building on this and the extensive experience of his Reputability partners, he helps organizations and their leaders identify and mitigate these risks. Anthony is co-author of *Roads to Ruin*, the seminal Cass Business School report on the deeper causes of corporate catastrophes for Airmic. He lectures extensively on reputational risk, is widely published in professional journals and is regularly quoted in the national and London press.

**Derek Atkins** BSc PhD MIMMM CEng FCIM FCII Chartered Insurer. After a long career in the City, Derek is a visiting Professor at the Cass Business School, University of London, teaching risk management, reputational risk and insurance, and a partner in Reputability LLP. He is co-author of a dozen books on risk management and insurance. He has been a member of two UK government working groups on risk-related issues and was involved in developing the corporate ethics codes for two professional institutes. He was awarded the Exceptional Service Medal of the Chartered Insurance Institute for his work in professional education. Like Anthony, Derek was trained as an engineer. He is currently a non-executive director of several international financial services firms and chairman of an insurance broker.

# INDEX

*Note*: Page numbers in **bold** indicate Glossary entries.